ARTISTS
AGAINST
WAR AND
FASCISM

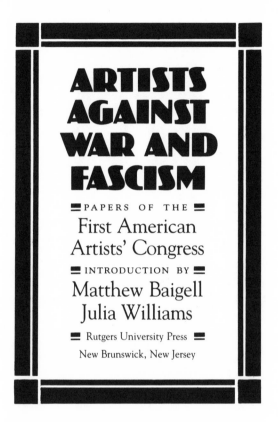

ARTISTS AGAINST WAR AND FASCISM

■ PAPERS OF THE ■

First American
Artists' Congress

■ INTRODUCTION BY ■

Matthew Baigell
Julia Williams

■ Rutgers University Press ■

New Brunswick, New Jersey

Library of Congress Cataloging in Publication Data

American Artists' Congress (1st : 1936 : New York, N.Y.)
Artists against war and fascism.

Originally published under title: Papers of the
American Artists' Congress.
Bibliography: p.
Includes index.
1. Artists—United States—Political activity—
Congresses. 2. Social realism—Congresses. 3. Communism
—United States—1917–   —Influence—Congresses.
4. Fascism and art—Congresses. I. Baigell, Matthew.
II. Williams, Julia. III. Title.
N6512.A585   1936A   701'.03   85-2335
ISBN 0-8135-1125-9

CONTENTS

LIST OF ILLUSTRATIONS

PREFACE

In February of 1936 a group of artists, meeting under the auspices of a new organization, the American Artists' Congress, filled the auditorium of Town Hall in New York City. There they listened to speeches and tried to decide how they, as artists, could respond to the two major crises of the 1930s: the Great Depression and the spread of fascism. In the view of most of these men and women, the times were so dangerous that working alone in a studio immune from the press of daily events was a luxury they could not afford. Many of these artists were political leftists, influenced by the Communist Party and its Popular Front strategy which sought to organize as many people as possible into visible anti-fascist organizations—such as the American Artists' Congress.

The papers presented at the first meeting of the congress were written by a variety of artists and observers of the art scene. They were collected and published by the congress as the *Papers of the American Artists' Congress*. This volume, one of the central artistic documents of the period, describes the thoughts, fears, intentions, and preoccupations of artists during a time of national and international crisis. The original edition, of which 3,000 copies were published, has never been reprinted. In books and articles about the art and artists of the 1930s, they are mentioned often, but rarely have they been seen in complete form. Fortunately, the papers are once again accessible. The Rutgers University Press is reprinting the papers to coincide with the fiftieth anniversary of the founding of the congress. The papers correspond to the original edition with misspellings and punctuation silently emended to enhance readability and with an occasional missing word editorially supplied within brackets to ensure clarity. To provide a context for the original essays, we have written a brief history of the congress. We have also included the texts of several catalogs from exhibitions sponsored by the congress, biographical sketches of the speakers at the first meetings, and a sampling of illustrations, most from congress-sponsored exhibitions, that suggest the range of artistic styles and interests of its members.

The essays recall the partisan politics of the 1930s. We hope their availability will contribute to the reevaluation of that turbulent period. Although they are now part of the history of American art, the essays also relate to more recent manifestations of political activism among American artists. In fact, the interests and activities of left-wing artists in the 1930s marked the first instance in this country of widespread activism among artists. In this regard, the papers are an important document in the political history of American art to which additional chapters have been added in the 1970s and 1980s concerning feminism, street art, racism, and criticism of United States policies concerning nuclear weapons and third-world countries.

·   We want to thank those who responded to our queries and those whom we interviewed in person. They include Rose Arenal, Peter Blume, Earl Davis, Dorothy Dehner, Harry Gottlieb, John Groth, Meyer Schapiro, Bernarda Bryson Shahn, Joseph Solman, Raphael Soyer, Harry Sternberg, May McNeer Ward, and Anna T. Zakarija. Howard L. Green made many useful suggestions.

We also want to thank Leslie Mitchner of the Rutgers University Press whose support and enthusiasm were crucial from the project's inception to its publication.

Matthew Baigell
Julia Williams

ARTISTS
AGAINST
WAR AND
FASCISM

1
INTRODUCTION

THE AMERICAN ARTISTS' CONGRESS:
ITS CONTEXT AND HISTORY

It is difficult to recreate the mood of a period, especially one as complex as the 1930s. But the following passage written by Max Weber in the summer of 1936 suggests some of the reasons for the creation and initial success of the American Artists' Congress. The sentence was part of a statement written in response to Francisco Franco's fascist-supported attack on the legitimate Spanish government.

> And while the serpentine Nazis and treacherous Fascists and traitors are sending bombs and other implements of destruction and war to the miserable traitors and agents under the despicable Franco, the working classes and the forward-looking masses of this and all other countries send their comradely greetings and good cheer to the fighting and bleeding masses of Spain and their elected democratic government . . . in the hope . . . that a sister Soviet Government will be born of this historic struggle in Spain.[1]

Emotional in its overall tone, but also calculated in the choice of adjectives, this sentence reflected the temper of both its author and like-minded artists who had been engulfed by the Depression, now six years old, and frightened by the rise of a repressive and brutal fascism in central Europe and by the outbreak of civil war in Spain.

Weber's sentence also recalls the language then being disseminated by the Soviet Union and national Communist parties, which had placed themselves, verbally at least, in the path of advancing fascism. Countering intimations of despair, Weber's aggressive rhetoric indicated the importance of a political community in which to find shelter and to grapple with the anxieties of the moment. Its message: a closing of the ranks might contain and even lead to the demise of fascism. Artists who shared Weber's concerns felt compelled to organize. So was born the American Artists' Congress.

For Weber and artists like him, working with organizations tied to the Communist Party U.S.A. and ultimately to the Soviet Union seemed a reasonable step in the fight against the fascists. Because the Soviet Union took the lead in the initial fight against Hitler's Germany, Mussolini's Italy and the militarists running Japan, its example was praised and its policies as well as politics supported, if not always agreed with. For Weber and others it was clear that the battle had started abroad and that a threat of home-grown fascism existed as well. Unless protective measures were taken, the position of artists would grow increasingly precarious. The American Artists' Congress, if it could not offer such protection, at least represented an organized forum that set as its responsibility the protection of American artists from destructive forces within the country and provided a platform from which artists could speak out about world affairs.

The history of the American Artists' Congress encompasses a seven-year period from its inception in 1935 to its dissolution in 1942. At its peak in 1939, the congress had about nine hundred members; it sponsored exhibitions and symposia across the country, and it lobbied for artists' rights, jobs, and economic security. Of several artists' organizations active during the mid-1930s, the American Artists' Congress was one of the few that tried to organize artists who worked in all styles and with all media. The congress tried to develop into an organization that could exert nationwide pressure to better the condition of artists.

At the same time the congress was a left-wing political organization that fought artistic and political repression at home and abroad. Despite its constant agitation over a variety of issues, the congress was silent on the type of art it preferred. Its political interests were well defined, but its artistic personality was purposely undeveloped. Esthetic concerns were secondary to the effort to organize and politicize artists because its leaders wanted to attract as many artists as possible to its ranks, regardless of stylistic preference. The unifying factor among participants in the congress was their adherence to the key ideas of the Soviet Union's Popular Front: the defense of peace and democracy, and the fight against war and fascism.

The Popular Front made its official appearance in August 1935, at the Seventh World Congress of the Communist International in Moscow. It was a political strategy designed to enlist Western democracies in the struggle against fascism in Italy and Germany, and in opposition to the rise of militarism in Japan. It had enormous implications for the history of American radicalism. Simply put, the Popular Front redirected the basic aims of international Communism. Before the Popular Front strategy was announced, the overarching issue for Communists was the conflict between socialism and capitalism. Writers and artists at such meetings as that in Kharkov of the Second International Conference of Revolutionary and Proletarian Writers in 1930 were urged to turn their art into a weapon in the class struggle, to emphasize proletarian themes, and to accept a proletarian point of view. In contrast, for the strategists of the Popular Front the central issue was the choice between war and fascism on the one hand, peace and democracy on the other. They chose to emphasize the fight against fascism rather than the fight against capitalism.

During the years before the Popular Front, John Reed clubs flourished in the United States. Founded in New York City in 1929 and tied to the Communist Party, about thirty clubs had been started around the country by 1934. Their purpose was to encourage the proletarianization of both literature and the visual arts. Exhibitions that began in December 1929 centered around themes such as "The Social Viewpoint in Art" (1933) and "Hunger, Fascism, War" (1934). At meetings and in its art school in New York City, the clubs taught artists that their interests were in harmony with those of the working class; therefore their art should advance the position of the working class as well as reflect the social conflicts of the day.[2] During this period—the early 1930s—the most militantly political art of the decade was created.

In 1934, the American Communist Party (CPUSA), reflecting a political shift in Moscow, decided it needed "to bring intellectuals into closer contact with the working class."[3] Accordingly, Alexander Trachtenberg, who represented the Central Committee of the CPUSA, suggested at the second national conference of the John Reed clubs in Chicago that a National Writers' Congress be held in the near future. Trachtenberg also called for "a similar action uniting American artists" to help, among other things, fight, referring to the artistic policy of the Public Works of Art Project, "the Roosevelt-fostered national chauvinist art." But, as one observer stated, Trachtenberg made "it clear that there could be no opposition between the intellectuals of our movement and the party organizers."[4] The National Writers' Congress, which was held on April 26–27, 1935, included among its resolutions the intention to struggle against war and fascism, to fight racial discrimination and the imprisonment of revolutionary writers and artists, to preserve civil liberties, and to defend the Soviet Union against capitalistic aggression as well as to strengthen the revolutionary labor movement.[5]

This first Writers' Congress, like earlier antiwar congresses abroad such as those initiated in 1932 by Willi Münzenberg, Henri Barbusse, and Romain Rolland, was not, properly speaking, part of the Popular Front; but it was part of a looser initiative known as the United Front. The United Front was antagonistic to the capitalist democracies, associating them with fascism. It openly supported the Soviet Union and wanted to increase "the issue of propagandist literature."[6] In its view, President Franklin D. Roosevelt was on par with Adolf Hitler or Benito Mussolini. The position of the United Front was clearly expressed in the Party magazine, the *Communist*, in March 1935. "The Party's general line in this period is to mobilize the masses against capitalist reaction and fascization, against war preparations, and for the defense of the Soviet Union, on the basis of the united front policy, seeking to lead the masses up to the revolutionary way out, to the struggle for a Soviet America."[7]

This position was reversed abruptly with the institution of the Popular Front in August 1935. The Soviet leadership developed the Popular Front strategy because it believed the war between Germany and Russia had become unavoidable. It feared that the Western nations might support Hitler or not hinder his expansionist policies. Through the Popular Front the leadership sought antifascist allies wherever they might be found—in government, major political parties, labor unions, and among the middle classes all over the world. This abrupt change of strategy called for working with people and organizations previously considered enemies: with anybody, even anti-Communists, sympathetic to the fight against fascism and for the preservation of culture.

In the United States the Popular Front attacked organizations and individuals that, in its view, were already leading the country toward fascism, such as the Liberty League, the hatemonger Father Coughlin, and the newspaper mogul William Randolph Hearst. The Front also tried to win over the middle class to its point of view. Intellectuals, writers, and artists, it was thought, could certainly play a significant role in its effort. William Z. Foster, an important CPUSA theoretician, held that professionals, if properly cultivated, could be useful in "carrying the Party's anti-fascist message to the ranks of the white collar middle class."[8] A variety of front organizations were subsequently established. One of them, the American League for Peace and Democracy, became an umbrella for 1,023 groups with 7.5 million members. "The fronts," as one historian has suggested, "sought to book famous names and exploit them for Communist causes by means of manifestoes, open letters, petitions, declarations, statements, pronouncements, protests and other illustrations of opinion groundswells in the land."[9]

The entire October 1935 issue of the *Communist* was devoted to this new strategy for developing an antifascist front. But cooperation did not imply capitulation. The editors published a resolution on the speech given by Georgi Dimitroff at the 1935 Moscow Congress that had instituted the Popular Front. It stated, in part, "Without for a moment giving up their independent work in the sphere of Communist education, organization and mobilization of the masses, the Communists, in order to render the road to unity of action easier for the workers, must *strive to secure joint action with the Social-Democratic parties, reformist trade unions and other organizations of the toilers against the class enemies of the proletariat, on the basis of short or long-term agreements.*" [10] The directions were quite clear: cooperation and control.

With this change in policy some Communist-led organizations were abandoned. For example, the John Reed clubs, too closely associated with the proletarian culture (Prolitcult) movement, became a casualty of the Popular Front. Their purpose had been, as one writer baldly stated, "to win writers and artists to the Revolution." [11] During the winter of 1935–1936, the clubs were summarily disbanded, and the art school in New York City was closed about February 1, 1936, all in the name of cooperation with the non-Communist, anti-fascist world. [12] Nevertheless, many of the people active in the John Reed clubs were instrumental in establishing the American Artists' Congress. In fact, the congress was formed at a club meeting. The new organization was intended to reflect completely the newly developed strategies of the Popular Front and it was among the first cultural organizations to do so.

Because of the lack of documentation as well as the number of years that have passed since the first organizational meetings of the Artists' Congress, we may never know the complete story of its inception or its daily operation. But, fortunately, much information is contained in the informal history of the American Contemporary Artists Galleries (ACA Galleries), the gallery in which most congress exhibitions were held, written in 1944 by its director Herman Baron, and in documents in the possession of Earl Davis, the son of Stuart Davis. [13]

A week or two after the National Writers' Congress met on April 26 and 27, 1935, Alexander Trachtenberg (whom Stuart Davis called "Comrade Trachtenberg") attended a John Reed Club meeting (which Davis called a "Club fraction") to discuss the formation of an artists' congress. [14] Trachtenberg wanted an organization that would include artists whom the John Reed clubs had failed to recruit. He said that the Writers' Congress demonstrated the possibility of organizing politically unaffiliated creative writers of proven reputation who could be brought "closer to the party and saved from irresponsible and obstructing acts." A committee of twelve club members was then appointed to consider forming such a congress. Several discussions were subsequently held and Stuart Davis accepted the position of executive secretary. Two courses of action were initiated simultaneously, the first to establish the nature and structure of an artists' congress and the second to seek artists outside of the John Reed clubs for membership.

The first organizational meeting, with twenty artists present, took place at the studio of Eitaro Ishigaki under Trachtenberg's guidance on May 18, 1935.[15] Trachtenberg was also present at the second meeting on June 10, when artists George Ault, Stuart Davis, Hugo Gellert, and Louis Lozowick, and critic Jerome Klein were asked to prepare a draft of the Call of the American Artists' Congress. Soon after, a draft prepared by Lozowick for this committee was accepted with some revisions. However, at the next meeting of the larger group, on June 24, Lozowick's draft was rejected for being "discursive and lacking the qualities of a manifesto." Another committee was formed, this time with Stuart Davis, Aaron Douglas, Hugo Gellert, Ben Shahn, William Siegel, and a person whose name appears as Schang (probably Saul Schary) to rewrite the call. This was done and found acceptable by early August. By this time fifty-six artists had become associated with the nascent congress.

While the structure of the congress was taking form at these meetings, the initial group of John Reed Club artists also began to reach out to the general artistic community. As early as May 31, an informal meeting was held at the home of Leon Kahn (who did not sign the call) on Ninth Street to discuss the congress.[16] Those present included George Ault, Herman Baron, Maurice Becker, Henry Billings, Arnold Blanch, Peter Blume, Nicolai Cikovsky, Hugo Gellert, Harry Gottlieb, Minna Harkavy, Eitaro Ishigaki, Jerome Klein, Louis Lozowick, Jan Matulka, Isamu

Noguchi, Saul Schary, William Siegel, Moses Soyer, Niles Spencer, and Harry Sternberg—a group that included Social Realists, Social Surrealists, Modernists, painters, sculptors, and art writers. Of this group, Gellert and Gottlieb had been very active in the Artists' Union and its newspaper, *Art Front*.

Through the summer, the planning committee met every Friday evening at the ACA Galleries. According to Herman Baron, Davis, Gellert, and Baron became "the regulars," but Baron also referred to Klein, Gottlieb, Blanch, Henry Glintenkamp, and Lynd Ward as dedicated workers. Among their first problems was membership. They decided that the congress, unlike the Artists' Union, should be limited to "artists of standing," which meant that an artist had to have an "important exhibition, an award or other professional achievement which gave him 'standing' in the opinion of the majority of the members present [when a vote was taken]." In November 1935, when the call for the first meeting was printed as part of a fund-raising exhibition, the congress had 114 members.[17] At its first meeting membership had climbed to 401; it surpassed 900 in 1939.

Members were recruited in a variety of ways. John Reed Club artists would have heard about the new organization through word of mouth. The congress was anxious to attract artists who had won prizes, for they added prestige to its roster. Often congress publications noted members' achievements. For example, in a brief note about the first congress meeting, a press release mentioned Peter Blume, who had won first prize at the Carnegie International Exhibition in 1934; Alexander Brook, who had won a prize in landscape painting at the National Academy of Design in 1935; and Ivan Le Loraine Albright, president of the Chicago Society of Painters and Sculptors.[18] Undoubtedly several artists were personally solicited to join the congress. Moses Soyer evidently asked Stuart Davis to invite modernist Max Weber to sign the call.[19]

We will probably never know the extent of Communist influence on the congress. Stuart Davis was assured that the Party would not interfere in congress activities, but it is possible that, as with the Artists' Union, a small, perhaps shifting, group of

Party members actually ran the daily affairs of the organization.[20] But toward the end of the life of the congress, Davis grew irritated with an active core group within the executive board that formed the de facto leadership of the organization. Besides Davis himself, these were (in 1940), Herman Baron, Arthur Emptage, Philip Evergood, Hugo Gellert, Harry Gottlieb, Zoltan Hecht, Marvin Jules, Jerome Klein, Louis Lozowick, Lincoln Rothschild, Alexander Stavenitz, and Lynd Ward. As Davis sarcastically observed,

> For reasons known to themselves, there has always seemed to be an enormous confraternity of opinion among the overwhelming majority of this little group of serious thinkers. Controversial issues seem to be amazingly simple of solution to many of these people. The breadth of their viewpoint knew no bounds. It was international in scope and included everything except the concrete problems and interests of a certain stratum of American artists, namely 'American artists of standing,' which supposedly has been the subject matter of the Congress's organization.[21]

Despite the emotional rhetoric that often characterized congress pronouncements and catalog statements (see List of Congress Exhibitions in New York City), its bylaws were written in moderate prose; the preamble was actually rather understated. It listed six reasons for the congress's formation:

1. to unite artists of all esthetic tendencies to enable them to attain their common cultural objectives;

2. to establish closer relationships between the artist and the people and extend the influence of art as a force of enlightenment;

3. to advocate and uphold permanent Governmental support for the advancement of American art;

4. to support other organized groups on issues of mutual interest in an effort to develop and maintain conditions favorable to art and human existence;

5. to oppose all reactionary attempts to curtail demo-

cratic rights and freedom of expression [in the United States]
and all tendencies that lead to Fascism;

     6. to oppose war and prevent the establishment of con-
ditions that are conducive to the destruction of culture and
detrimental to the progress of mankind.

The preamble provided the context in which the congress
operated. The congress fought to protect the artists' ability to survive financially as well as to maintain artistic freedom both in
America and abroad. Actually, it operated in three contexts: economic, artistic, and political. As Stuart Davis said, juggling these
contexts, "We are confronted with the high probability of a world
cataclysm, threatening creative workers with the enforced role of
instruments of barbarous destruction. Within this country, not
only is the great body of American artists harassed by economic
insecurity, but they have just cause for alarm in the rapidly increasing attacks upon the liberty of honest artistic expression." [22]

    When art magazines and political journals carried news about
the newly formed congress, their tone varied, depending on their
own political slant. The *New Masses*, an organ of the CPUSA,
argued that ideological realignments were taking place in the artistic community because of economic problems and that the
congress should "consolidate ranks into an ever wider front as an
unwavering bulwark against the destructive forces of war and fascism." *Art Front*, the newspaper of the Artists' Union, tried to
define complementary spheres of activity for the two groups. The
union would stick to economic issues, encouraging the congress
to "take the initiative in defense of civil liberties, for freedom of
expression in art, and against any manifestation of fascist tendencies. The congress must do everything possible to forestall war,
and should be in the vanguard of this movement." The more conservative *Art Digest*, on the other hand, adopted a wait-and-see
attitude toward the congress, but it did publish articles and letters
that attacked the notion of collective action for artists. [23]

    The first meeting of the congress opened on February 14,
1936, at Town Hall in New York City. Sessions continued on the

following two days at the New School for Social Research. Three hundred seventy-eight people had signed the call. Membership at the time of the meeting numbered 401 and came from 28 states. All but 41 members attended, along with artists from Mexico, Peru, and Germany.[24]

The papers presented at the congress illuminate a moment in the history of American culture. They are an undiluted product of the Communist Party's Popular Front strategy against war and fascism. As mentioned, this strategy was first articulated in the Soviet Union, but the eagerness with which it was implemented in the United States suggests that it touched a deep chord in members of the CPUSA. Judging from the response to this new tactic for fighting the spread of fascism, this approach must have appealed to many others as well. The Popular Front provided the American left with an opportunity to end its political isolation. By building an alliance among Communists, Socialists, independent leftists, and Democrats, artists could feel as if they were part of American society. The shared fascist enemy unified the left and helped Communists work with people whose politics they had previously scorned. Sectarian differences and political purism were, for the time being, overshadowed by the urgency of the cause and the necessity of unity.

For artists and writers of the left, the Popular Front strategy of cooperation with the mainstream of American culture meant a profound change. Previously, for a variety of reasons, serious American artists had chosen to stand apart from their society. The bohemian model for the artist, imported from Europe in the late nineteenth century, had isolated artists from the mainstream. This isolation was strengthened when, in the 1920s, American intellectuals and artists accepted an image of America as the land of Babbitt. However, in the late 1920s and early 1930s some radical artists became social critics. Artists such as Joe Jones and Harry Gottlieb observed the world around them and reported its injustices in their paintings, hoping to move people to action with their art. Yet at the first congress this role for the radical artist was downplayed. Meyer Schapiro argued in his paper, "The Social

Bases of Art," that artists and their work were defined by the society of which they were a part. Schapiro urged artists to cease standing in opposition to their society and instead to recognize their links to the world around them. From the sense of community that replaced self-conscious alienation, artists would find, in Schapiro's phrase, "the courage to change things." Furthermore, he suggested, artists might turn their art away from studio problems and "aesthetic moments," and toward more humane concerns.

An overarching Popular Front theme was the great necessity of presenting a united face to the world. Reading these papers one is struck by how carefully areas of possible disagreement among artists are avoided. Over and over again issues that might have caused discord were skirted or glossed over quickly. In fact, there was remarkably little specific talk about art. There were few, if any, discussions of what or how to paint, sculpt, or print. Although the underlying consensus was that art should have "social value," even this topic was not emphasized, evidently from a desire not to alienate the abstractionists or the academic artists.

An example of curtailing such discussion is seen in Aaron Douglas's paper, "The Negro in American Culture." In it he criticizes "socially conscious" artists for their manipulative use of American blacks as symbols. "It is when we come to revolutionary art," says Douglas, "that we find the Negro sincerely represented, but here the portrayal is too frequently automatic, perfunctory and arbitrary. He becomes a kind of proletarian prop, a symbol, vague and abstract." But, in the spirit of the congress, Douglas mutes the impact of his critique of revolutionary artists by praising them for "pointing a way and striking a vital blow at discrimination and segregation, the chief breeding ground of Fascism." As if to cement the solidarity of the artists present, Douglas reminds his audience of their common enemy, fascism.

Speakers were so anxious to minimize differences among artists that even the generally scorned Regionalist or American Scene painters were relatively safe from attack. These artists, whom some leftist publications such as *Art Front* had treated as crypto-fascists, received little attention at the congress. (The attacks in *Art Front* had been so vicious that both John Curry and Thomas Hart Benton defended themselves in the journal.[25]) There were, to be sure, several critical inferences such as Francis Robert White's assurances that "Iowa is not 100% Regionalist, publicity to the contrary not withstanding. A majority of the recognized artists of this state repudiate Regionalism with its theme of opposition between city and country." But despite this veiled suggestion of a shared hostility toward Regionalism, the papers of the congress were free of outright attack on any American artists or their work.

This was not the case for artists who openly served the fascist governments of Italy and Germany. In his opening speech Stuart Davis attacked F. T. Marinetti, quoting his infamous remark, "War is the only world hygiene." Marinetti and other Futurists who had embraced Mussolini were also attacked by Margaret Duroc, who accused them of naked opportunism by using their art to glorify Mussolini and improve their positions. Artists who capitulated to or served these governments were, Duroc argued, partners in the destruction of the cultural heritage of their nations. She demonstrated the way a seemingly apolitical activity such as archeology was put to ideological ends in Italy by promotion of the "slogan that Fascist Italy is a continuation of the ancient Roman Empire and the glorious Italian Renaissance." She further reported that the Italian government had commissioned artists to create a new history of Italy, remaking the past to serve the state.

An exiled artist from Nazi Germany reported to the congress that the Germans were remaking history as well. The author of this paper remained unidentified, perhaps out of fear of Nazi reprisals. His anonymity may have added to the drama of his message; the effect upon an audience composed of people who believed they might share his fate under similar circumstances must have been chilling. The author argued that as in Italy, the German government used art to further its policies. The Nazis encouraged "national themes" presented in a naturalistic manner, a "steel-blue and hard romanticism" as a Nazi art critic described it. The exile then detailed the methods by which the German fascists dealt with unacceptable art: book burning, censorship, and discrimination against artists of minority races, religions, or nationalities. Artists were sent "to prison, committed suicide, [or] died of hunger." The lucky ones went into exile. He also described the 1933 Nuremburg "Chamber of Horrors," a propaganda exhibition of art disapproved of by the Nazi government. Stories such as these were familiar to the artists at the congress, but they must have had great impact.

The congress was called to fight fascism at home and abroad. Each speaker in the opening session reminded the audience of the horrors of fascism, and most suggested, as did Stuart Davis, that "we are confronted with the high probability of a world cataclysm." [26] This overwhelming sense of imminent danger of "world catastrophe" must be recalled when reading these papers. The perception of emergency influenced all discussion at the congress, especially that dealing with repression or censorship. In fighting repressive censorship artists believed they were resisting the tide of fascism. The proceedings were littered with references to the dangers of censorship. Specific cases were recounted. They ranged from well-known episodes such as the destruction of Diego Rivera's Rockefeller Center mural (illustration 1), or rejection of Ben Shahn's murals for the prison on Riker's Island, New York City (illustration 2), and the covering up of Gilbert Wilson's murals in the Woodrow Wilson Junior High School in Terre Haute, Indiana (illustration 36) to lesser-known incidents such as an attack by the Los Angeles police on a John Reed Club exhibition. More subtle examples were discussed as well, such as the exclusion of works from gallery or museum exhibitions because of content or proposed revisions in government murals.

In significant contrast to the reports of repressive manipulation of the arts in Italy, Germany, and the United States came glowing reports on the state of the arts in the Soviet Union. Margaret Bourke-White described her experiences in Russia, emphasizing the artists' "freedom to experiment," their economic security, and their respected role in Soviet society. Louis Lozowick made similar observations. Mexican representatives to the congress reported on the generally healthy situation of the arts in their country and made suggestions as to how the Mexican system might be duplicated in the United States.

But if the Congress had been called to organize artists into an antifascist opposition, except by resisting censorship, how could the American artist fight fascism? This was a question to which congress participants turned again and again. Lewis Mumford suggested that artists were central to the opposition. "Dictatorships fear artists," he claimed, "because they fear free criticism. They rightly believe that if the forces represented by the artist are allowed to exercise their free will, they will disrupt the Fascist regime. The irrepressible impulse of Art may upset the whole Fascist program."

Whether or not artists could topple fascism by the "exercise of their free will," it was generally accepted that art could be used to influence the public. In deference to the overall quest for unity at the meeting, few specific suggestions were made as to the appropriate subject matter or plastic form for the artist. However, a major part of at least one session was devoted to the problem of the "artist and his audience." At this session Max Weber gave perhaps the most emotional speech at the congress. He argued that a "truly modern art is yet to come" because it requires the revolutionary transformation of the whole society. In the meantime he urged artists to "bring new light and hope to the masses." In one of the congress's few strong endorsements of a specific type of work, Weber counseled artists against abandoning the "innovative and contributive in modern art." He felt they should strive to make modern art "with greater appeal to a much vaster and more eager audience," avoiding work that interested only the "few esthetic art hair-splitters." Artists should do this, according to Weber, "because we are in a struggle between darkness and light. . . . Let us turn to the gladiatorial heroism, ambition and tempo of modern beneficent and yielding industry, science and technology, to scenes of joy and verve of happy toilers in their own made environments, to the new home-life, nursery and school, to the new comradeship and brotherhood hitherto unknown." Interestingly, the art Weber described, although realistic in form and based on scenes in daily life, was not typical of left-wing art of the period, which generally depicted scenes of back-breaking labor, poverty, disease, and ill treatment of racial minorities. Instead Weber called for art that "springs from, interlocks with, and serves the new humanity." He envisaged an art that inspired with ideas of new possibilities, rather than an art that aroused through anger and outrage. In this way Weber thought artists could play a role in facing the "great and impending danger" of fascism.

Other papers that dealt with this subject, mundane in comparison to Weber's, were more representative. For example, Gilbert Wilson's enthusiasm for the work of the Mexican muralists was shared by many artists in the 1930s. (The enthusiasm that George Biddle expressed in his influential letter to President Roosevelt on the Mexican muralists and their work was well-known.)[27] The idea that murals allowed a new relation between artist and audience was much discussed in the 1930s. Wilson saw the mural as an art form that could break down barriers between art and life: "a real, vital, meaningful expression, full of purpose and intention, having influence and relations to people's daily lives." For Wilson, "Fascism sinking its ugly roots more deeply into almost every part of the world" was a reality; so art must be turned to the "task of applying its powerful influence to the creating of an awareness in the mass mind—an emotional awareness—of the significance of the great forces of social and economic change that are current in today's tempo."

John Groth addressed the special circumstance of artists employed by magazines. Though he spoke of the necessity of constant compromise, he argued that "veiled, though none-the-less evident criticism of an inequitable social order" was possible. He urged artists "in the fight against War and Fascism" to work for the popular press because through "innuendo it is possible to reach a larger and an otherwise misdirected and misinformed audience." His message was clear: the artist should accept compromising circumstances when they provide good opportunities to influence the public.

Reaching a wide audience was also of interest to Harry Sternberg, who spoke on the graphic arts. The "progressive" artist must break with the elitist "cult of rare prints," Steinberg claimed. Artists should be producing prints "rapidly and inexpensively in large quantities [so they] can be widely distributed at low cost." In fact the American Artists' Congress actively distributed graphic arts, by sponsoring print exhibitions that were shown around the country.

Besides the artists' fight against war and fascism, another large issue received attention at the First Artists' Congress: the economic situation of the artist during the Depression. Though other groups were addressing the special economic concerns of artists, many participants felt the congress should do so as well. Most notable among the organizations taking up the problem of earning a living was the Artists' Union, an organization that represented artists working on government art projects. Although the group had branches in several cities, it was most active in New York. Another group actively addressing specific economic concerns of artists was the American Society of Painters and Gravers (ASPG). Both groups sent representatives and speakers to the congress. Katherine Schmidt of the ASPG proposed that a modest rental fee be paid artists whose work was exhibited at museums. Though Schmidt concisely argued her case and emphasized the small amount of the proposed fee, the idea caused an uproar in museum circles. It was hotly debated at meetings throughout the 1930s. Artists were encouraged by the ASPG, by the congress, and by the Artists' Union to boycott exhibitions where no fee was to be paid. A few museum administrators tried to comply with the request, but others adamantly opposed it. The idea eventually faded away.[28]

Other proposals for dealing with the economic plight of American artists were discussed at the congress. Harry Gottlieb, a member of the National Executive Committee of the congress reported on a project of the Artists' Union to establish a municipal art gallery for New York City. According to Gottlieb, the need for such a gallery was evident because dealers and museums, artists' usual sources of revenue, were inadequate during the Depression. To fill the gap, he urged the creation of municipal art centers to serve three purposes. The "centers would stimulate public interest in contemporary art," which in turn would generate sales for living artists. Gottlieb argued that in hard times private galleries and museums preferred to emphasize old masters and safe, uncontroversial artists. He also thought municipal art centers could serve social functions, providing artists with a place to meet one another and an agency through which they could associate with the public. He further suggested the centers could provide studio and exhibition space, as well as places for lectures and classes.

The plan for a municipal art gallery in New York had been first proposed in February 1934, by the Artists' Committee of Action (ACA), formed in response to the destruction of Diego Rivera's mural at Rockefeller Center. That same month, just weeks after the destruction of the mural, a large show organized by Holger Cahill opened at Rockefeller Center. Hailed by its organizers as the first municipal art exhibition, a group of artists protested the location of this show, arguing that artists were being used to give the "censors" at Rockefeller Center legitimacy as patrons of the arts. Out of this protest grew the ACA whose initial demand was for an exhibition space that it could control. At an ACA rally in the summer of 1934 an elaborate plan was presented to Mayor Fiorello La Guardia. He appointed a committee to make recommendations on the matter. The mayor's group announced in December 1935 that a temporary exhibition space had been found, and it distributed applications to artists for the inaugural show. But the applications excluded noncitizen artists such as Yasuo Kuniyoshi. Once again the artists protested. The administration of the gallery was pressured to remove that requirement. The gallery opened in December of 1935 without the exclusionary clause, just a few months before the meeting of the congress. At the time of the congress's first meeting, the Artists' Union (the ACA disbanded in early 1935) was still urging changes in the administration of the center. It wanted the center to be run by artists and wanted its services expanded to include a rental library of works of art, "a school and a discussion forum." Gottlieb, in his speech, called for "municipal art centers in every city in the United States."

Many speakers at the congress called for a more radical change in the structure of the art world: substantial government patronage of the arts. Though government projects had been initiated only a short time before the congress first met in 1936, the idea of government support for the arts had taken hold very quickly among artists. Government projects received praise for saving artists from financial catastrophe, for bringing art to a popular audience, and for relating art to the life of the community.

The papers contain several calls for the establishment of permanent government art projects. (The Artists' Union had made the same demand in the spring of 1935, even before the creation of the Works Progress Administration [WPA], Federal Project One in October.) Boris Gorelick reported from the Artists' Union to the congress that "the creation of these [art] projects recognized the major principle of our organization: The government assumed responsibility for the welfare of the artist." Widespread implementation of this kind of proposal would have meant a dramatic restructuring of the art world. Ready acceptance of the idea was bolstered by the rosy descriptions that the congress heard of artists' circumstances in countries where the government did support its artists. Louis Lozowick and Margaret Bourke-White wrote glowing reports of artists in the Soviet Union, who were "paid so well that artists, together with writers form the highest salaried class in the country." American artists were attracted to the fact that in the Soviet Union and Mexico artists held prominent positions. Lozowick may not have foreseen the implications when he illustrated the degree to which the Soviets appreciated their artists by his uncritical endorsement of artists as the "highest salaried class." Certainly the high salaries do not reflect a particularly egalitarian vision of the new society. In fact they prefigure precisely the criticism Yugoslavian Milovan Djilas was to offer of Communist society in his work, *The New Class*.

The reports from the Mexican delegation must also have encouraged American artists to hope for more government patronage, although one of the messages from the Mexican artists contained a proposal for a different method for funding art. Mexican artists at their own antifascist congress, the National Assembly of Artists, had abandoned the idea of government support of the arts. Like many on the left, they believed the key to resisting fascism lay in a strong trade union organization. The Mexican delegation urged artists to forge an alliance with the trade union movement in order to participate in the fight against fascism. They proposed that artists' organizations provide cultural services to trade unions: theater productions, books, lectures, mural decorations, and so on. These services would be paid for by the trade unions by means of a monthly assessment paid by each member. There is no evidence that this proposal was discussed by the congress. Francis Gorman, the only representative of a union that did not represent artists, sent a paper in which he urged artists to join their own unions and to support the formation of a labor party, an idea then current among some leftist trade unionists.

Despite the great enthusiasm for government patronage as an idea, congress participants had serious reservations about the way existing programs had been implemented in the United States. Boris Gorelick, the Artists' Union representative, recounted how his union had had to fight unfair selection processes, censorship, low wage scales, and cutbacks on various projects. Waylande Gregory, although recognizing the benefits of the WPA to sculptors, had several suggestions for changes in the organization of sculpture programs.

These criticisms notwithstanding, the members of the congress essentially accepted the New Deal's art programs. We might ask whether one can really be in fundamental opposition to the government to which one is appealing for permanent art projects. While several of the speakers at the congress demonstrated the uses to which a government (as in Italy and Germany) might put artists and their work, few mentioned the possibility their own government might make ideological use of the art it commissioned. In "Government in Art," the authors suggest, "It was in the blackest depths of the crisis that the government manifested this sudden interest in art. The administration was rousing despairing, demoralized millions to new hope with the prospect of regeneration and security through the New Deal. Unquestionably, it must have been felt in administration circles that artists could help fill out this promising picture." But they conclude, "Artists could find no objection to aiding the government's program, if given full right to express themselves, plastically and socially."

This is a naive, if not contradictory, position. That is, the artists indicated that they would allow the government to use their art to promote their programs as long as they could paint anything they liked, in whatever way they liked, however critical their message. Surely, if one recognized that the government might find art useful, then one could expect the government to attempt to influence the content of the art that it financed. But the disputes that might have arisen from such a contradiction between artists' desires for free expression and the government's political uses of official art were to a large extent circumvented by the nature of the Popular Front itself.

At the first meeting, the large attendance combined with the general agreement on goals so easily arrived at created a euphoric atmosphere. Both Stuart Davis and George Biddle, then president of the Mural Painters' Society, thought the congress to be the greatest event in American art since the Armory Show.[29] Other responses, no less positive, were generally communitarian. They emphasized the pleasure of realizing that artists were finally collectively confronting the realities of current economic and political life and that artistic independence might best be achieved through group effort. Several resolutions were passed, many of which are included in the final section of the papers. But there were others, including condemnation of the ban on the motion picture production of Sinclair Lewis's novel, *It Can't Happen Here*; condemnation of the police detention of left-wing New York City congressman Vito Marcantonio for participating with dissatisfied relief workers in a political demonstration; a request that more artists sit on the juries of government-sponsored art competitions; and a refusal to exhibit works at the Olympic Games in Berlin in 1936. Seven members of the congress refused to exhibit at the Venice Biennale because of the issue of fascism and because of the lack of a rental fee.[30]

To continue the work of the congress after the three-day meeting, an executive committee of fifty-seven members was formed with Stuart Davis as the national executive secretary. Max Weber was installed as chairperson.[31] In addition to the branch in New York City, others were established in Cleveland, St. Louis, New Orleans, and Los Angeles, and, though slightly later, Chicago. (In 1937, the national leadership separated from the New York City chapter for organizational reasons.) The various talks delivered at the meeting were collected and published in an edition of 3,000 which sold for fifty cents a copy.[32] Symposia and exhibitions were organized and presented (see List of Congress Exhibitions in New York City). Among the exhibitions, one of the most ambitious was the print show entitled "America—1936" which opened simultaneously in thirty cities. The works of one hundred printmakers were shown and published in the book *America Today: A Book of One Hundred Prints*. Annual exhibitions were also coordinated in several cities simultaneously. Throughout the history of the congress, the leadership kept up a steady drumbeat of reports and memoranda to its members.

The congress took an energetic role in public affairs. It championed the Artists' Union and lobbied strenuously for the passage of the Coffee-Pepper Bill that would have established a permanent federal arts program. Sponsored by Representative John Coffee (Democrat, Washington) and Senator Claude Pepper (Democrat, Florida), the bill was introduced in the House in August 1937, and in the Senate in January 1938, but it did not pass. In the spring of 1937 the congress tried to organize a campaign to change the terms of the donation of the Mellon Collections to the National Gallery of Art, according to which a self-perpetuating board of trustees would run the gallery. The congress also fought for the inclusion of contemporary art exhibits at the New York World's Fair, which opened in 1939.[33]

Ever alert to international events, in spring 1937 the congress helped form the American Artists and Writers Ambulance Corps under the Medical Bureau of the American Friends of Spanish Democracy. Earlier, in October 1936, it had organized an exhibition entitled "To Aid Democracy in Spain," raising over seven hundred dollars. The exhibition, held at the same time as the second congress meeting in December 1937, was called "In Defense of World Democracy: Dedicated to the Peoples of Spain and China." Late in 1937 the congress objected to the inclusion of German artists in the International Exhibition of Lithography and Wood Engraving at the Art Institute of Chicago, since those artists would have been acceptable to the Nazi leadership. A year later, the congress charged the Metropolitan Museum of Art with "helping to subsidize Nazi industry" through the sale of color reproductions made in Germany for Christmas cards. (The Metropolitan Museum's position was that the United States was still on friendly terms with Germany.)[34]

The congress did not neglect its own members, either. It organized campaigns, usually unsuccessful, to protect artists, particularly muralists, from overzealous administrators and boards of trustees that wanted to remove, change, or tamper with mural paintings. These included supporting Leo Katz, whose mural in the Frank Wiggins Trade School, Los Angeles, was removed in the summer of 1935 and Rockwell Kent from whose mural in the Post Office Building, Washington, D.C., the following words, written in Eskimo, were removed late in 1937: "To the people of Puerto Rico, our friends. Go ahead, let us change chiefs. That alone can make us equal and free."[35]

Within months of the first meeting in February 1936, the congress became, in effect, the most vocal defender of artists throughout the country, as well as a noisy voice, though lacking in power, in left-wing political affairs. By the time the second annual meeting took place on December 17 and 18, 1937, it was acknowledged as a major artistic organization involved in both exhibitions and public affairs, the result of long hours spent by various committee members in meetings, drafting letters, formulating petitions, writing memos, and lobbying in New York City and Washington, D.C. The second meeting, not as ambitious as the first, also addressed a variety of topics of concern to artists. The list of speakers and their subjects included: for the meeting on December 17, Pablo Picasso, "The Defense of Culture in Spain"; Mayor Fiorello H. La Guardia, "New York as a Cultural Center"; Max Weber, "Reasons for an Artists' Congress"; George Biddle, "The Artist Must Organize: A Realistic Approach"; Erika Mann, "A Message from Thomas Mann"; Representative John Coffee, "The Federal Arts Bill"; and Martha Graham, "The Dance, an Allied Art"; and for the meeting on December 18, Jerome Klein, "The Artist in the World Today"; Lynd Ward, "Government Support of Art and the Fight against Fascism"; Harry Gottlieb, "The Profit System and Art"; Ned Hilton, "The Cartoon in the Fight against War and Fascism"; Holger Cahill, "Cultural Aspects of Government Support of Art"; Philip Evergood, "The Federal Arts Bill"; Doris Krans, "Public Uses of Art"; Gwendolyn Bennett, "The Negro Artist"; Paul Burlin, "Rental and Museum Policy"; Arthur Emptage, "Copyrights and Royalties"; Hugo Gellert, "The World's Fair"; and Ralph Pearson, "The World's Fair." Unlike the papers presented at the first meeting, these papers were not published.

Unfortunately for congress members, because of illness Picasso's message was relayed from Switzerland by an assistant; and neither Mayor La Guardia nor Representative Coffee appeared. Still, the fact that support from Picasso as well as public officials was sought and gained attests to the aggressiveness of the congress leadership and to the acceptance of its Popular Front activities. The talks, if their titles are accurate indicators, covered much of the same ground as those of the previous year, but the resolutions were even more wide ranging. In international affairs, the congress condemned German and Italian intervention in Republican Spain, as well as Japan's attack on China. It asked for an economic boycott of Japanese goods and sought in broad terms a greater collective effort against fascist intervention. In domestic affairs, it called for an end to discrimination against minorities and condemned the curbing of freedom in specific localities (Jersey City, New Jersey, and Quebec). It attacked any limitation on picketing. It supported an antilynching law and the freeing of radical labor leader Tom Mooney from prison. (He was released in 1939.) For artists, the congress favored, once again, the passage of the Federal Arts Bill and called on artists to join the trade union movement. (Philip Evergood announced in his talk that the Artists' Union had joined the Congress of Industrial Organizations (CIO) as the United American Artists.) The congress also urged the officials of the New York World's Fair to exhibit works by contemporary artists when the fair opened in 1939. Finally, it criticized museum administrators for indifference and paternalism to living artists, charging that museums preferred familiar styles by dead artists to work by contemporary artists. To carry out policies for the coming year, Max Weber, the former chairperson, became honorary chair; Stuart Davis became chair; and Arthur Emptage replaced Davis as executive secretary.[36]

Following its resolutions on international affairs, in the spring of 1938 the congress called for the lifting of the embargo on shipping war supplies to Republican Spain. It wanted the Neutrality Act revised so that countries such as Spain, a victim of fascist aggression, could have access to American markets. The congress sought an embargo on war supplies and raw materials to aggressor nations (Germany, Italy, and Japan). And it asked for a people's boycott of trade with aggressor nations. On the domestic front, the congress continued its organizing activities by establishing with the United American Artists a group called the Young American Artists in the spring of 1938.[37]

Through the remainder of 1938 and 1939, the congress continued its lobbying, organizing, and exhibition activities. It played an instrumental role in bringing Picasso's *Guernica* to New York City where it was exhibited at the Valentine Gallery in May 1939 (coinciding with the third annual meeting), and in raising funds for the relief of Spanish War refugees. The principal theme of this third meeting was to organize a loosely knit fraternal body of the progressive artists of the world, including the Chinese Artists' National Federation and the Artists' International Association in London.[38]

But at the same time, the congress had become increasingly subject to charges from the right of Communist control. The editor of the *Art Digest*, Peyton Boswell, Jr., a supporter of Regionalist art, had, at the inception of the congress in 1935, published articles and letters to the editors attacking the notion of group action by artists. By 1938, he had begun to raise the specter of Communist control. For instance, in a reprint of an article written by Arthur Millier for the *Los Angeles Times*, the concluding sentence stated: "Artists of sense ought to wake up and realize that the American Artists' Congress is a potential tool of the Communist Party." And in a subsequent issue, Boswell published a letter from an artist named Raymond O'Neill, an "early defector" from the congress who had wanted to read a paper at the first meeting in 1936 and offer a resolution attacking not only fascism but also Communism, "the other totalitarian twin," but was prevented from doing so.[39]

Of course, the congress was open to such attacks, and in several of its reports it referred to political red-baiting, but its handling of the matter did not help its reputation. For instance, in the winter issue for 1937 of the *American Artist*, the news bulletin of the congress, an elaborate, but evasive, answer was given to a hypothetical midwestern artist who wanted to know if Communism would be destroyed once fascism was eliminated. The answer included the following points: that the congress was not a political organization; that members held wide ranging political views; that the congress was concerned with the immediate problems of artists as well as "with the conditions in the world about us that made for the growth of art or that hinder it." The congress, according to the answer, wanted freedom and a government art program and was in favor of "forthright opposition to the forces of reaction here in America." In other countries, these forces had "crystallized into a political and economic system known as Fascism." The next several sentences were devoted to attacks on Germany, Italy, and Japan. Finally, the issue of Communism was confronted, only to be deflected. "As far as 'Communism' is concerned, it is equally plain that the phrase is invariably a bugaboo raised by opponents of progress to confuse believers in democracy such as yourself about the real situation." The answer then ended on a sarcastic note by stating that Roosevelt, the Tennessee Valley Authority, and the CIO, and other individuals and institutions had been labeled Communist so often that the word had become meaningless. The midwestern artist never received an answer to his question but was told instead that the congress represented his interests and was fighting for decency, liberty, and freedom. He might have been better served by the kind of straightforward argument offered by many non-Communists, such as poet Archibald MacLeish, who said he was willing to work with Communists in the struggle against fascism.[40]

In the end, attacks from the non-Stalinist left were more damaging than from any other quarter and ultimately led to the disintegration and final dissolution of the congress in 1942. Confidence in the Communist Party was undermined by events that challenged the beliefs of all but the most faithful supporters of the Soviet Union. First, between August 1936 and March 1938, Stalin purged the Communist hierarchy; second, modernist influences were officially banned from Russian art in 1938;[41] third, Hitler and Stalin agreed to a nonaggression pact on August 23, 1939; fourth, the Russians fought the Finns from December 1939 to March 1940.

The Moscow Trials clearly challenged the assumptions, or, at least, the hopes of those who thought the Soviet government was minimally democratic. Still, many in the congress were reluctant to argue openly with the Stalinist position that Trotsky and others were shameless traitors. After all, no other country seemed to be opposing fascism so vigorously. In response to the two volumes produced by John Dewey's commission to study the fairness of the trials—*The Case of Leon Trotsky* (1937) and *Not Guilty, Report of the Commission of Inquiry* (1938)—a round-robin letter defending Soviet tactics, initiated by Stuart Davis and Paul Strand, among others, was published in the *New Masses* on May 3, 1938. Signers included Arnold Blanch, Stuart Davis, Philip Evergood, Hugo Gellert, Harry Gottlieb, William Gropper, Joe Jones, Louis Lozowick, Raphael Soyer, Paul Strand, Nahum Tschabasov, and Max Weber. A year later, however, a letter published in the *Daily Worker* on August 14, 1939, denying that Russia and totalitarian states were alike, was signed by many of the same figures, but not by Stuart Davis.[42]

By that date, Davis, and others, had grown less accommodating to Communist tactics. Davis, especially, was incensed by the block-voting habits of congress board members.[43] Furthermore, Davis and the artistic community in general would also have become aware of the American Committee for the Defense of Leon Trotsky, formed in 1936, which, renamed the Committee for Cultural Freedom and Socialism, became a focal point for left-wing opposition to Stalinist control of the Communist Party. Whatever the private conversations among artists concerning the true nature of Stalinist Russia, the discussions became public when in the summer 1939 issue of *Partisan Review*, the league published a strong statement condemning intellectuals who no longer protested repression in the United States or in Russia and attacking the "spurious anti-fascist unity" of front groups. "Pretending to represent progressive opinion," the league stated, "these bodies are in effect but apologists for the Kremlin dictatorship. They outlaw all dissenting opinion on the left."[44] Signers of the league's statement included critics Clement Greenberg and Harold Rosenberg, along with art historian Meyer Schapiro and Fairfield Porter, both of whom had signed the original call of the congress in 1936.

In August 1939, shortly after the statement was published in *Partisan Review* and barely a week after the letter denying similarities between fascist states and the Soviet Union appeared in the *Daily Worker*, Hitler and Stalin agreed to a nonaggression pact. The League for Cultural Freedom responded to this shattering event by addressing a letter to the League of American Writers, the official organ of the American Writers' Congress in the next issue of *Partisan Review*. The letter pointedly addressed the issue of the Hitler-Stalin agreement and asked how the League of American Writers, which once wanted to fight fascism, could now support the agreement and, particularly one of its clauses, the partition of Poland between Germany and the Soviet Union.[45] The letter implied that the writers' group was following the Stalinist position.

The letter did not mention the fact that since Germany and the Soviet Union had become allies, responsibility for the outbreak of war now belonged to England and France. This issue seems to have been raised at Artists' Congress meetings because the leadership was subsequently accused of "implicitly [defending] Hitler's position by assigning the responsibility of the war to England and France." Furthermore, it seemed strange that an organization proclaiming both its own independence and its willingness to fight for artistic independence everywhere should revise its boycott policy of German and Italian exhibitions, on the basis that participation was a matter of personal taste. Finally, the congress leadership was questioned on its lack of response to a German-Russian meeting of art officials and official artists concerning exchange exhibitions.[46]

Stuart Davis, still national chairperson, tried to diffuse the situation late in 1939 by asking the congress to concern itself exclusively with cultural affairs. A compromise was arranged, but the flash point was reached over congress policies toward Finland in the Russo-Finnish War of 1939–1940. Evidently, the congress refused to respond to a request for funds from the Hoover Committee for Finnish Relief. Pressure was exerted by a group within the congress led by Meyer Schapiro, who in a letter dated February 24, 1940, to executive board member Ralph Pearson, asked if the congress were following the Stalinist line and requested an open discussion of congress policies.[47] Davis tried to deflect the confrontation by calling for a further study of the issues. The executive committee, at its meeting on March 14, 1940, refused to discuss the Finnish matter for two reasons: following Davis's lead, it decided to consider only cultural matters, and the short war with the Soviet Union had been concluded.

Further discussion was set for the membership meeting on April 4, at which time Lynd Ward was to give a personal account of the Finnish matter. At that meeting, he said that the congress should remain neutral, but he approved of the German-Soviet pact and the invasion of Finland. He also argued for maintaining American neutrality in the coming war, a position also held by the League for Cultural Freedom to which Schapiro belonged. But the mutually held position of the congress and the League on neutrality did not mitigate the attitudinal difference concerning Stalinist control of the congress. The vote to approve Ward's assessment passed by a vote of 125 to 12. Schapiro claimed the meeting had been packed. The next day, April 5, Stuart Davis resigned. About thirty members followed suit within the next two weeks, prompted in part by the circulation of the Minority Report accusing Ward and the congress of following the Stalinist line. The report proposed either the reorganization of the congress to remove the Stalinist leadership, which it considered to be a minority faction, or the resignation of all those opposed to present congress policies.[48] By June 1940, the dissidents had formed a counterorganization, the Federation of Modern Painters and Sculptors, to promote "the welfare of free progressive artists working in America."[49]

At this point, the congress stopped functioning as a significant force in the art world. But despite defections, it still existed. Henry Glintenkamp became national chairperson and called for a meeting to take place on June 6–8, 1941, at the Hotel Commodore in New York City. This meeting was sponsored by the congress and by the United American Artists. To the extent possible, its call avoided the political situation abroad by concentrating on the presumed fascist threat in America and on the economic plight of artists. The signers of the call, who were many fewer than those who signed the original call in 1936, included Peter Blume, Philip Evergood, Robert Cronbach, Adolph Dehn, William Gropper, Helen West Heller, Georges Schreiber, Charles Sheeler, Raphael Soyer, William Steig, Lynd Ward, and Art Young.

CALL FOR A CONGRESS
OF AMERICAN ARTISTS 1941

In this grave hour, mindful of our responsibility to the art of our time and conscious of the dangers that increasingly threaten both our heritage of freedom and our growing democratic culture, we issue this Call to a Congress of American Artists.

Five years ago we met in the First American Artists' Congress. We proclaimed there our passionate opposition to Fascism, both at home and abroad. We saw in Fascism not only the destruction of culture in those countries in which it had come to power, but the ominous promise of war involving the whole world.

Through our work as artists as well as through the organizational programs of the United American Artists and the American Artists' Congress, we sought to make people aware of the nature of the Fascist threat, in terms of America as well as the then more remote parts of the world. We warned of the consequences of "nonintervention" in Spain, of continued economic support of aggressors there and in China, and of the glittering promise of Munich.

We urged upon all artists the necessity of concerted action for peace in the world, and of common action for those conditions in America in which artists can live and work. We saw the promise of democratic culture in the renaissance of popular art: the awakened interest in new technical forms and the growth of wider and more vital audiences for painting, sculpture and graphic arts. We called for the extension of government support for art, for freedom from censorship of the artist's concept or suppression of the finished work. At a time when the world stood aghast at the Fascist burning of books abroad, we opposed the destruction of art here in America as well. We pointed out parallels between repressive actions at home and the rise of Fascist forces abroad noting similar assaults on living standards and civil liberties, on labor organizations and political minorities.

Today, the Fascist threat has come full circle. In a traditionally free and liberty loving America, Fascism comes in the name of Anti-Fascism. All the enemies of progress suddenly become defenders of democracy. Our liberties are destroyed to defend liberty and the policies to which our people are committed by their government, in the name of peace, border ever closer on overt war.

Artists are always among the first to feel the impact of crisis. Our lives and our work are at stake as never before. With the steady decline of the private market and a simultaneous choking off of the government's art program, the economic problem of the artist becomes increasingly acute. Artists find ever fewer opportunities for the exercise of their profession and the promise of yesterday is negated in the spreading cultural blackout of today.

We believe that the defense of America begins not with steps towards war and dictatorship but with the defense of our basic liberties, standards of living and cultural opportunities. Because we know that our work as free artists is indissolubly linked with continuing peace and the dominance in American life of democratic principles, we call our fellow artists to this Congress to consider the following questions:

1. What can artists do to oppose the high-pressure drive towards war and the increasing use of Fascist solutions for the problems facing the American people [?]

2. What can be done to expand and make permanent the government art program, stimulate the private market

and provide more opportunities for artists to work at their profession [?]

3. How can we aid the development of a genuine cultural interchange between the peoples of the Americas [?]

4. How can we preserve the widespread community interest of the past decade and further develop the new audiences that have played so important a role in the renaissance of American culture [?] [50]

One of the resolutions passed by this congress in 1941 condemned the European war as a "brutal shameless struggle." Just two weeks after the congress met, on June 22, 1941, Germany invaded the Soviet Union. Almost at once the congress reversed its position and called for American aid to those fighting fascism, as it had done before the Hitler-Stalin agreement of 1939. [51]

The congress continued to function through 1941 and the beginning of 1942, but primarily in conjunction with other organizations. On December 17, 1941, soon after the United States entered the war, the congress participated in a mass meeting called by the Artists' Societies for National Defense, which established, on January 19, 1942, the Artists' Council for Victory, an umbrella organization of twenty-three artists' societies. But the days of the congress were numbered. In a letter to congress members, dated April 11, 1942, the executive board recommended merging forces with the United American Artists to form the Artists' League of America. [52]

Yet another call was issued by this group "to set up a new organizational structure committed to the destruction of Fascism abroad, to the defeat of the friends of Fascism at home, to the safeguarding of our cultural heritage, to the maintenance of our cultural values in the present struggles, and to the development of the strongest possible relationship between the artist and society in the world of the future." [53] And so, the fight against fascism and for economic security continued into the 1940s, though the congress lacked influence and had little hope of being effective. In truth, the demise of the congress had occurred in April of

1940 at the time of the first mass resignations. It was an offshoot of the Popular Front; as that strategy failed, the Artists' Congress failed with it.

For all of its rhetoric about foreign and domestic affairs, the congress had little to say about art because proclaiming a strong preference for socially realistic or proletarian art might have excluded the politically uncommitted and those favoring abstract styles. Artists associated with the congress articulated a less class-based concern for subject matter in contrast to the insistent demand for developing proletarian themes associated with the artists of the John Reed clubs. Perhaps the stated intentions of the John Reed Club school of art and the subsequent American Artists' School (the faculty of which included many congress members) most clearly symbolizes this difference. The guiding philosophy of the former held that the interests of all artists were in harmony with those of the working class. It claimed to be "perhaps the only [school] in the country that endeavors specifically to prepare the art student to express in his work the political and social conflicts of the day," and to advance the interests of the working class.[54] By contrast, the American Artists' School was premised on the belief "that artists who can clearly see the complicated structure of America and pick out its basic social pattern, who are sympathetic to its people and its culture and traditions, who are interested in the psychology of its classes and groups have the basis for saying something about America."[55] Compared to any statements issued by the John Reed clubs, intentions are more guarded in this statement, which is calculated not to frighten anybody. To be sure, the school offered a class called "Composition through Social Research" which explored social and historical forces of present-day American as the primary subject for study, but in a decade when realistic art was quite popular, this course might have seemed entirely reasonable.

The Communist Party leader Earl Browder showed how even the Communist Party willingly tolerated nonproletarian art in the cause of unity against fascism. In a speech before the Second American Writers' Congress on June 4, 1937, he made a statement that was applicable to visual artists as well as to writers. Although he said that "writers cannot contribute anything to literature . . . except in service of the people against reaction, fascism and war," he argued that the Party was not interested in turning writers into union organizers or regimenting them in any way. Some writers, he felt, would find their best material through participation in social struggle, but all would have to find such material in their own way. The artist chose his or her own content but was responsible for work that served "the common cause." He said that he wanted no privileges for Party writers but rather sought cooperation and openness.[56] The key phrase, "the common cause," could be interpreted to mean anything so long as it did not reflect a fascist position.

One of the slogans of the Popular Front, "Communism is Twentieth-Century Americanism," also served to diffuse and inhibit a politically radical content in art, since it helped open up the more progressive aspect of the American past to artists in search of a usable heritage. Although figures such as Thomas Hart Benton and Grant Wood, along with the xenophobic critic, Thomas Craven, were still castigated by left-wing artists, the American scene was being reclaimed from their chauvinistic clutches. (As late as February 1940, "the absurd theories of Craven and his reactionary followers [were] analyzed and properly classified" at a Congress symposium.)[57] No less a figure than Max Weber, certainly one of the most experienced and educated artists in the congress, invoked the style and tone of Walt Whitman's *Democratic Vistas* (1871) in a speech reminiscent of the interests of such artists and writers as Benton, Charles Sheeler, and William Carlos Williams who in the early 1920s were discovering source material in the American environment.[58]

World culture and art are in a very critical condition, and it seems to me that this era calls for a new aggressive and independent art which should serve as a dominant educational force, an art that will cope and interlock with the rapidly changing philosophy of life, and art that will extricate itself slowly from intellectual squander, abuse, and economic and academic servility. An art for all,—for men and women who toil and create real wonder and wealth of modern times, and live and hope by the sweat of their brow. Their dreams, their environment, their happiness should be our human concern and artistic inspiration. Conscious searching of the sub-conscious were affectation and pretense, and inevitably leads to impasse and error. What we need today is an American art that will express the Whitmanesque spirit and conception of democracy, an art as heroic and prophetic as the undying *Leaves of Grass* in literature and philosophy of the new world.[59]

Weber's own style in the middle 1930s might most accurately be termed figurative expressionism. His subjects included workers and religious figures. He influenced other artists, but neither his work nor that of any other artist can be said to be central to an Artists' Congress style. In fact, there was no style. From the first exhibition to the last, works in virtually all styles, from academic to abstract, were shown, and subjects ranged from the politically militant to the traditional, from strikers to innocuous still lifes. The first competitive annual exhibition in June 1936, included a Precisionist painting by Ralston Crawford, and the first national membership annual exhibition contained academic works by Paul Manship and Leon Kroll, Regionalist paintings by Doris Lee and Paul Cadmus, and satirical works by Peggy Bacon. These early exhibitions set the general tone for subsequent shows—unless an exhibition was built around a particular theme. Generally, however, the earlier shows contained more political works concerned with economic and social conditions, but as the tenets of the Popular Front displaced those of the proletarian movement, such themes either disappeared or were turned into more generalized images. Scenes of broad humanitarian concern replaced those with specific political messages. For instance, coal-mining scenes, very popular in 1936 and 1937, changed from studies of the hardships of men and women in coal-mining towns to coal-mining landscapes or works in which design and composition were more important than the subject matter. Overall, artists created their most politically trenchant work in prints. In these the rhetoric of political militancy was most effectively translated into visual images.

By 1939 and 1940, critics began to complain about the decline in quality of congress exhibitions, especially the annuals, suggesting that major figures sent lesser pieces to these shows. The annuals had, by that time, turned into catchall exhibitions with little control exerted by the exhibition committees. Without the strong political guidance of the John Reed clubs and with major figures exhibiting their minor work, the congress could not provide guidance of any sort. George L. K. Morris, a nonobjective painter, observed, in a review of a congress show in 1939, that despite the surprising technical freedom of many artists, the special character of the exhibition stemmed from the "social satires" that "demonstrate the unavoidable effect of violent subject-matter upon artists who have never become grounded in an authentic tradition of their own. The very language of painting by which literary ideas can be made plastically credible, has been laid aside."[60] In other words, since no indigenous politically radical art tradition had existed in the United States, the congress could not create one, especially since its own official points of view were controlled by forces exterior to itself. In effect the congress told artists to believe as it believed, but paint as they wished. It is therefore reasonable to conclude that the congress, in the cause of unity against fascism, contributed to the eclipse of Social Realism in painting in the late 1930s, making radical political art a victim of a left-wing artists' group. Ironically, for an artists' congress, its words, not its images, are of interest today.

Notes

1. Article with statements by several artists entitled "Viva España Libre!" *New Masses* 20 (August 18, 1936):12.

2. *New Masses* 5 (December 1929):20, and 10 (January 2, 1934): 27; *Creative Arts* 12 (March 1933): 216; *Art Digest* 8 (January 1, 1934): 14, and 9 (October 1, 1934): 26; *Art Front* 1 (January 1935):3.

3. Irving Howe and Lewis Coser, *The American Communist Party: A Critical History (1919–1957)* (Boston: Beacon Press, 1957), p. 312.

4. Orrick Johns, "The John Reed Clubs Meet," *New Masses* 13 (October 30, 1934):26. See also Walter Rideout, *The Radical Novel in the United States* (Cambridge, Mass.: Harvard University Press, 1956; reprint ed., New York: Hill and Wang, 1966), pp. 147–148; Daniel Aaron, *Writers on the Left* (New York: Harcourt, Brace and World, 1961; reprint ed., New York: Avon, 1965), pp. 298–299; Howe and Coser, *The American Communist Party*, p. 312.

5. See n. 4 and Lawrence H. Schwartz, *Marxism and Culture: The CPUSA and Aesthetics in the 1930s* (Port Washington, N.Y.: Kennikat Press, 1980), p. 61; *New Masses* 14 (January 22, 1935):20.

6. "On the Main Immediate Tasks of the CPUSA: Resolution of the Central Committee Plenum, January 15–18, 1935," *Communist* 14 (February 1935):126. See also Aaron, *Writers*, p. 172; Daniel Bell, *Marxian Socialism in the United States* (Princeton: Princeton University Press, 1952; reprint ed., 1973), p. 147.

7. Alex Bettleman, "Report to the National Agitation and Propaganda Conference, January 18, 1935," *Communist* 14 (March 1935):240.

8. William Z. Foster, "The Communist Party and the Professionals," *Communist* 17 (September 1938):806. See also Schwartz, *Marxism and Culture*, pp. 55–56.

9. Bell, *Marxian Socialism*, p. 147.

10. "The Offensive of Fascism and the Tasks of the Communist International in the Fight for the Unity of the Working Class against Fascism (Resolution on Georgi Dimitroff's report adopted at Seventh Congress of the Communist International, August 20, 1935," *Communist* 14 (October 1935):929. See also Georgi Dimitroff, *The United Front: The Struggle against Fascism and War* (New York: International Publishers, 1938), pp. 9–93.

11. Orrick Johns, "The John Reed Clubs Meet," *New Masses* 13 (October 30, 1934):26.

12. *New York Times*, 26 January 1936, sec. 9, p. 10; *Art Front* 2 (February 1936):11; Helen A. Harrison, "John Reed Club Artists and the New Deal. Radical Responses to Roosevelt's Peaceful Revolution," *Prospects* 5 (1980):249.

13. ACA Galleries Papers, Archives of American Art, microfilm roll D 304, frames 639 to 663. References to the Archives of American Art will be abbreviated as AAA and followed by roll and frame designations. After this introduction was completed, Earl Davis donated his documents to the AAA.

14. From penciled notes in Stuart Davis's handwriting, in Davis's Collection, donated to the AAA.

15. From a typed report in the Davis Collection.

16. Copy of a letter from Stuart Davis to Mabel Dwight, May 23, 1935, in the Davis Collection. See also Baron Papers, AAA, roll D-304, frame 639.

17. The call was printed in the *New Masses* 17 (October 1, 1935): 33.

18. *Art News* 34 (October 12, 1935):12.

19. Max Weber Papers, AAA, roll N69–86, frame 199, letters from Stuart Davis to Max Weber, August 29, 1935, and January 4, 1936.

20. Gerald M. Monroe, "The Artists' Union of New York" (Ed.D. diss., New York University, 1971), pp. 135–136.

21. Copy of a letter from Stuart Davis to Edward Bieberman, April 24, 1940, in the Davis Collection.

22. *Art Digest* 10 (October 1, 1935):7.

23. *New Masses* 17 (October 1, 1935):33; *Art Front* (February 1936):5; *Art Digest* 10 (November 15, 1935):19.

24. *Art Digest* 10 (March 15, 1936):25.

25. *Art Front* 1 (April 1935):1–2; *Art Digest* 9 (March 15, 1935): 20, and 9 (September 1, 1935):29. Much of this material is reproduced in David Shapiro, ed., *Social Realism: Art as a Weapon* (New York: Frederick Ungar, 1973), pp. 95–107.

26. *Art Digest* 10 (October 1, 1935):7.

27. George Biddle, *An American Artist's Story* (Boston: Little, Brown, 1939), p. 268.

28. *New Republic* 85 (December 4, 1935):104, and 86 (February 26, 1936):62; *New Masses* 18 (February 18, 1936):19–20; *New York Times* February 14, 1936, p. 17.

29. *Art Digest* 10 (March 15, 1936):25; Biddle, *An American Artist's Story*, p. 293.

30. *New York Times*, March 1, 1936, sec. 9, p. 10, February 15, 1936, p. 13, and April 23, 1936, p. 25; *Parnassus* 8 (March 1936):31; *American Magazine of Art* 29 (March 1936):193.

31. Lynd Ward Papers, AAA, roll 141, frames 1176–81, "Report to Membership," November 1, 1936.

32. *New York Times* May 31, 1936, sec. 10, p. 7.

33. Max Weber Papers, AAA, roll 69–86, frames 262–63, Letter from Stuart Davis to National Executive Committee, March 3, 1937; *American Artist* [news bulletin of the American Artists' Congress] 1 (Spring 1937):1–4; *New York Times*, March 21, 1937, sec. 11, p. 9, Letter to the Editor from the heads of the American Society of Painters, Sculptors, and Gravers, An American Group, the Artists' Union, and the American Artists' Congress.

34. Max Weber Papers, AAA, roll 69–86, frame 246, "Report to Membership," November 1, 1936, and frame 263, letter from Arthur Emptage to Max Weber, January 5, 1939; *American Artist* 1 (Spring 1937):1, and 1 (Winter 1937):3; *New York Times*, December 22, 1938, p. 10.

35. *American Artist* 1 (Spring 1937):2; *New York Times*, November 3, 1937, preserved in Harry Gottlieb Papers, AAA, roll 343, frame 69, on a mimeographed sheet from the American Artists' Congress concerning censorship, c. November 10, 1937.

36. Weber Papers, AAA, roll 69–86, frame 303, letter from Lynd Ward to members, December 23, 1937; *Magazine of Art* 30 (December 1937):747; *New Republic* 93 (December 29, 1937):212; *New York Times*, December 18, 1937, p. 22, December 20, 1937, p. 25, and December 21, 1937, p. 27; *Twelve Twelve* [news bulletin of the Artists' Union of Philadelphia] 1 (December 1937):n.p.; a press release of the American Artists' Congress in Gerald Monroe Papers donated to the AAA (not microfilmed).

37. *American Artist* 2 (Spring 1938):8; Weber Papers, AAA, N 69–112, frames 343–45, "A Call to Young Artists and Art Students," March 30, 1938.

38. Weber Papers, AAA, roll 69–86, frames 365–67, "Report to Membership," January 1939.

39. *Art Digest* 12 (January 15, 1938):12–13, and 12 (February 1, 1938):8. See also *Art Digest* 13 (November 15, 1939):15.

40. Norman Holmes Pearson, "The Nazi-Soviet Pact and the End

of a Dream," in *America in Crisis*, ed. Daniel Aaron, (New York: Knopf, 1952), pp. 337–340.

41. *Art Digest* 13 (October 1, 1938):3.

42. *New Masses* 27 (May 3, 1938):19; Bell, *Marxian Socialism*, p. 151; Howe and Coser, *The American Communist Party*, p. 300; Donald Drew Egbert, *Socialism and American Art* (Princeton: Princeton University Press, 1967), p. 101.

43. Gerald M. Monroe, "The American Artists' Congress and the Invasion of Finland," *Archives of American Art Journal* 15, no. 1 (1975): 17.

44. "Statement of the League for Cultural Freedom and Socialism," *Partisan Review* 6 (Summer 1939):126.

45. "A Letter to the League of American Writers," *Partisan Review* 6 (Fall 1939):12–28.

46. *New York Times*, April 17, 1940, p. 25; *Art Digest* 14 (May 1, 1940):14.

47. Copy of letter from Meyer Schapiro to Ralph Pearson, February 24, 1940, in the Davis Collection.

48. Typescript of the Minority Report in the Davis Collection.

49. *Art Digest* 14 (June 1, 1940):8; Hermon Baron Papers, AAA, roll D-304, frames 659–61; Lynd Ward Papers, AAA, roll 141, frame 1282, *Artists' Congress News* (April 1940):2; *New York Times*, April 14, 1940, sec. 9, p. 9, April 15, 1940, p. 19, April 17, 1940, p. 25, and April 21, 1940, sec. 9, p. 9; *Art Digest* 14 (April 15, 1940):9, and 14 (May 1, 1940):14.

50. Weber Papers, AAA, roll N 69–86, frame 286, a typescript; *Art Digest* 15 (June 1, 1941):22.

51. Egbert, *Socialism and American Art*, p. 116n; account of the meeting of October 6, 1941, in the Monroe Papers, AAA.

52. *American Artists' Congress Bulletin* (March 1942):1, and letter to congress members, April 11, 1942, both in the Monroe Papers (see n. 36); Monroe, "The Artists' Union in New York," 241; Monroe, "The American Artists' Congress and the Invasion of Finland," 20.

53. Gottlieb Papers, AAA, roll 343, frame 22, *Joint Bulletin* [of the American Artists' Congress and United American Artists] (May 1942): 1–2.

54. *Art Front* 1 (January 1935):3; *Art Digest* 9 (October 1934):26.

55. Philip Evergood, "Building a New Art School," *Art Front* 3,

no. 3 (1937):21; *American Magazine of Art* 29 (November 1936):758.

56. Earl Browder, *The People's Front* (New York: International Publishers, 1938), pp. 276–281.

57. Cited in *Art Digest* 14 (February 1, 1940):13, from *Daily Worker*, January 23, 1940.

58. Matthew Baigell, "Recovering America for American Art: Thomas Hart Benton in the Early Twenties," in *Thomas Hart Benton: Chronicler of America's Folk Heritage* (Annandale-on-Hudson: Blum Art Institute of Bard College, 1984), pp. 13–31.

59. Weber Papers, AAA, roll 69–86, frame 321. An attached note states that this was from a speech read at Carnegie Hall on December 17, 1938. This is probably in error, since the second congress meeting took place on December 17, 1937.

60. George L. K. Morris, "Art Chronicle," *Partisan Review* 6 (Spring 1939):63.

2
FIRST AMERICAN
ARTISTS' CONGRESS

CALL FOR THE
AMERICAN ARTISTS' CONGRESS

THIS IS A CALL to all artists, of recognized standing in their profession, who are aware of the critical conditions existing in world culture in general, and in the field of the Arts in particular. This Call is to those artists, who, conscious of the need of action, realize the necessity of collective discussion and planning, with the objective of the preservation and development of our cultural heritage. It is for those artists who realize that the cultural crisis is but a reflection of a world economic crisis and not an isolated phenomenon.

The artists are among those most affected by the world economic crisis. Their income has dwindled dangerously close to zero.

Dealers, museums, and private patrons have long ceased to supply the meager support they once gave.

Government, State and Municipally sponsored Art Projects are giving only temporary employment—to a small fraction of the artists.

In addition to his economic plight, the artist must face a constant attack against his freedom of expression.

Rockefeller Center, the Museum of Modern Art, the Old Court House in St. Louis, the Coit Memorial Tower in San Francisco, the Abraham Lincoln High School, Riker's Island Penitentiary—in these and other important public and semi-public institutions, suppression, censorship or actual destruction of art works has occurred.

Oaths of allegiance of teachers, investigations of colleges for radicalism, sedition bills aimed at the suppression of civil liberties, discrimination against the foreign-born, against Negroes, the reactionary Libery League and similar organizations, Hearst journalism, etc., are daily reminders of fascist growth in the United States.

A picture of what fascism has done to living standards, to civil liberties, to workers' organizations, to science and art, the threat against the peace and security of the world, as shown in Italy and Germany, should arouse every sincere artist to action.

We artists must act. Individually we are powerless. Through collective action we can defend our interests. We must ally ourselves with all groups engaged in the common struggle against war and fascism.

There is need for an artists' organization on a nation-wide scale, which will deal with our cultural problems. The creation of such a permanent organization, which will cooperate with kindred organizations throughout the world, is our task.

SIGNERS OF THE CALL

Berenice Abbott
Yarnall Abbott
Albert Abramovitz
Harry Ackerman
Bertrand Ruben Adams
Kenneth M. Adams
Lawrence Adams
Ivan le Lorraine Albright
Rafea Angel
Annot
George Ault
Milton Avery

Peggy Bacon
Phil Bard
Will Barnet
Herman Baron
Thomas W. Barrett, Jr.
Victor Basinet
A. S. Baylinson
Maurice Becker
Norman Bel Geddes
Ben Benn
Ahron Ben-Shmuel
E. M. Benson
Bernece Berkman
Saul Berman
Lucian Bernhard
Henry Bernstein
Theresa Bernstein
Jolan Gross Bettelheim
Edward Biberman
George Biddle
Joseph Biel
Henry Billings
Emil Bisttram
Arnold Blanch

Lucille Blanch
Lou Block
Peter Blume
Walter Bohanan
Aaron Bohrod
Ilya Bolotowsky
Cameron Booth
Henry Albert Botkin
Louis Bouche
Margaret Bourke-White
Julian Bowes
Ernest Brace
Edith Bronson
Alexander Brook
Sonia Gordon Brown
George Byron Browne
Beniamino Bufano
Jacob Burck
Paul Burlin
Dorothy Randolph Byard

Paul Cadmus
Alexander Calder
Kenneth Callahan
Florence Cane
Frank Carson
Dane Chanase
Warren Cheney
Nicolai Cikovsky
Minna Citron
Grace Clements
Hy Cohen
Sonya Cohen
Howard Cook
Ralston Crawford
Francis Criss
Robert M. Cronbach

Adelyne Schaefer Cross
Beatrice Cuming
John Cunningham

Leon Dabo
Vincent D'Agostino
Gustaf Dalstrom
Morris Davidson
Helen S. Davis
Lew E. Davis
Stuart Davis
Horace Talmadge Day
Alice Decker
Jose De Creeft
Julio De Diego
Adolf Dehn
Phyllis De Lappe
Joseph De Martini
Nathaniel Dirk
Isami Doi
Thomas Donnelly
Aaron Douglas
Milton Douthat
Ed Dreis
Werner Drewes
Margaret Duroc
Mabel Dwight

Stuart Edie
Camilo Egas
Dorothy Eisner
Paula Eliasoph
Charles Ellis
Arthur Emptage
Philip Evergood

William Sanders Fanning
Lorser Feitelson

Duncan Ferguson
Louis Ferstadt
Earl T. Fields
Ernest Fiene
Furman J. Finck
Peter Fiordalisi
Ed Fisk
Eugene C. Fitsch
Frank Fleming
Angel Flores
Hans Foy
Karl Free
Maurice Freedman
Arnold Friedman

Wanda Gag
Todros Geller
Hugo Gellert
Eugenie Gershoy
Lydia Gibson
C. Adolph Glassgold
Enrico Glicenstein
Maurice Glickman
H. Glintenkamp
Aaron Goodelman
Boris Gorelick
Mordecai Gorelick
Adolph Gottlieb
Harry Gottlieb
John D. Graham
Blanche Mary Grambs
D. S. Greenbaum
Grace Greenwood
Marion Greenwood
Waylande Gregory
William Gropper
Chaim Gross
John Groth
Bernar Gussow
James Guy

Alex Haberstroh
Thomas Handforth

Murray Hantman
Minna Harkavy
Louis Harris
Abraham Harriton
Bertram Hartman
Theodore G. Haupt
Alonzo Hauser
Zoltan Hecht
Albert Heckman
Harry Hering
Eugene Higgins
Hilaire Hiler
Stefan Hirsch
Albert Hirschfeld
Carl Hoeckner
Carl R. Holty
Emil Holzauer
John Langley Howard
Loretta Howard
Leo T. Hurwitz

Eitaro Ishigaki

Rudolph Jacobi
Herbert Kent Jennings
Grace Mott Johnson
Mary O. Johnson
Sargent Claude Johnson
Harry Donald Jones
Joe Jones
Mervin Jules

Jacob Kainen
Louis Kamm
Martha Ryther Kantor
Morris Kantor
Philip Kaplan
Sam Karp
Leo Katz
Irving Katzenstein
Valeria Kaun
Rockwell Kent
Frank C. Kirk

Jerome Klein
Karl Knaths
Frederic Knight
Benjamin Kopman
Eve Kottgen
Yankel Kufeld
Yasuo Kuniyoshi

Chet Harmon La More
Edward A. Landon
Edward Laning
Sidney Laufman
Adelaide J. Lawson
Myron Lechay
Doris Lee
Margaret LeFranc
Julien E. Levi
A. F. Levinson
Lewis Jean Liberté
Russell Limbach
Sidney Loeb
John Lonergan
Erle Loran
Barbara Lotham
Margaret Lowengrund
Louis Lozowick
Eugene Ludins
Ryab Ludins
Helen Lundenberg
Gwen Lux

Peppino Mangravite
Abraham Manievich
Helen Mann
Paul Manship
Berta Margoulies
Herman Maril
Jack Markow
Jan Matulka
Austin Mecklem
Joseph Meert
Paul R. Meltmer
Maurice Merlin

Knud Merrild
William Meyerowitz
Edward Millman
Winifred Milius
Florence Minard
David Mintz
Bruce Mitchell
Ross Moffett
Peter Paul Mommer
Barbara Brooks Morgan
Eugene Morley
Peter Muller-Munk
Lewis Mumford
Helen McAuslin
Miriam McKinnie

Thomas Nagai
Reuben Nakian
Willard A. Nash
Barney Nestor
J. B. Neumann
Isamu Noguchi

Paul O'Higgins
Elizabeth Olds
Moses Oley
John Opper
Sam Ostrowsky
Peter Paul Ott
William Owen

Jose M. Pavon
Ralph M. Pearson
Anne Merriman Peck
Augustus Hamilton Peck
Fritz Pfeiffer
Esther Phillips
Girolamo Piccolli
George Picken
Hobson Pittman
Joseph Pollet
Fairfield Porter
Austin Purves, Jr.

Walter Quirt

Saul Raskin
A. Redfield
Anton Refregier
Bertram Reibel
Philip Reisman
Louis Ribak
Maurice Ritman
Boardman Robinson
Gilbert Rocke
Kurt Roesch
Robert Bruce Rogers
Elsa Rogo
Emanuele Romano
Arnold Ronnebeck
Doris Rosenthal
Theodore Jay Roszak
Lincoln Rothschild
Andrée Ruellan

William Sanger
Leo Sarkadi
Concetta Scaravaglione
Meyer Schapiro
Saul Schary
Katherine Schmidt
Arthur Julian Schneider
Georges Schreiber
Alfred A. Sessler
Ben Shahn
Frederick E. Shane
Louis Shanker
Joseph M. Sheridan
William Siegel
Bernice Singer
William Earl Singer
Mitchell Siporin
Clara Skinner
Jean Paul Slusser
David Smith
Jacob Getlar Smith
Miron Sokole

Serge Soudeikine
Moses Soyer
Raphael Soyer
Walt Speck
Niles Spencer
Max Spivak
Benton Spruance
Maxwell B. Starr
Alexander Stavenitz
William Steig
Ralph Steiner
Joseph Stella
Algot Stenbery
Harry Sternberg
Louis King Stone
Paul Strand
Jay Sutton
Sakari Suzuki
James Johnson Sweeney
Sam Swerdloff

Chuzo Tamotzu
Rudolph F. Tandler
Jack W. Taylor
Prentiss Taylor
Eve D. Teitel
E. Oscar Thalinger
Cleon Throckmorton
Jennings Tofel
Morris Topchevsky
Abram Tromka
Ernest Sergei Trubach
Tschacbasov
LeRoy Turner

Walter Ufer

Jara Henry Valenta
Stuyvesant Van Veen
John Vassos
Charmion von Wiegand
Joseph P. Vorst
Vaclav Vytlacil

Anna Walinska
Abraham Walkowitz
Lynd Ward
Max Weber
Louis Weiner
Charles S. Wells
Nat Werner
Harold Weston
Warren Wheelock
Francis Robert White

Donald Williams
Barbara Willson
Gilbert Wilson
Arnold Wiltz
Caleb Winholtz
Jan Wittenber
Ann Wolfe
Hamilton Achille Wolf
Adolph Wolff

Chikamichi Yamasaki
Art Young

Bernard B. Zakheim
Carl Zigrosser
Gyula Zilzer
Santos Zingale
Nicola Ziroli
Marguerite Zorach
William Zorach

INTRODUCTION

The first American Artists' Congress against War and Fascism, held in New York City at Town Hall and the New School for Social Research, February 14, 15 and 16, 1936, was a unique event in the history of American art. Through this Congress more than 400 leading American artists, academicians and modernists, purists and social realists, were brought together on a platform in defense of their common interests. The event has already had far-reaching consequences.

The Congress was not a mere spontaneous explosion. On the contrary, it was the result of nearly a year of meetings and planned effort by a group of New York artists who took the initiative in searching for a way out of the economic and cultural impasse confronting virtually all artists. Among the initiators who met in May 1935 were George Ault, Arnold Blanch, Henry Billings, Peter Blume, Maurice Becker, Nicolai Cikovsky, Aaron Douglas, Stuart Davis, Adolph Dehn, William Gropper, Hugo Gellert, Harry Gottlieb, Minna Harkavy, Eitaro Ishigaki, Jerome Klein, Louis Lozowick, Jan Matulka, Saul Schary, William Siegel, Niles Spencer, Harry Sternberg, and Moses Soyer.

These artists drew up a Call for an American Artists' Congress and through its publication the original group was soon rapidly augmented by artists from all over the United States.

With a widespread response to the Call assured, the task of planning topics of discussion for the Congress itself became the objective of the weekly meetings. The problem of giving clarity of form to the ideas which had brought these artists together proved a tough one. The artists were masters of their own mediums, but not of words. Jerome Klein, writer and lecturer on art, gave invaluable guidance at this time in simplifying and clarifying the ideological content of papers brought forward by the artists. As the date of the Congress approached the meetings were increased to two or three a week, and finally to daily "jam-sessions," the results of which form the contents of this volume.

The Congress was attended by 360 members representing many states, and in addition a delegation of 12 from Mexico, including José Clemente Orozco and David Alfaro Siqueiros. Julia Codesido represented the artists of Peru. There were also many guest delegates from schools, colleges, artists' unions and student bodies.

At the Congress the members voted unanimously to form a permanent organization, which is called the American Artists' Congress. Its national headquarters are in New York City.

The purpose of this organization is to achieve unity of action among artists of recognized standing in their profession on all issues which concern their economic and cultural security and freedom, and to fight War, Fascism and Reaction, destroyers of art and culture. Its work is carried on through symposia, publications and special exhibitions, and its effectiveness is proportionate to the degree of unity which it can establish among the artists of the United States regardless of race, esthetic creed or color.

Information regarding membership and activities of the organization may be had by communicating with Stuart Davis, National Secretary, American Artists' Congress, Box 12, Station O, New York City.

Stuart Davis

PREFATORY NOTE

In organizing the material of the Congress for publication in its present form, the Editorial Committee has made no attempt to reconcile opposing views, or to develop further statements that are incomplete or confused. The task of editing has been conceived as that of making the material readable and compact, of keeping to the fore the issues that dominated the Congress, and of portraying faithfully the character of the participation, without violation of personal viewpoints. The book stands thus as a significant record of the response of representative artists to problems of vital immediate concern.

THE EDITORIAL COMMITTEE
Jerome Klein, *Chairman*
E. M. Benson
Margaret Duroc
Louis Lozowick
Ralph M. Pearson

CONTENTS

First Closed Session

THE ARTIST IN SOCIETY

Second Closed Session

PROBLEMS OF THE AMERICAN ARTIST

Third Closed Session

ECONOMIC PROBLEMS OF
THE AMERICAN ARTIST

Fourth Closed Session

REPORTS AND RESOLUTIONS OF DELEGATES AND PERMANENT ORGANIZATION

AMERICAN ARTISTS' CONGRESS
Stuart Davis, National Executive Secretary
National Executive Committee

NEW YORK

Peter Blume
Margaret Bourke-White
Boris Gorelick
Katherine Schmidt
Paul Manship
Alexander Brook
E. M. Benson
Hugo Gellert
Aaron Douglas
Louis Lozowick
George Biddle
Rockwell Kent
Max Weber
William Gropper
Yasuo Kuniyoshi

Joseph Sinel
Aaron Goodelman
Arnold Blanch
Alexander Stavenitz
Jerome Klein
Harry Gottlieb
Lewis Mumford
Henry Billings
Lynd Ward
Ralph M. Pearson
Lucien Bernhard
Lincoln Rothschild
John Cunningham
Niles Spencer

Herbert Jennings, *Philadelphia, Pennsylvania*
Gilbert Wilson, *Terre Haute, Indiana*
Joe Jones, *St. Louis, Missouri*
Robert F. White, *Cedar Rapids, Iowa*
Alfred Sessler, *Milwaukee, Wisconsin*
Nicolai Cikovsky, *Cincinnati, Ohio*
Morris Topchevsky, *Chicago, Illinois*

NATIONAL EXECUTIVE COMMITTEE

Erle Loran, *Minneapolis, Minnesota*
Philip Kaplan, *Cleveland, Ohio*
Karl Knaths, *Provincetown, Massachusetts*
Walter Ufer, *Taos, New Mexico*
John L. Howard, *Santa Fe, New Mexico*
Mervin Jules, *Baltimore, Maryland*
Walt Speck, *Detroit, Michigan*
Grace Clements, *Los Angeles, California*
James Pfeufer, *Boston, Massachusetts*

Public Session
Town Hall, New York City
February 14th, 1936

OPENING ADDRESS
Lewis Mumford

Friends, comrades, ladies and gentlemen:

Herewith we open the first American Artists' Congress. On this occasion we are buoyed up and stimulated by a number of fraternal greetings from all parts of the world. I won't read them in detail, but we have one from the Artists' International Association of London, one from the International Writers' Association, another from the Artists' Association of Michigan, and a greeting from the *New Masses* encouraging us in our step. I have the double duty as a member of the American Writers' League and as chairman, tonight, to read the greeting of the American Writers' League. It was through this organization and through the unity demonstrated last April by the American Writers' League that the artists became conscious of their own needs and their opportunity.

Now, the question has perhaps occurred to you as you sat here tonight waiting for the Congress to open—Why is it that there has not been an American Artists' Congress before this? I have asked myself this question and the only reply I have is a very simple one. It sometimes takes a universal catastrophe before people begin to act normally. In New York an apartment house fire is necessary before a man can get to know his own neighbor. Or a ship has to sink and cause many to lose their lives before people learn to cooperate with each other.

We are gathered together tonight for the first time partly because we are in the midst of what is plainly a world catastrophe, and we have to realize what our position is, and do our best to put our hands to the oar and do whatever else is necessary to face this emergency.

The catastrophe is with us—no doubt about that! There is the economic depression which has been with us for six or more years. A depression marked for the artist not merely by his usually meager diet, but sometimes by the inability to get so much as the bare food necessary for life. And there is imminent another large catastrophe, on even a larger scale, even more dire in its threat, and that is the threat of war. Soldiers have a very simple cure for economic crises—it consists of shooting everyone who does not share their limited opinions and their bellicose attitudes. We have seen in our country, as people have seen in other countries, that depression and repression go hand in hand. When the economic situation gets so bad that people's minds must be moved from their own desperate plight, there is nothing so effective as to give them something else to think about, namely, a war. As you know, it is a sort of counter-irritant.

That is one alternative. Now let us look at the other alternative that is being presented to us by some people: Fascism. Look Fascism in the face and what do you discover: that it has one common animus with war, and that is the ruling class notion of exterminating every other type of personality and every kind of social and political group.

Unfortunately, people who like extermination dislike culture. They wish to simplify matters by solving the differences within a society by use of force. They resent arts-and-science people as they resent thought itself—chiefly because the latter stirs them up, irritates them, makes them feel inferior. In a Fascist form of government some one person, usually with a silly face, a Hitler or a Mussolini, becomes the model which every subject must imitate and salute. Anyone who dares to dislike that sort of uniformity, that sort of standardization, is regarded by Fascists as an enemy of society. Anyone who laughs at those stupid mugs, or incites other people to laugh at them, is a traitor.

I think that is the reason why dictatorships fear artists. They fear them because they fear free criticism. They rightly believe that if the forces represented by the artist are allowed to exercise their will, they will disrupt the Fascist regime. The irrepressible impulse of Art may upset the whole Fascist program.

The forces that are bringing on war, that are preparing for larger and better economic depressions in the future, are at odds with all the forces of human culture. The time has come for the people who love life and culture to form a united front against them, to be ready to protect, and guard, and if necessary, fight for the human heritage which we, as artists, embody.

WHY AN ARTISTS' CONGRESS?
Stuart Davis, Secretary, American Artists' Congress

The American Artists' Congress is unique in the history of American art. That it takes place now is no accident. For it is the response of artists to a situation facing them today. How can we describe this situation?

Its immediate background is a depression unparalleled in the history of this country. The cracks and strains in the general social fabric resulting from the economic crisis inevitably reached the world of art, shaking those psychological and esthetic certainties which had once given force and direction to the work of artists.

In order to withstand the severe shock of the crisis, artists have had to seek a new grip on reality. Around the pros and cons of "social content," a dominant issue in discussions of present day American art, we are witnessing determined efforts by artists to find a meaningful direction. Increasing expression of social problems of the day in the new American art makes it clear that in times such as we are living in, few artists can honestly remain aloof, wrapped up in studio problems.

But the artist has not simply looked out of the window; he has had to step into the street. He has done things that would have been scarcely conceivable a few years back.

Nearly two years ago prominent New York artists started a campaign through the Artists' Committee of Action for a Municipal Art Gallery to provide a badly needed outlet for the artists of this city.

When the city administration finally took up the idea, without recognition of the Artists' Committee of Action, it opened a gallery in a remodelled private house early in 1936, on a basis of discrimination against non-citizens and censorship of art disapproved by the administration. Such reactionary ideas could never have been introduced under a truly democratic management of the Municipal Gallery by the artists themselves, which the Artists' Committee of Action had repeatedly called for.

What's more, leading New York artists, together with the Artists' Union, showed that they would not stand for such practices by making a prompt and emphatic protest. The result was an immediate victory! Both citizenship and censorship clauses were speedily withdrawn.

Sharp necessity likewise drove the most hard-pressed artists into organized efforts for Federal Government support. Their opportunity had come through the initiation of a limited Government art project in December, 1933. This project was no more than a liberal gesture, employing a select few, and ignoring the dire distress of the great majority of American artists.

But that move of the liberal New Deal Government awakened artists to the realization that they had every right to go to the Government when all other resources and prospects had been exhausted, to demand support for their continued functioning as creative workers.

Artists at last discovered that, like other workers, they could only protect their basic interests through powerful organizations. The great mass of artists left out of the project found it possible to win demands from the administration only by joint and militant demonstrations. Their efforts led naturally to the building of the Artists' Union.

The relatively greater scope of the present art projects is due, in large measure, to the militant stand of the various artists' unions, on behalf of all unemployed artists.

The unions have also gone a long way toward showing that the best American art cannot be developed by merely encouraging a hand-picked few. Their insistence on a democratic extension of Government support to young and unknown artists has brought out a vast variety of talent completely ignored by private patronage and commercial galleries. For the young generation of American artists there is no visible hope except continuation and expansion of Government art projects.

Growing economic insecurity cannot be ignored by even the

most firmly established American artists, those who contribute regularly to the big museum exhibitions. Now they are organizing to gain at least a minimum compensation for their important contributions through the loan of contemporary art to museums. They are requesting that the museums pay a small rental fee for the use of their work.

The hostility of most museum officials, and their boards of trustees, to the proposals of the American Society of Painters, Sculptors and Gravers is indicative of their indifference to the needs of artists.

In the struggle around the rental policy, the American Society has found its campaign can only be advanced through the active cooperation of other artists' societies and the Artists' Union. Here is a concrete instance of how great numbers of American artists are drawing together on an ever widening front for mutual support against exploitation.

But we can give no adequate picture of the extreme urgency for concerted group action of all progressive American artists, an urgency which is tangibly demonstrated by the gathering of representative artists from all sections of the United States, from Mexico, Cuba and even from South America, here in this Congress, unless we portray realistically the possibilities contained actually within the situation in the United States and throughout the world today.

The increasingly open drive of arch reactionaries like William Randolph Hearst and the American Liberty League to promote so-called recovery at the expense of the living standards and freedom of expression of the great masses of American people is a direct menace to the whole body of American artists.

It is Hearst's *Daily Mirror* that launches the most vicious attack against the artists on Government projects, calling them "Hobohemian chiselers" and "ingrates ready to bite the hand that feeds them."

It is probably no accident that a prominent art critic, associated with the Hearst press, writes of his disgust with the work produced on the projects. He advises the young artists to disperse, return home, admit they were not intended to be artists, and take up pursuits more suited to their abilities.

Hearst, today the spearhead of the sharpest attacks upon intellectual freedom in this country, focuses his drive against the artists at just that point where they have made their only real advance toward economic security, namely, the Government projects.

This attack is part of a general drive by powerful vested interests to perpetuate exploitation by smashing the efforts of the underprivileged American masses to gain security and a decent living standard. The goal of entrenched interests is a regime founded on suppression of all those liberties which Americans fought to establish and are today struggling to maintain. This goal is shrewdly screened with such slogans as "Back to the Constitution" and "Save America for Democracy," and hypocritical appeals to Americanism and love of country.

The examples of the so-called national resurgence that were accompanied by the most brutal destruction of the economic and cultural standards of the masses of people in Italy and Germany through the introduction of Fascism should warn us of the real threats that lie behind the rabidly nationalistic movements in this country.

There is a real danger of Fascism in America.

How Fascism is plunging headlong toward a devastating new World War is evident to every reader of the daily press. Fascists have no other solution for the crying needs of their people than an outburst of war.

To carry out their program of death and destruction they would enlist the services of even the artists. Here is how Mussolini employs an artist, F. T. Marinetti.

"We, Futurist poets and artists," Marinetti says, "have recognized for 27 years that war is the only world hygiene. War is beautiful because it creates new architectures, as the heavy tank. It creates the flying geometries of the aeroplane, the spiral smoke of burning villages. War is beautiful because it completes the beauty of a flowery meadow with the passionate orchids of machine-gun fire. War is beautiful because it serves the greatness of great Fascist Italy."

That is the way a Fascist artist speaks.

The talents of many American artists were employed to whip up the war psychology essential to win over the mass of Americans to support participation of the United States in the last World War.

It is because artists do not want their creative talents perverted and used to mask a barbaric war that they have signed the Call for an American Artists' Congress and come together here to show their solidarity. And this struggle against war cannot be divorced from the struggle against every manifestation of warmongering reaction.

The members of this Congress who have come together to discuss their problems in the light of the pressing social issues of the day are representative of the most progressive forces in American art today. The applicants for membership were accepted on the basis of their representative power, which simply means that they had already achieved a degree of recognition and esteem as artists in the spheres in which they function.

We, members of the Congress, have recognized that we are not alone in this fight. We recognize that our basic interests are not remote from those who do the work of the world. And with this recognition comes the realization that if we are to be serious, we can only attack even the most highly specialized problems that confront us, in relation to our main objective, which is to build a bulwark for the defense of intellectual freedom, for economic security.

Even if we were to rally all the American artists to our cause, we would achieve little working as an isolated group. But we have faith in our potential effectiveness precisely because our direction naturally parallels that of the great body of productive workers in American industrial, agriculture and professional life.

The Congress will enable us to focus our objectives.

To realize them, we plan to form a permanent organization on a national scale.

It will not be affiliated with any political group or clique of sectarian opinion.

It will be an organization of artists which will be alert to take action on all issues vital to the continued free functioning of the artist.

It will be alert to ways and means for extending this freedom and for making contact with a broader audience.

It will be a strengthening element to the whole field of progressive organization against War and Fascism.

It will be another obstacle to the reactionary forces which would rob us of our liberties.

I call on all artists of standing to join the permanent organization which will carry out the program planned by the succeeding sessions of the Congress.

WHAT IS WORTH FIGHTING FOR?
Rockwell Kent

During the Franco-Prussian War our General Sheridan was attached to the Prussian army as military observer for the United States. His eminence as a general was due not only to his courage and personal magnetism but to his ability as a strategist; and his knowledge of the nature of war had been gained by long experience. He instructed the Prussian General Staff in the strategy of war: "The proper strategy in war," he said, "is to inflict as much suffering as possible upon the civil population of the enemy. They should be left with nothing but their eyes to weep with." That was half a century ago and the means for thoroughly strategic warfare were far from well developed. The World War lent a great impetus to the advancement of war strategy; and we are led to believe that by recent developments in flying and chemistry the next war will prove to be a veritable soldier's dream.

Artists *should* be active in the movement against war, for artists, of all people in the world, are most concerned with life. It is by virtue of their love of life in all its manifestations, their love of the life-giving sun, of the moon that is so potent in the tides of living organisms, of the stars and the depths of the heavens toward which the living soul projects itself, of spring, summer, autumn, winter, because these are seasons in the life of mankind's world, in the seven ages of man as he observes them in the generations about him, in all living creatures, for they are, in a measure, his kindred. The living world is beautiful to him: therefore he loves it. It is by virtue of their love of life that men are artists.

It is by virtue of their insight into the phenomena of life, their instinctive understanding of the significance of the phenomena, their instinctive true appraisal of values and proportions, their feeling for the enduring and eternal qualities in life, that some of them achieve what we call immortality. For beneath the veneers of civilization, throughout the never-ending surface changes of custom, manner and fashion that mankind affects, there are enduring human values; there is a residue which we may say is *Man*. Of this essential kinship of all human life, of the kinship of the ancients and the moderns, of the Latin and the Nord, of the Jew and the Gentile, of the primitive and the European or American, of the black, red, yellow and the white, the artist is profoundly aware; his art records the fact. Man needs to be continually reminded of this, to have it printed in books, painted upon walls and canvas, sculptured in stone, sounded in music, put before his eyes, dinned into his ears. To write it, paint it, carve it, play it, din it, is the artist's job.

I happen to be one who is peculiarly fitted by experience to judge whether or not this universal kinship that is felt by artists is a fact; for I have lived in many places on the globe, have known, with some intimacy, two races historically and culturally almost as widely separated as any on the earth today. I was born and reared an American, a New Yorker, and I have lived among a brown race just emerging from the stone age. There is one thing that life among the Eskimos has shown me; it is that in all essential human things, in their laughter and tears and what they laugh or cry about, in the quality of their affections, in all the human qualities that love and friendship are premised upon, we and the brown-skinned, stone-age Eskimos are one. Loving the most remote of our human relatives because of their identity with myself, ourselves, I can't believe that there can be found on the face of the earth a race so different from ourselves that we should hate it.

And, in fact, except in the heat of wartime hysteria—or of the comparable Nazi hysteria in Germany—no one asserts that we should hate a race. They tacitly admit, who feel the possibility or probability of war, that it must be, on our part, in defence of our institutions, of our culture, of the American ideal, of civilization. These things, our institutions, our culture, the American ideal, civilization, sky scrapers, automobiles, airplanes, subways, railroads, bath tubs, gadgets, jazz, I know, have never in the period in which we have enjoyed them, nor in the centuries through which we have advanced toward their enjoyment, added, and can never add, one thing to Man that in the sight of God is worth His blessing, or a tinker's damn, or war.

The traveller is often called upon to tell about the foreign countries that he knows. "Tell us about Greenland," say my friends. And I tell them of how six-sevenths of Greenland is buried under thousands of feet of ice, of how people only live on a narrow fringe of shore; that North Greenland is so sterile that no trees can grow; that the people there, living in scattered isolated communities, eke out the barest subsistence on the seals and fish of their depleted waters; that the most a good hunter can earn in a year is $100; that few of them earn that much; that they are often hungry and often, thanks to civilization, cold; but that they are always happy and that there is no unemployment. It is a short story, the resources of the Greenlanders, but the story of their happiness is long.

When I go to Greenland I am, to the people there, a traveller from a remote and almost unknown world. They want to hear about my world. I tell them that America is the greatest and richest country on the globe; that its resources are almost unlimited; that we have factories and machinery for producing almost everything in almost unlimited quantities; and roads and trains and motor cars for transporting it. And stores for selling it. That American women are the most beautiful in the world and the most intelligent; that American men are the handsomest, bravest, noblest, most brilliant, energetic in the world; that we admit all this, and that we now have an average of almost ten million people out of employment, all of whom would starve to death but for the charity of those who work. That with people starving we pay farmers to destroy their crops. I tell them that if I planted a thousand acres of corn, paid men to plant it and harvest it, and then, piling it up in the middle of my acres, poured hundreds of barrels of kerosene on it and, even with people who needed the corn watching me over the fence, set fire to it, I would be considered a great public benefactor. I tell them that in America we are all educated—or most of us; that we have beautiful schools and universities; and that when our sons have at last after years of schools and colleges been graduated with fancy degrees, they can, if they are lucky, get just such a job in a filling station as an Eskimo could get and fill it exactly as well. When I have told the Eskimos, the primitives, about America, they all begin to laugh. "Greenland," they say, "is good enough for us."

But I am a traveller who has returned home, and I may say that before we consider imposing our splendid civilization upon others, or concerning ourselves with defending it against outside attack, we establish in America a civilization that is not a funny story to tell to primitives. Let us, following the counsel of Voltaire's philosopher Pangloss, turn to the cultivation of our own gardens. And let me, now, as a traveller who has seen and partaken of other civilizations, and as an artist who, like all artists, is concerned above all with the more enduring values of human life, counsel you that you take as your ideal such happiness and love of peace as is enjoyed by our brothers the Eskimos of Greenland, and that you seek justification for war only after you shall have established here in America such a paradise for all as may truly deserve the shedding of blood for the preservation of its integrity. That Paradise, to win it and to keep it, is a thing worth fighting for.

REPRESSION OF ART IN AMERICA
Joe Jones

So long as the overwhelming majority of American artists were concerned only with the creation of individual art works with no predetermined destination, censorship or repression of art was no problem in this country. If works made for hypothetical buyers found no takers, the artist could only complain of being neglected or not appreciated. And there the matter ended.

But with the depression came a new interest in art with a social, a general public bearing. And with the expression of this interest came reactionary efforts to stifle freedom of thought.

In the worst depths of the crisis, in 1933, the Rockefellers found it expedient to make a liberal gesture toward the distressed masses of the country by employing Diego Rivera to paint a mural in Rockefeller Center showing "Man Standing at the Crossroads, Looking to the Future with Uncertainty but Hope." When Rivera expressed more certainty than the Rockefellers had bargained for by including a portrait of Lenin in his prospect, he was asked to remove this detail, and on his refusal was ordered off the scaffold. Widespread protests were made against the stoppage. Several months later, the Rockefellers had the unfinished mural completely destroyed, an act characterized by outstanding liberal artists as "vandalism."

The Museum of Modern Art, where the Rockefellers are also active, had attempted censorship of work by Ben Shahn, William Gropper and Hugo Gellert in its mural show on the ground that attacks against living Americans in their works were unpermissible. In this case J. P. Morgan, one of those caricatured, preferred letting the pictures hang to getting unfavorable publicity, and for this reason censorship was not finally imposed.

A cooperative mural done in the old court house of St. Louis by Negro and white students under the direction of Joe Jones was saved from destruction for a year and a half through mass defense by the workers. Finally the administration succeeded in closing the room to the public.

The first censorship of art on government projects was the case of the Coit Tower murals in San Francisco, where artists were forced to efface the title of a worker's newspaper, *The Western Worker*, and other symbols before authorities would permit the public showing of the paintings.

The most openly Fascist act, however, took place in Los Angeles, where Police Captain Hynes and his notorious Red Squad broke into a John Reed Club exhibition, smashing sculpture and portable murals. To show their feelings they put bullet holes through the heads of Negroes portrayed in the murals, but spared two figures, a Ku Klux Klan member and a judge.

On a number of government art projects artists have been ordered to make all sorts of changes to blunt or polish up the plain truths of the situations they were painting before they were found acceptable to the reactionary administrators. A mural by Michael Loew for Textile High School in Brooklyn was found unsatisfactory by the Board of Education because workers leaving a factory looked too serious, whereas "they should have been smiling." Also the massing of workers left possible the inference that it was a strike walkout, according to the educators, who ordered the number of workers reduced. Another high school mural by Louis Ferstadt was rejected because it did not conform to the "taste" of the principal.

The splendid mural designed by Ben Shahn and Lou Block for the Riker's Island Penitentiary in New York, contrasting brutal methods of penal institutions under backward administrations with the technique of modern scientific penology, a work widely praised, was rejected by the Muncipal Art Commission as "psychologically unfit." This phrase might better have been applied to the commission itself, as a poll of the prisoners showed an intelligent response. Jonas Lie, at the time a member of the commission, described this progressive work as "anti-social"!

Most significant is the fact that the reactionary moves toward censorship and repression have even extended to the field of private easel painting. The mere showing of a few realistic or highly personal expressions in the last annual exhibition of contemporary American art at the Chicago Art Institute brought indignant protests and threats of withdrawal of contributions to the museum from a number of "art benefactors."

These cases need no further elaboration. They indicate plainly how the widespread growth of reaction in the United States is affecting liberty of artistic expression. Powerful protest actions have already done much to prevent stifling of our liberties. It is up to the American Artists' Congress to give impetus to the movement for the defense of our rights as artists and Americans.

THE NEGRO IN AMERICAN CULTURE
Aaron Douglas

In the United States there are twelve to fifteen million Negroes, or more precisely, people of African descent. From colonial days to the present a black skin has been taboo by the white man of America. After the Civil War the Negroes became a lost submerged group, the forgotten men of America. Whenever they were for one reason or another forced on the attention of the nation, it was almost never in connection with the cultural life of the country, and almost always in association with crime and vice. I have no intention of putting on sack cloth and ashes and reciting the woes and lamentations of the Negro. I should like, however, to make an exception to the above mentioned rule in the hope of calling attention to a much neglected people and, further, to introduce to this congress a group of Americans that has a chance to contribute so much of value to the arts of painting and sculpture.

It is often said, and with considerable truth, that anytime four Negroes are together, there you have a quartet. This, of course, is an exaggeration, but it does serve to focus our attention on the Negroes' extraordinary sense of rhythm and harmony. This talent is brought out fully in the field of music where the Negro has created the spiritual, a distinctly new type of folk music.

The Negro musician has amused and entertained America for a century. As early as 1870 the Fisk Jubilee singers and other groups began their travels through America and Europe singing the spirituals and sorrow songs of the former slaves. This small voice has grown in beauty and volume to the point where Negroes are no longer ashamed to sing the spirituals and white America is willing to concede [them] an important place in the musical expression of the country.

The Negro has dominated the form and direction of modern popular music with its explosive, staccato-like syncopation and intricate melodic patterns. Jim Europe, Noble Sissle, Cab Calloway and Duke Ellington are known throughout the world, but in spite of [the] wide popularity of these bands they rarely, if ever, get the big contracts that come to white organizations of the same rank. Roland Hayes, Paul Robeson and Marion Anderson have stood in the first rank of American concert singers for a decade.

In the theatre the Negro has taken advantage of all the opportunities offered. These, I regret to say, have been few, distasteful, and very far between. Because of his economic position and by reason of color, the Negro has been held in very restricted limits in the American theatre. The greed of producers and managers prevented the development of the Negro actor in the traditional sense. Little more was expected of him than to transfer the atmosphere of Mobile or Charleston or Harlem to the Broadway stage. Such irrelevancies as dramatic technique were never considered. In spite of these severe handicaps and limitations, we have developed some notable figures in the theatre.

Fifteen years ago Charles Gilpin thrilled America with his magnificent portrayal of the Emperor Jones. But that was his first and last role. Paul Robeson, for all of his voice, scholarship, physique and personal charm, can't play Othello, a black man's role, in his own native America. The great tragedy of the late Richard B. Harrison, who created the role of "de Lord" in Green Pastures, was that he had to wait forty years for a part that coincided with his color. A still greater tragedy was his utter silence in face of the miserably low pay of most of the cast and the awful working conditions on tour.

The dance offered a field for the unrestricted expression of the Negroes' creative passion. Here were no expensive instruments to be purchased, no weird symbols to be mastered, no unfamiliar tools and stubborn material to be overcome, only swift feet, strong legs, a lust for life and a soaring imagination. With this limited equipment the Negro has kept folk dancing alive in America when it has died almost everywhere else in the world. He has not only kept the dance alive, but in a spontaneous, revolutionary, creative state.

The spirit of the Gay Nineties was never more beautifully expressed than in the Negro dance, the "Cake Walk." There was also the "Buck and Wing," the "Pigeon Wing," and later the "Dog Walk," the "Eagle Rock," and "Balling the Jack." Soon after the War the Ghetto-like bonds of Negro life were momentarily burst asunder by the most sensational Negro dances, the "Charleston." After the "Charleston" we had the "Lindberg Hop," the "Black Bottom," the "Shim, Sham, Shimmie" and finally "Trucking." As there were no known creators of spirituals there are no individual creators of Negro dances. After the essential steps or movements are once mastered each dancer goes on to give his own interpretation, adding and eliminating at will.

It would be interesting to trace in detail the characterization of the Negro in literature and the drama but time forbids. Suffice it to say that in all the American drama, there is scarcely a Negro role that might be called intelligent, sympathetic or lovable. In the movies he is invariably represented as a docile lackey, a bombastic fool or an unbelievable monster. Occasionally some genius comes along and wraps all these misrepresentations into one, as for example Eugene O'Neill's "Emperor Jones." In the last Negro number of the *New Theatre Magazine*, George Sklar makes the following very pertinent observation:

"For the American theatre has never really given up its minstrel-show conception of the Negro. The fiction of that conception has continued from the first 'burnt-cork' end-man down to Amos and Andy today. It was the fiction which played up the mythical idiosyncrasies of color and made those idiosyncrasies a butt for the white man's laughter. It was the fiction of Sambo, the lazy good-for-nothing, crap-shooting, razor-toting, ghost-ridden, sex-hopped Negro. And although the long tradition of the white actor in blackface was finally broken and the Negro himself allowed to appear on the stage, that fiction still prevails. Cork or no cork, it was still the white man's fabrication of the Negro. And it will persist when you see an Ethel Waters on the stage, a Buck and Bubbles in vaudeville, a Cab Calloway in a night club, or a Stepin Fetchit in the movies. These performers have, consciously or unconsciously, allowed themselves to fall in with that fiction and to be utilized in this way because the commercial theatre allows for no other conception."

When we come to painting and sculpture, the arts which concern us here, we get an entirely different picture of the Negro's role in American culture. In all the fifteen million Negroes there aren't more than a dozen painters and less than a half dozen sculptors of outstanding attainment. This is a very peculiar situation. A record, I should say, and one that can't be matched anywhere excepting among those people who have banned art on religious grounds. Nor may we get consolation by turning to semi-civilized and uncivilized peoples.

What then are the causes for such an unusual distortion in the cultural development of the American Negro? A partial answer is to be found in his peculiar historical-economic development. When Eli Whitney invented the cotton gin and large areas of the south were placed under cotton cultivation, the Negro was pushed down from the position of a bond servant, in many ways similar to that of white indentured servants, to that of a thing, chattel, a machine.

Even before the wide-spread use of the Negro as a human machine, other important differences besides his color separated him from white bondsmen. From the very beginning he was divested of his African religions, a terrific blow to a primitive people. These religions were rich in spirits that symbolized intimate alive contacts between man and nature, both animate and inanimate. He was also stripped of his languages, rich in tribal history and folk lore. In short, his was the Herculean task of giving creative expression to a traditionless people brought face to face with nature and the unyielding hostile attitude of his fellow-men. Naturally his music and dances were banned from the beginning and held up as savage and therefore indecent and unthinkable in a striving and progressive, civilized society. What is more important for us here is the complete suppression of his arts and crafts which seemed to have been at a high level in Africa at the beginning of Negro slavery in America.

European civilization, predominantly feudal, was rapidly disintegrating and passing into a stage of active revolution. The over-whelming power and authority of the church, active in every relationship existing between men, was being challenged at every turn. In America where this control had been most successfully checked, religion was reduced to a one-day affair, Sunday. This left six days for men to carry on their every day man-to-man relationships without divine interference.

No new opportunity for plastic expression was afforded the Negro by this Protestant Christianity. Proscribing religious art as wasteful and profane, Protestantism provided the moral basis for the sober, industrious life of a pioneering people with no leisure for art.

So every sculptor that chanced to survive the gruelling ordeal of the "Black Passage" became at least a humble picker of cotton or tobacco.

It was not until about 1920 that we began to notice something like a continuous cultural movement among Negroes. This was soon thought of as a renaissance. But where were the artists, the painters, and sculptors? The critics and interpreters of this new expression set out to remedy the defect. Harlem was sifted. Neither streets, homes nor public institutions escaped this frenzied search. When unsuspecting Negroes were found with a brush in their hands they were immediately hauled away and held for interpretation. They were given places of honor and bowed to with much ceremony. Every effort to protest their innocence was drowned out with big-mouthed praise. A number of these people escaped and returned to a more reasonable existence. Many fell in with the game and went along making hollow and meaningless gestures with brush and palette.

But in spite of the critics, interpreters, and so-called friends of Negro art, the Negro artists have emerged. Without support, without well-defined objectives, they have been suspended in mid-air between the hostility of most whites and the almost total ignorance of their own people.

What the Negro artist should paint and how he should paint

it can't be accurately determined without reference to specific social conditions. Although in a sense we are the proletarians of the proletariat, our chief concern as a group has been with segregation and discrimination (manifestations of economic exploitation) rather than with exploitation as such. We have only held jobs considered unfit for the rest of the proletariat. We have held some property but only with a very thin thread. Our chief concern has been to establish and maintain recognition of our essential humanity, in other words, complete social and political equality. This has been a difficult fight as we have been the constant object of attack by all manner of propaganda from nursery rhymes to false scientific racial theories. In this struggle the rest of the proletariat almost invariably has been arrayed against us. Some of us understand why this is so. But the Negro artist, unlike the white artist, has never known the big house. He is essentially a product of the masses and can never take a position above or beyond their level. This simple fact is often overlooked by the Negro artist and almost always by those who in the past have offered what they sincerely considered to be help and friendship.

In spite of the crushing ostracism and exploitation, a few Negroes here and there have arrived at a fair mastery of the painter's craft. Of all the Negro artists, H. O. Tanner is the best known; William Johnson, Hal Woodruff, and Archibald Motley are possibly the most accomplished of our younger painters. Among our young artists of sound talent and definite promise are Wells, Porter, Alston, Banarn, Hardwick and Bearden. The well known cartoonist E. Simms Campbell, the recent winner of Hearst's contest, is at present our most successful artist. In sculpture Sargent Johnson, Richmond Barte and Augusta Savage have done important work.

Before closing this paper, I think there are some other factors that should be mentioned. One of the most interesting is the manner in which the Negro has been treated in American art. Before the beginning of the present century, the Negro was rarely considered a serious subject in American art. He was occasionally represented, but quaintness, picturesqueness, or brutishness be-

AARON DOUGLAS

came the subject rather than the Negro per se. In the Metropolitan Museum of Art there is a room devoted to modern American masters. Not one Negro face is represented. It is when we come to revolutionary art that we find the Negro sincerely represented, but here the portrayal is too frequently automatic, perfunctory and arbitrary. He becomes a kind of proletarian prop, a symbol, vague and abstract. Revolutionary art should be praised, however, for pointing a way and striking a vital blow at discrimination and segregation, the chief breeding ground of Fascism.

I should like to close this paper with a sincere appeal to every artist of this congress and to every lover of liberty and justice, everywhere, to fight against the rising tide of Fascism. If there is anyone here who does not understand Fascism let him ask the first Negro he sees in the street. The lash and iron hoof of Fascism have been a constant menace and threat to the Negro ever since his so-called emancipation.

In America, race discrimination is one of the chief props on which Fascism can be built. One of the most vital blows the artists of this congress can deliver to the threat of Fascism is to refuse to discriminate against any man because of nationality, race, or creed.

AN ARTIST'S EXPERIENCE
IN THE SOVIET UNION
Margaret Bourke-White

Visiting Soviet Russia as an industrial photographer, I was very quickly made the guest of the government and given papers that would allow me to travel and to get help anywhere. The papers even said that I could "command." I never had to "command," needless to say, for I found the greatest spirit of helpfulness everywhere. This had nothing to do with me. It was simply because I was taking industrial photographs—something they believed in—and they wanted to help me get my work done. I am by no means an exception. The French architect Lurçat has been working in Russia for some years. The man I consider their greatest movie photographer—the greatest in the world perhaps—is Eisenstein's cameraman, Tisse. Tisse is not a Russian but a Swede.

The same spirit of hospitality extends with Russia to the various national minorities. In the days of the czars, their art was suppressed. Now it is encouraged to a high degree. National academies have been established in Kazan, Tiflis, Tashkent, and many other cities. National arts are flourishing.

The party and government lay down no method of technique, no laws of esthetics. All types of art are found—abstract, cubist, surrealist. Every artistic experiment that individual artists wish to carry out they can. People in general have the notion that there is an art line laid down by the government but this is not true.

This freedom to experiment—and the opportunity to experiment without worrying about the rent and the grocery bill—points up, more sharply than anything else I can think of, the tremendous difference between the opportunities of the artist under a system like that in the Soviet Union and the situation here.

Despite difficulties due to limited availability of equipment and materials, all kinds of creative work go forward. There must be some reason. The excellence of this work is no accident. There is something that happens to the minds of these men because they have found freedom to think.

And there is something else too that comes into this picture. That is the artist's audience.

Who are the audiences of artists in this country? For easel artists the audiences are esthetes and rich patrons, some of whom have good taste, and some of whom have very bad taste. If the artist is a commercial illustrator, his audience includes everyone who reads the current magazines and newspapers. But rarely do the limitations imposed upon the artist in commercial work permit him to do a free creative job.

That is a terrible thing—bad for artists, bad for our artistic growth, bad for those who, theoretically at least, look at our pictures.

But in Soviet Russia the artist is needed. He assumes a place of importance in Soviet life. He is paid while he is learning, paid while he is experimenting, paid for his finished work. If his work is reviewed, he is even paid for the use of his picture in that magazine or paper where the review appears. He is paid so well that artists, together with writers, form the highest salaried class in the country.

And not only is the artist being educated, but his audience is being educated as well. The circulation of books is tremendous, and book illustrators reach an audience that runs into millions.

The need for muralists is greater than the supply, and all the good ones have signed contracts for two, three, sometimes five years ahead.

Mass education of the entire population extends to all the artistic fields. I would like to see a time in this country when workers have such cultural opportunities.

WHY ESTABLISHED ARTISTS SHOULD OPPOSE WAR AND FASCISM
Paul Manship

The purpose of the Congress is to organize artists in the interests of peace and in the defense of culture. We have seen in Europe the working of forces to destroy this culture. By united action we may do much for the preservation of this peace and culture which is of such inestimable value to us all.

From time immemorial the struggle for freedom of expression has been part and parcel of the accomplishment of great art. In relation to his environment the artist of all times has been the exponent of spiritual and social concepts and ideals and in large measure has been the prophet and interpreter of popular aspirations. Freedom of expression is an all-important factor in art, and the artist, as the revealer of it to the people, should be one of the first to sense danger to this freedom. One calls to mind the struggle of Michelangelo to maintain his spiritual liberty as voiced against the authority of the church, or the liberty of action, and freedom of thought of such artists of genius as Rembrandt and Brueghel, or, in more modern times, the devotion to artistic independence by such men as Goya and Courbet. Jacques Callot, the French engraver, devoted his energies to depicting the horrors of war. The liberty of expression in France in his day permitted Daumier to make his highly vitalized drawings for the public press; obviously in a Fascist country this would have been impossible for both the artist and the press.

Artistic freedom of expression may take the form of creating in pictorial or sculptural form those enthusiasms and beliefs which the artist holds nearest and dearest to him, whether they be abstractions in form or color, or dealing in the subject matter of the prevalent religious or social themes. In various epochs and different countries the artist has interpreted for his audience those beliefs and ideals in the terms of his cultural background. He is naturally in harmony with and part of the life currents of his day. Freedom of expression of the artist in ancient Greece may have been one of interpreting in form the current religious ideals, or on the other hand he may have belonged to the school which treated in abstract [the] representation of the human figure. In the middle ages the artist helped to visualize to the public the ideas of Christianity in Europe, or of Buddhism in Asia, they being philosophies of which he was the sympathetic exponent, or inspiration may have been found in the beauty of nature from the hillsides of China or Tuscany. His freedom of expression has been the essential factor without which his inspiration and enthusiasm would have had no outlet.

There are artists today who live in comparative economic security. That they may be threatened with the loss of that security as well as their artistic independence is not obvious to them. It may not occur to them that their economic condition, as well as their spiritual freedom, is subject to the tendencies of political forces. They are not politically minded and their education probably is against their being so, as they have concentrated in a single direction, and lived for, and by, their art. It is mainly in the group of those who are economically affected that the awareness takes place.

The artists to whom the horrors and destruction of war are abhorrent and whose entire lives and processes of thought are bound up with the forces of liberty and benevolence, whether they realize it or not, should at least join openly and whole heartedly this movement for peace for the preservation of their liberties.

In times of war the artist who is not in accord with the philosophies and policies of the controlling power of government is in an unhappy condition indeed. He may be sent to a prison camp, and, if he is not opposed to those philosophies and policies the best he may hope for is the trenches, or that his services will be useful to the controlling powers to camouflage and conceal implements of destruction. This is contrary to the sentiments of humanity and spiritual enlightenment of which the artist should be the torch bearer.

PAUL MANSHIP

When people say there is no danger of Fascism in this country it seems to me to mean that they are not conscious of the great and inevitable shaping of forces in that direction going on in the world today. They think America is isolated and uninfluenced politically by those forces. In Europe we have seen the beginnings of those movements which have ended in the seizure of power, then the militarization and regimentation of the people, with the accompanying stifling of democratic and cultural liberties.

We have seen the great state of Louisiana become subservient to the whims of a demagogue and many of the established constitutional rights of free expression suppressed.

Artists in Fascist countries, because of economic depression and expenditures for war, have lost their private patrons except in the case of the favored few, and the meager support of the government is conditional to complete acceptance of the acts and policies of the government. The forces of Fascism so confuse the fundamental issues that the unthinking man risks to be herded like sheep into the corrals of a Fascistic state unless consciousness of the danger of loss of his freedom is brought before his eyes.

The artist, through organization, will serve culture and may do much to keep the beacon of warning alight to show the threat to liberty, democracy and peace.

ARTISTS' BOYCOTT OF
BERLIN OLYMPICS ART EXHIBITION
George Biddle

The subject on which I was asked to speak to you is the appropriate and necessary reasons why the united artists of America should pass a resolution protesting our participation in any exhibition in connection with the Olympic games in Berlin, sponsored by the present Nazi government.

Such a resolution is only effective if we, ourselves, clearly understand the basis of such protest and its practical significance to our life and growth as American artists.

As with many of us, my own art development had its roots in Europe. Twenty-five years ago I studied in Germany and Italy. I have today the deepest respect and gratitude for the high professional standards of art and for the liberal inheritance which these two countries have given us. I am personally happy that a few of my closest friends are German and Italian artists.

The truth of the matter is this: any nation, be it of little consequence or be it one of those favored few which have contributed most generously to the world's happiness, has within its body both the seeds of liberalism and the germs of bigotry, suppression and hatred. Italy had its renaissance. Today it has in it the seeds of science and enlightenment. Germany has given its music and its philosophy. Today it has in it the seeds of liberal progress. America has had its William Penns, its Franklins, its Paines, its Jeffersons and Justice Holmes. It has also in its heritage witch burnings, Ku Klux Klans, Vigilantes and lynchings. Today they are with us. Tomorrow they can ride us in the saddle.

As individual artists we have been invited to participate in an exhibition by a government which sponsors the destruction of all freedom in art. This invitation directly challenges the professional code of ethics of American artists. If no such code exists, it is urgent that we adopt one. As a congress of American artists we can emphatically state our attitude toward such an invitation.

GEORGE BIDDLE

Our protest is not against a form of government, which to us, as Americans, is abhorrent. Our protest is not against Germany or Italy as such. As realistic American artists we protest against participation with a government, which sponsors racial discrimination, the censorship of free speech and free expression, and the glorification of war, hatred and sadism.

There is an urgent need today that we align ourselves in conformity with such policies as we feel necessary to our professonal self-preservation. There is a living danger, today greater than ever, that the germs of intolerance may so infect our system that the ends and conditions of life, which are most essential to us as artists, may be smothered in the general sickness of our social system.

I therefore move that "whereas the present German government, judged by the statements of their own leaders, has suppressed freedom of religion and freedom of thought, and

Whereas they have exiled or caused to live in exile, many of their greatest scientists, writers and artists—

Be it now resolved that the Members of the Artists' Congress will take no part in the exhibition of paintings to be held in concurrence with the Olympic games in 1936, and they further urge all other American art societies and individual artists to refuse to exhibit in Germany, as a protest against the spiritual intolerance and suppression of free thought, which the present German government not only condones but openly boasts of."

(*This resolution was unanimously adopted.*)

ARTISTS MUST ORGANIZE
Heywood Broun

I want to talk of the undoubted fact—of the vital fact—that the artists and writers of America must organize, and organize along trade union lines and principles. It is good to have meetings in which the artist gets up and states his opposition to Fascism. To make that opposition good, he must make good through organization; and I see no other way except the organization through labor lines. I think it is enough to say that the future of art in America must come through a closer contact with labor.

I would not say that there had not been certain notable things done in art by Americans, but I am disappointed on the whole. I wrote a column the other day in which I stated, perhaps erroneously, that as soon as you cross the border in Mexico, you find wherever there is a broad wall four or five Mexican artists to paint on it. I thought perhaps that was due to a certain native genius in the Mexican artist. I am probably wrong about that. The reason seems to be in the unity of purpose art has with labor in Mexico. This statement is probably true because Mexican art exemplifies the life and thought of the Mexican people as a whole.

I wonder whether American art might not begin to step with labor. The highest prize to an artist this year was a prize given to him by the United Mine Workers of America. As labor moves along the economic and the political front, it moves along the cultural front at the same time. There is the goal of the American artist.

What is the American artist fed on today? He is fed on what is called taste—the taste of the American people. I think we must get back to something better, greater than taste, and that is

emotion; and where do you get emotion except out of the masses?
So I say as a fellow artist, get together with labor. Get to know
the aspirations, the ideals of the masses, and then art will be put
back on earth. Then art will go ahead, lickety split, buckety
bucket, here in America!

ARTISTS AND TRADE UNIONS
Francis J. Gorman, Vice-President,
United Textile Workers of America

Too long have the professional man and woman considered themselves apart from the sordidness of this world's economic chaos!
Too long have the artist, the doctor, the dentist, the engineer
and the architect allowed themselves to be exploited in precisely
the same manner which the unorganized worker is today exploited in industry, simply because the professionals have considered themselves "above" organization.

This present crisis, however, and the rapid advance of the
forces of reaction in the form of destruction of our democratic
and economic rights, have begun to teach the professional workers, and the hitherto un-class-conscious white-collar workers that
if they are to protect themselves, they must enter into the political and economic scene with a group organized of and by themselves. This group, however, if it is to serve as protection must act
in conjunction with other groups, and thus present to the forces
of reaction which seek to compel the people of the United States
to accept the decadence and destruction of our present order,
with a united people's group, ready to demand its rights and protect the few vestiges of democracy left us.

This, it seems to me, is particularly important for the artist
and for the writer. These two professions are among those most
ruthlessly attacked when they are not organized into economic
and political groups for their own protection. It is in the miser-
able rewards for culture that we find some of the most blatant
forms of exploitation. The rich throw crumbs from their tables to
the living artists and writers in order to pacify their "cultural
whims" while they put millions of dollars into the purchase of
dead artists' pictures, because the premium has gone up with the

---

Mr. Gorman, unable to attend the Congress, sent in this paper which
arrived too late to be read at Town Hall.

centuries. It must not be thought that I deprecate the culture of the ages, nor that I feel that pictures of Old Masters are not worth handsome prices. It merely occurs to me that the living artist might well demand his share of the bounty also. It occurs to me that the artists today have not taken advantage of the opportunities to organize and demand a living in return for their works which enrich civilization culturally.

My interest in the organization of professional men and women is not wholly an unselfish one. The professional* is more and more making inroads on the living standards of the workers, many of whom have protected their wages and working conditions for years by dint of hard effort to form trade unions. Furthermore, the unorganized sections of our exploited classes form the most fertile field for the advancement of reaction and fascism. And with fascism comes the end of trade unionism and all democratic rights.

We cannot under-estimate the danger of fascism. Nor can we under-estimate the unconscious part which unorganized professional workers play in helping the advent of fascism. It is historically a fact that the bulk of the mass support of Italian and German fascism lay amongst the professional and intellectual class together with the vast, dispossessed middle class. That is what any believer in democracy must prevent in those countries where the formal forces of democracy still exist.

It is time that the artist came down from his aloof position, and soiled his hands with helping his fellow-workers struggle for a living wage. His fellow-workers will then help him in the same struggle. For too long has the artist and the intellectual professed disinterestedness in political and economic matters. But artists and intellectuals are beginning to realize that as the economic crisis deepens, and the entire economic structure begins to wobble under the weight of decay, that they, too, must organize to protect themselves.

Though the first attack upon democracy comes with the destruction of the trade-union movement, it is followed quickly by

---

* Unemployed and unorganized. —[Original] Editors

the suppression of freedom of expression in cultural fields as well. How many German and Italian artists, writers, philosophers and intellectuals have had to flee from their native countries with the advent of the barbaric regimes of Mussolini and Hitler? How many people felt like weeping as the giant funeral pyre of the intellectual contributions of Germany's foremost artists and writers wrote the bloody story of Hitler across the midnight sky?

The same fate awaits us in the United States if we do not act now to prevent it. Events are moving swiftly in that direction. Our foremost middle-class champions and writers have discarded the outmoded liberal theory of "It can't happen here" in favor of the grim, realistic realization that it not only *can* happen here, but that it *is* happening here. One of the first steps to be taken in the prevention of this mass enslavement is the militant organization of professional workers and intellectuals. I cannot stress this point too much. It is a vital necessity if we are to win over decadence and the rebirth of the Dark Ages.

There is a second step to be taken also. It must come closely on the heels of the solidification of a strong economic organization of artists. It might even come simultaneously with economic organization. This second, or simultaneous step, is the organization of the artists, together with the entire mass of under-privileged and dispossessed, into a political front—into a militant, determined Labor Party.

We are beginning to discover in the trade-union movement that our trade unions, our economic organizations, are no longer sufficient protection for us. We cannot, indeed, even continue with our trade unions if we do not also band together in political unity. Big Business and the controlling financial and industrial interests are making organization harder and harder. They are turning more and more to the use of troops in times of strike; to the hiring of the industrial spy to break up trade unions; to the persecution, framing and murder of trade-union leaders. State legislatures are passing sedition bills. War becomes an ever-nearer menace. These things, this terrible march of events, have as vital a meaning to the artist as they have for the textile worker, the miner or the garment worker. For all of us are treated with the same ruthless cruelty in concentration camps; all of us, no matter whether we be textile workers or artists, feel the vigilant terror of storm troop activity.

My message, then, to the artists of the United States is two-fold. I would urge the immediate strengthening of an artists' union, all-inclusive, embracing every artist, whether he be the "successful" artist or the struggling, unrecognized artist. I would hope, also, that this artists' front would include also provisions for unity with all working-class organizations, organizations of unemployed and consumer and other professional groups in the common struggle for a decent standard of living and for other economic rights.

Next, I would urge that the artists not confine themselves to activity in the economic field alone. For this, we believe, is now inadequate in the face of the marching legions of fascism. Therefore, I would hope also that the artists will unite their organization with the thousands and thousands of other organizations now behind the movement for a Labor Party for the United States.

With the workers, the small business men, the bankrupt farmers, the professionals and intellectuals banded together first in strong, militant economic organizations, and finally coalesced into a powerful political vanguard, there is no way that the fascist bands can invade our ranks. We will present to the agents of re-action a solid, invincible front, and defy them to invade our ranks with the destruction of a dictatorship of dying capitalism!

THE ARTIST MUST CHOOSE
Peter Blume

A few years ago, no one could ever have gotten the artists of America together to discuss anything. There never was, in fact, a common basis that many artists could get together on. They would have been prejudiced against the idea of holding a congress to talk about esthetic problems, for instance, because they considered this a private matter for individual artists to solve for themselves. Yet that was about the only thing they could have found to talk about. As a class they were broken into mutually antagonistic little groups, each trying to defend [its] own interests.

The astonishing thing is that American artists have changed in the past five years. This Congress Against War and Fascism would have been impossible before. Now they have come together, almost spontaneously, from every part of the country because they fear that their integrity as artists is being threatened and because they realize that their whole existence is tied up with the economic crisis of the entire world.

Many artists today, even in the face of these conditions, still view the fundamental problem with apathy and distrust. They consider themselves immune to the conditions in society. But as a matter of fact, all their peculiarities, their traditions, their general social outlook, are symptoms of how social conditions have molded them. Changes in the order of society have not only affected their style and technique, but have actually caused them to take sides in the economic struggle and to develop peculiar class prejudices.

The economic changes are clearly recorded in their work. The history of art and esthetics can be taken as a guide to the history of mankind, as everybody knows. If we had no other evidence of European civilization during the past 500 years, we could get a very good picture of this whole period through its art. It would give us not only a visual sense of how people lived, dressed, and were governed, but also the most subtle interpretations of how they thought and felt.

The artists were among the first to be affected by the change in the structure of society from Feudalism to bourgeois aristocracy. The artists became individualistic and remote from the active world around them. Their whole function in society altered. Patronage was shifted from Church and State to private individuals. The artists ceased to play a part as important vehicles for the communication of ideas, and became instead, decorators engaged to glorify the personal greatness of their patrons. They became utterly dependent on this class for their economic and artistic welfare.

For several centuries, in various corners of Europe, art followed the erratic course of business and trading activity. It flourished during prosperity and declined during business depressions. Under adverse economic conditions whole schools became static or extinct. Art was a product of abundance, to be enjoyed by the few who could afford it. This transformation of a work of art from a part of a social system into a luxury product, exploited by wealthy individuals, has given art and the personality and tradition of the artist much of their present unearthly characteristics.

The upheavals caused by the industrial revolution upset the precarious relationships the artist had with this class. The new economic forces that came in completely changed the aspect of wealth. It developed entirely new symbols of power. The display of luxury became unnecessary.

The artists were left high and dry, abandoned without anchorage anywhere. They had lost their privileged position, and they became the misfits of society, maladjusted to the economic laws and hostile to its philosophy. The artists were forced to retreat to a cloistered world of their own—into a Bohemia, under cover of defiance, because they could not reconcile themselves to the new situation nor accept the prevailing philistine tastes and standards.

In the latter half of the nineteenth century, an artist's greatness came to be measured not by his ability to express the ideals and aspirations of society, but in proportion to the cultural gap that existed between him and the standards of his time. To be in tune with the times was to be condemned to mediocrity; there was no way in which an original work of art could be made to fit into the scheme of things. Artists *were* misunderstood, and their audience was progressively narrowed.

The artist became a peculiar spectacle, a spiritual exile, a hobo in a materialistic world, wandering about in search of enduring truth. They scorned the idea of men finding their way to a better life through politics, for they were preoccupied only with the eternal qualities which no political circumstance could alter. They believed their art could function under any form of government.

The contradictions of this position soon became manifest. The artists had their own highly specialized set of values. The art they produced in an atmosphere of isolation became more introverted and more devoid of human meaning. They had shut themselves off from the world and now realized that they would have to find their way back into it again. They were weary of their own effeteness and longed for some direction.

At this point they put themselves into a position which would have led them straight to Fascism. They felt that a new social adjustment was imperative, but they were not in any way prepared to make a direct approach to the people. Their prejudices against the philistine mob impelled them in the opposite direction. Instead of coming down to earth, they retreated into the dead past. They looked for something authentic and they finally found it in the idea of an "intellectual aristocracy." The function of this august body of dilettantes was to give the artists a criterion of values, to maintain, by their authority, a high cultural level, and to arbitrate matters of esthetic dispute. The artists resolved that this was the only way out of the impasse that individualism had led them into.

They flirted with a whole variety of causes, such as Humanism, Monarchism and Medievalism in an attempt to give their idea social plausibility. They felt that authority and discipline could be restored once more only through a rigid hierarchical system.

The prevailing motive was a hatred of democracy, as the leveler of culture and the root of all evil, and a profound contempt for the masses as the despoilers of culture. These were causes artists could subscribe to and still remain aloof. They saw no paradox in the position they took against democracy. They simply argued that culture had to be concentrated in order to flourish.

This typically Fascist idea of a large subject class dominated by a highly civilized minority was enormously popular with the esthetes of the late Twenties. The artists had become so antisocial that they would have been ready to accept all the tenets of Fascism, though few were aware of its implications.

When the economic crash came, this elaborate scaffolding of ideas built upon their faith in a leisure-class culture collapsed. The artists didn't really descend from their Olympian heights and their ivory towers—they were thrown out. The depression helped to dispel their sacred illusions that they belonged to a privileged and sheltered class. Their low economic level was forced still lower. They found themselves side by side with the lowliest victims of the depression. It took more imagination than even artists possessed to cling to their illusions of grandeur, in the midst of unemployment, breadlines and bank failures, and what looked like the imminent fall of the whole economic system. We artists could see now that we would have to reach out for a more honest and more solid social relationship.

We were afforded a concrete example of how our old ideas worked out in real life—what a return to medievalism was like in a modern state—during the reign of terror when the Nazis came into power in Germany. We could not remain complacent at the sight of a government persecuting its artists and sending them into exile and imprisonment. It shamed us to think how near we once came to being Fascists ourselves, and how we had cherished a belief in the choice place we would have in an established aristocracy with its perfectly balanced social hierarchies.

We became aware of the threat of Fascism as an international menace. We could see its economic impulses operating everywhere, under the stress of economic crisis; its brutality, its racial and religious prejudices parading under the flag of reaction. We recognized it as the real enemy of culture, and we saw its portentous beginnings right here in the United States, in the violations of civil liberties, in acts of censorship and in the destruction of works of art.

We are aware that these violations of human liberties can no longer be minimized. These are not mere scarecrows invented by radical propagandists to mislead loyal Americans, but the recognizable symptoms of incipient Fascism, increasing daily in frequency and boldness and condemned by every decent civil and religious organization in America.

We have called this Congress Against Fascism and War to discuss the threat that has arisen to our liberties and our future as artists, and to add our weight in the united struggle against it. We know that there is no retreat for the artist, no ivory tower we can hide away in for protection, and no promise, as we have seen in the countries where Fascism has triumphed, that our sensitivity will be in any way regarded. Fascism is a desperate method of making us mute automatons in a dying order. Fascism means the death of culture. We must oppose it now, or be destroyed by it. There is no other choice.

A few years ago, the advent of Fascism seemed inevitable. We now know that it cannot triumph against a united opposition; that Fascism can be and has been stopped. The world we live in is a modern world, torn by opposing forces and moving with ever greater intensity and violence towards a crisis—a crisis culminating with Fascism and war. We must fight against both for our own salvation. We, as artists, must take our places in this crisis on the side of growth and civilization, against barbarism and reaction, and help to create a better social order.

THE ARTIST IN SOCIETY
First Closed Session
New School for Social Research
Henry Glintenkamp, Chairman

━━━━━━━━━━━━━━━━━━━━━━

THE SOCIAL BASES OF ART
Meyer Schapiro

When we speak in this paper of the social bases of art we do not mean to reduce art to economics or sociology or politics. Art has its own conditions which distinguish it from other activities. It operates with its own special materials and according to general psychological laws. But from these physical and psychological factors we could not understand the great diversity of art, why there is one style at one time, another style a generation later, why in certain cultures there is little change for hundreds of years, in other cultures not only a mobility from year to year but various styles of art at the same moment, although physical and psychological factors are the same. We observe further that if, in a given country, individuals differ from each other constantly, their works produced at the same time are more alike than the works of individuals separated by centuries.

This common character which unites the art of individuals at a given time and place is hardly due to a connivance of the artists. It is as members of a society with its special traditions, its common means and purposes, prior to themselves, that individuals learn to paint, speak and act in the current manner. And it is in terms of changes in their immediate common world that individuals are impelled together to modify their no longer adequate conceptions.

We recognize the social character of art in the very language we use; we speak of Pharaonic art, Buddhist art, Christian art, monastic art, military art. We observe the accord of styles with historical periods; we speak of the style of Louis XV, of the Empire style and the Colonial style. Finally, the types of art object refer to definite social and institutional purposes—church, altarpiece, icon, monument, portrait, etc. And we know that each of these has special properties or possibilities bound up with its distinctive uses.

When we find two secular arts existing at the same time in the same society we explain the fact socially. We observe, this is a peasant art, this is a court or urban art. And within the urban art, when we see two different styles, it is sometimes evident without much investigation that they come from different groups within the community, as in the official academic art and the realistic art of France in 1850. A good instance of such variety rooted in social differences are the contemporaries, Chardin and Boucher, an instance already grasped in its own time.

There is overwhelming evidence which binds art to the conditions of its own time and place. To grasp the force of this connection we have only to ask whether Gothic sculpture is conceivable in the eighteenth century, or whether Impressionist (or better, Cubist) painting could have been produced in African tribal society. But this connection of time and place does not by itself enable us to judge what conditions were decisive and by what necessities arts have been transformed.

But all this is past art. The modern artist will say: yes, this is true of Giotto who had to paint Madonnas because he worked for the Church. But I today take orders from no one; my art is free; what have my still life paintings and abstract designs to do with institutions or classes? He will go even further, if he has thought much about the matter, and say: yes, Giotto painted Virgins for the Church, but what has that to do with his art? The form of the work, its artistic qualities, were his personal invention; his real purpose was to make formal designs or to express his personality; and if we value Giotto today, if we distinguish him from the hundreds of others who made paintings of the same subject for the Church, it is because of his unique personality or design, which the Church certainly could not command or determine.

If—disregarding here the question of Giotto's intentions—we ask the artist why it is then that the forms of great artists today differ from the forms of Giotto, he will be compelled to admit that historical conditions caused him to design differently than one does today. And he will admit, upon a little reflection, that the qualities of his forms were closely bound up with the kind of objects he painted, with his experience of life and the means at his disposal. If Giotto was superior to other painters, his artistic superiority was realized in tasks, materials, conceptions and goals, common to the artists of his immediate society, but different from our own.

If modern art seems to have no social necessity, it is because the social has been narrowly identified with the collective as the anti-individual, and with repressive institutions and beliefs, like the church or the state or morality, to which most individuals submit. But even those activities in which the individual seems to be unconstrained and purely egoistic depend upon socially organized relationships. Private proeprty, individual competitive business enterprise or sexual freedom, far from constituting non-social relationships, presuppose specific, historically developed forms of society. Nearer to art there are many unregistered practices which seem to involve no official institutions, yet depend on recently acquired social interests and on definite stages of material development. A promenade, for example (as distinguished from a religious procession or a parade), would be impossible without a particular growth of urban life and secular forms of recreation. The necessary means—the streets and the roads—are also social and economic in origin, beyond or prior to any individual; yet each man enjoys his walk by himself without any sense of constraint or institutional purpose.

In the same way, the apparent isolation of the modern artist from practical activities, the discrepancy between his archaic, individual handicraft and the collective, mechanical character of most modern production, do not necessarily mean that he is out-side society or that his work is unaffected by social and economic changes. The social aspect of his art has been further obscured by two things, the insistently personal character of the modern painter's work and his preoccupation with formal problems alone. The first leads him to think of himself in opposition to society as an organized repressive power, hostile to individual freedom; the second seems to confirm this in stripping his work of any purpose other than a purely "aesthetic" [one].

But if we examine attentively the objects a modern artist paints and the psychological attitudes evident in the choice of these objects and their forms, we will see how intimately his art is tied to the life of modern society.

Although painters will say again and again that content doesn't matter, they are curiously selective in their subjects. They paint only certain themes and only in a certain aspect. The content of the great body of art today, which appears to be uncon-cerned with content, may be described as follows. First, there are natural spectacles, landscapes or city-scenes, regarded from the viewpoint of a relaxed spectator, a vacationist or sportsman, who values the landscape chiefly as a source of agreeable sensations or mood; artificial spectacles and entertainments—the theatre, the circus, the horse-race, the athletic field, the music-hall—or even works of painting, sculpture, architecture and technology, experi-enced as spectacles or objects of art; the artist himself and indi-viduals associated with him; his studio and its intimate objects, his model posing, the fruit and flowers on his table, his window and the view from it; symbols of the artist's activity, individuals practising other arts, rehearsing, or in their privacy; instruments of art, especially of music, which suggest an abstract art and im-provisation; isolated intimate fields, like a table covered with pri-vate instruments of idle sensation, drinking glasses, a pipe, play-ing cards, books, all objects of manipulation, referring to an exclusive, private world in which the individual is immobile, but free to enjoy his own moods and self stimulation. And finally, there are pictures in which the elements of professional artistic discrimination, present to some degree in all painting—the lines, spots of color, areas, textures, modelling—are disengaged from things and juxtaposed as "pure" aesthetic objects.

Thus elements drawn from the professional surroundings and activity of the artist; situations in which we are consumers and spectators; objects which we confront intimately, but passively or accidentally, or manipulate idly and in isolation—these are typical subjects of modern painting. They recur with surprising regularity in contemporary art.

Modern artists have not only eliminated the world of action from their pictures, but they have interpreted past art as if the elements of experience in it, the represented objects, were incidental things, pretexts of design or imposed subjects, in spite of which, or in opposition to which, the artist realized his supposedly pure aesthetic impulse. They are therefore unaware of their own objects or regard them as merely incidental pretexts for form. But a little observation will show that each school of modern artists has its characteristic objects and that these derive from a context of experience which also operates in their formal fantasy. The picture is not a rendering of external objects—that is not even strictly true of realistic art—but the objects assembled in the picture come from an experience and interests which affect the formal character. An abstract art built up out of other objects, that is, out of other interests and experience, would have another formal character.

Certain of these contents are known in earlier art, but only under social conditions related to our own. The painting of an intimate and domestic world, of moments of non-practical personal activity and artistic recreation (the toilette, the music-lesson, the lace-maker, the artist, etc.), of the landscape as a pure spectacle with little reference to action, occurs, for example, in the patrician bourgeois art of Holland in the 17th century. In the sporadic, often eccentric, works of the last three centuries in which appear the playing cards, the detached personal paraphernalia, the objects of the table and the artistic implements, so characteristic of Cubism, there we find already a suggestion of

Cubist aesthetic—intricate patterns of flat, overlapping objects, the conversion of the horizontal depth, the plane of our active traversal of the world, into an intimate vertical surface and field of random manipulation.

Abstract forms in primitive societies under different conditions have another content and formal character. In Hiberno-Saxon painting of the 8th century the abstract designs are not freshly improvised as in modern art, as a free, often grotesque, personal fantasy; but are conceived ornamentally as an intricate, uniformly controlled and minute, impersonal handicraft, subject to the conventional uses of precious religious objects. Hence in these older works, which are also, in a sense, highly subjective, there is usually a stabilizing emblematic form, a frequent symmetry and an arrangement of the larger units in simple, formalized schemes. In modern abstract art, on the contrary, we are fascinated by incommensurable shapes, unexpected breaks, capricious, unrecognizable elements, the appearance of a private, visionary world of emerging and disappearing objects. Whereas these objects are often the personal instruments of art and idle sensation described above—the guitars, drinking vessels, pipes, books, playing-cards, bric-a-brac, bouquets, fruit and printed matter—in the older art such paraphernalia is completely absent. A more primitive and traditional content, drawn from religion, folklore, magic and handicraft—Christian symbols, wild beasts, monsters, knotted and entangled bands, plait-work and spirals— constitutes the matter of this art.

A modern work, considered formally, is no more artistic than an older work. The preponderance of objects drawn from a personal and artistic world does not mean that pictures are now more pure than in the past, more completely works of art. It means simply that the personal and aesthetic contexts of secular life now condition the formal character of art, just as religious beliefs and practices in the past conditioned the formal character of religious art. The conception of art as purely aesthetic and individual can exist only where culture has been detached from practical and collective interests and is supported by individuals alone. But the mode of life of these individuals, their place in society, determines in many ways this individual art. In its most advanced form, this conception of art is typical of the rentier leisure class in modern capitalist society, and is most intensely developed in centers, like Paris, which have a large rentier group and considerable luxury industries. Here the individual is no longer engaged in a struggle to attain wealth; he has no direct relation to work, machinery, competition; he is simply a consumer, not a producer. He belongs to a class which recognizes no higher group or authority. The older stable forms of family life and sexual morality have been destroyed; there is no royal court or church to impose a regulating pattern on his activity. For this individual the world is a spectacle, a source of novel pleasant sensations, or a field in which he may realize his "individuality," through art, through sexual intrigue and the most varied, but non-productive, mobility. A woman of this class is essentially an artist, like the painters whom she might patronize. Her daily life is filled with aesthetic choices; she buys clothes, ornaments, furniture, house decorations; she is constantly re-arranging herself as an aesthetic object. Her judgments are aesthetically pure and "abstract," for she matches colors with colors, lines with lines. But she is also attentive to the effect of these choices upon her unique personality.

Of course, only a small part of this class is interested in painting, and only a tiny proportion cultivates the more advanced modern art. It would be out of place here to consider the reason for the specialized interests of particular individuals; but undoubtedly the common character of this class affects to some degree the tastes of its most cultivated members. We may observe that these consist mainly of young people with inherited incomes, who finally make art their chief interest, either as artists and decorators, or as collectors, dealers, museum officials, writers on art and travellers. Active business men and wealthy professionals who occasionally support this art tend to value the collecting of art as a higher activity than their own daily work. Painting enters into little relation with their chief activities and everyday standards, except imaginatively, insofar as they are conscious of the individual aspect of their own careers and enjoy the work of willful and inventive personalities.

It is the situation of painting in such a society, and the resulting condition of the artist, which confer on the artist today certain common tendencies and attitudes. Even the artist of lower middle-class or working-class origin comes to create pictures congenial to the members of this upper class, without having to identify himself directly with it. He builds, to begin with, on the art of the last generation and is influenced by the success of recent painters. The general purpose of art being aesthetic, he is already predisposed to interests and attitudes, imaginatively related to those of the leisure class, which values its pleasures as aesthetically refined, individual pursuits. He competes in an open market and therefore is conscious of the novelty or uniqueness of his work as a value. He creates out of his own head (having no subject-matter imposed by a commission), works entirely by himself, and is therefore concerned with his powers of fantasy, his touch, his improvised forms. His sketches are sometimes more successful than his finished pictures, and the latter often acquire the qualities of a sketch.

Cut off from the middle class at the very beginning of his career by poverty and insecurity and by the non-practical character of his work, the artist often repudiates its moral standards and responsibilities. He forms on the margin of this inferior philistine world a free community of artists in which art, personalities and pleasure are the obsessing interests. The individual and the aesthetic are idealized as things completely justified in themselves and worth the highest sacrifices. The practical is despised except insofar as it produces attractive mechanical spectacles and new means of enjoyment, or insofar as it is referred abstractly to a process of inventive design, analogous to the painter's art. His frequently asserted antagonism to organized society does not bring him into conflict with his patrons, since they share his contempt for the "public" and are indifferent to practical social life. Besides, since he attributes his difficulties, not to particular historical conditions, but to society and human nature as such, he has only a vague idea that things might be different than they are; his antagonism suggests to him no effective action, and he shuns the common slogans of reform or revolution as possible halters on his personal freedom.

Yet helpless as he is to act on the world, he shows in his art an astonishing ingenuity and joy in transforming the shapes of familiar things. This plastic freedom should not be considered in itself an evidence of the artist's positive will to change society or a reflection of real transforming movements in the everyday world. For it is essential in this anti-naturalistic art that just those relations of visual experience which are most important for action are destroyed by the modern artist. As in the fantasy of a passive spectator, colors and shapes are disengaged from objects and can no longer serve as a means in knowing them. The space within pictures becomes intraversable; its planes are shuffled and disarrayed, and the whole is reordered in a fantastically intricate manner. Where the human figure is preserved, it is a piece of picturesque still-life, a richly pigmented, lumpy mass, individual, irritable and sensitive; or an accidental plastic thing among others, subject to sunlight and the drastic distortions of a design. If the modern artist values the body, it is no longer in the Renaissance sense of a firm, clearly articulated, energetic structure, but as temperamental and vehement flesh.

The passivity of the modern artist with regard to the human world is evident in a peculiar relation of his form and content. In his effort to create a thoroughly animated, yet rigorous whole, he considers the interaction of color upon color, line upon line, mass upon mass. Such pervasive interaction is for most modern painters the very essence of artistic reality. Yet in his choice of subjects he rarely, if ever, seizes upon corresponding aspects in social life. He has no interest in, no awareness of, such interaction in the everyday world. On the contrary, he has a special fondness for those objects which exist side by side without affecting each other, and for situations in which the movements involve no real interactions. The red of an apple may oppose the green of another apple, but the apples do not oppose each other. The typical human situations are those in which figures look at each other or at a landscape or are plunged in a revery or simulate some kind of absorption. And where numerous complicated things are brought together in apparent meaningful connection, this connection is cryptic, bizarre, something we must solve as a conceit of the artist's mind.

The social origins of such forms of modern art do not in themselves permit one to judge this art as good or bad; they simply throw light upon some aspects of their character and enable us to see more clearly that the ideas of modern artists, far from describing eternal and necessary conditions of art, are simply the results of recent history. In recognizing the dependence of his situation and attitudes on the character of modern society, the artist acquires the courage to change things, to act on his society and for himself in an effective manner.

He acquires at the same time new artistic conceptions. Artists who are concerned with the world around them, its action and conflict, who ask the same questions that are asked by the impoverished masses and oppressed minorities—these artists cannot permanently devote themselves to a painting committed to the aesthetic moments of life, to spectacles designed for passive, detached individuals, or to an art of the studio.

There are artists and writers for whom the apparent anarchy of modern culture—as an individual affair in which each person seeks his own pleasure—is historically progressive, since it makes possible for the first time the conception of the human individual with his own needs and goals. But it is a conception restricted to small groups who are able to achieve such freedom only because of the oppression and misery of the masses. The artists who create under these conditions are insecure and often wretched. Further, this freedom of a few individuals is identified largely with consumption and enjoyment; it detaches man from nature, history and society, and although, in doing so, it discovers new qualities and possibilities of feeling and imagination, unknown to older culture, it cannot realize those possibilities of individual develop-

ment which depend on common productive tasks, on responsibilities, on intelligence and cooperation in dealing with the urgent social issues of the moment. The individual is identified with
the private (that is, the privation of other beings and the world),
with the passive rather than active, the fantastic rather than the
intelligent. Such an art cannot really be called free, because it is
so exclusive and private; there are too many things we value that
it cannot embrace or even confront. An individual art in a society where human beings do not feel themselves to be most individual when they are inert, dreaming, passive, tormented or un-
controlled, would be very different from modern art. And in a
society where all men can be free individuals, individuality must
lose its exclusiveness and its ruthless and perverse character.

RACE, NATIONALITY, AND ART
Lynd Ward

Our multitudinous theories of race and nationality in art have
their source in the obvious fact that differences exist—that Chinese painting, for example, is different from the painting of Renaissance Italy, which in turn is different from that of modern
France. If we are to account for these differences, it can be by
only one of three possible explanations: first, it may be that there
is something in the blood stream of the individual and of the race
to which he belongs that makes it inevitable for him to produce
work with a specific quality, that no one in whose veins that particular blood does not flow can hope to achieve that quality. Or
second, it may be that within the boundaries of geographic areas
a people develop a unique feeling that results in a distinct flavor
in their art product. Or as a third alternative, it may be that the
character and qualities of the artist's work are determined not at
all by his blood, only incidentally by his geography, and predominantly by a combination of forces in the cultural environment
and the social situation in which he finds himself. It will be seen
that the first of these imposes inviolable categories on the artist
on the basis of accident of birth, that the second gives him a
static, geographically-determined character, and that the third
makes him a free agent reacting to an environment in which the
elements are in process of change and continual rearrangement.
This question is not an academic one. It is of vital importance to
artists because in many ways the character and scope of American
art in years to come will depend on our understanding of racial
differences, here where the pattern of growth has brought together some of all the peoples of the earth.

The easiest way is to assign the reason for all differences to
blood. It is the one that involves the least mental activity, and a

The writer wishes to acknowledge his indebtedness to Mr. Meyer Schapiro
for part of the material contained in this paper.

clear-cut division is made immediately. But because it rests on a very vague base, hypotheses can be built on it by anyone who chooses. On the one hand you are told that there are innate abilities that make the Italians great painters; on the other it is claimed that Italy's greatest paitners, specifically Giotto, da Vinci, Raphael, and Titian, were not of Italian blood at all, but were Nordic, their ancestry going back to the Nordic invaders of Italy. Regarding the Negro, it is maintained that when white and black are crossed there is always a reversion to what these white theoreticians call the lower racial strain, and the resultant hybrid can never be anything but a Negro. But on another occasion, if a Negro makes a definite cultural contribution, it is because his germ-plasm is predominantly white. Or it is said that while the English have demonstrated great abilities in literature and drama, they have no ability in painting. On the other hand it will be seriously proposed that the only hope for the development of an American art lies in the development of the Anglo-Saxon elements in the population.

What is there behind this maze of contradictory claims for the part blood heritage plays in the creative activity of man? Is there any evidence that biological differences exist, as the proponents of racial superiorities insist?

The testimony on this point is very explicit. All responsible anthropologists agree that there is no acceptable scientific foundation for the belief that one race is more primitive, basically inferior or fundamentally different in mind from another. This being the case, the unique qualities of African tribal art, for example, must proceed not from the blood stream but from cultural circumstances that stem originally from geographic and climatic conditions. The Negro who is born into that isolated culture becomes a part of it not because of special capacities in his bloodstream, but by the mere circumstance of birth, and a Negro who is born into another culture must, if he is to function validly, become part of it. There are no mystical blood lines leading back to Africa.

What then are we to think of certain leaders of Negro art

who would put the Negro artist in America to work in the forms of African tribal art, seeking thereby to develop his "unique racial qualities"? Surely they are playing into the hands of those whites who for economic reasons are anxious to deny to the American Negro the benefits of the only culture with which he has had any contact for hundreds of years, the only culture of which he could ever become a valid part.

On the question of racial purity, the testimony is equally clear. Not only is there no sharp dividing line between the different skin-pigmentations, but even within the white race itself, to speak of pure racial types is meaningless. From a scientific point of view there is no such thing as a French, German or Italian type. The three general strains that are found in Europe run in striations from east to west. From the racial angle, then, what similarity and unity can be conjured up is greater between the north of France and the north of Germany than it is between Northern and Southern extremities within each country, and so on. What this does to the suppositions of racial characteristics in the arts of these countries is easily seen.

But even if there is no ground for a structure of racial differences in Europe, the theorists of blood chemistry will still point to the Jewish race as evidence of the persistence of unique qualities that can be traced to blood alone. They hold it to be self-evident that the Jewish race has definite physical characteristics and equally characteristic cultural qualities, and the one stems from the other. But here again the inquiries of science tend to demolish the structure.

The concept of a Semitic race is a myth. Arabs and Jews are usually assumed to compose it, and Arabic and Hebrew both belong to the Semitic classification in languages. But when you come down to physical types, Arabs are almost exclusively Mediterraneans, whereas a minority of Jews are Mediterraneans, and the type that occurs most frequently is the Alpine. Wide studies have shown the greatest range of variation in physical characteristics, and the one thing that seems to emerge is a tendency for those of the Jewish religion to approximate the physical types of the people among whom they live. Almost all anthropologists agree that a scientifically-distinguishable Jewish race cannot be found. The cultural corollary of this lies in the fact that the Hebrew painted manuscripts of the Middle Ages showing clearly the style of the geographic region in which they have their origin. In Paris they are Parisian, in the Rhineland, Rhenish, in Venice, Venetian. In our own time we have the same of lack of evidence as regards a common blood and culture. Rothenstein is English; Pisarro, French; Soutine, Russian; Pechstein, German; Modigliani, Italian. Who can point to anything in the work of these men that can be said to be common to all of them, not found in the work of their contemporaries, and therefore a Jewish characteristic?

Here again the import of this has a direct bearing on our problems as American artists, for if there is not one iota of evidence acceptable to scientists that will support a claim of uniqueness in the Jewish blood stream, then we must read out of court all propositions based on it, such as the condemnation of Alfred Stieglitz's place in American art because he is a Hoboken Jew.

What of the second alternative, that a people living within given geographic boundaries develop a national character in their art product that can be easily identified over long periods of time. This means that whatever the racial strains in France, for example, there is a French quality that you can put your finger on all through the development of French art. But as soon as you begin to examine this, it starts to dissolve in thin air. Who is your Anglo-Saxon, Hogarth or Aubrey Beardsley? Who is your Frenchman, Daumier or Fragonard? Differences in time manifest much greater variations than do differences in national location. Thus Gothic sculpture in the Cathedral at Lübeck is much closer to French sculpture of the same period than it is to the Romantic historical painters of the eighteenth century in Germany. Polite court art in England in the seventeen hundreds bears more resemblance to polite court art in France at the same time than it does to anything else.

Moreover at any given point in time, the unity assumed

within such a national group is a fictitious one. German peasant art of the eighteenth century has greater kinship with French peasant art than it has with the art created for the German nobility. Today academic painting in England, France and Germany has a similarity regardless of national boundaries and is equally antithetical to the modern painting found in the same countries.

All this leaves us with no possible inference except that theories of differences based on nationality are untenable. If we require any further comment on this point it need only come through an analysis of the national composition of the most recent French schools. Of the Impressionists, Monet was from the North of France, Degas had a Creole mother and a father whose parentage was half Italian, Sisley was English and Pisarro was a West Indies Jew. The French Neo-Romantic school numbers one Frenchman, three Russians and one Dutchman. The leaders of the Paris-born Surrealist movement are four Frenchman, two Spaniards, one Swiss and one German.

If differences in art are not to be accounted for on the basis of racial inheritance or national composition, can they be explained by the concept of a human being, endowed with certain impulses toward visual expression, reacting to the social situation in which he finds himself? This would mean that what we habitually refer to as racial and national differences are social habit-patterns proceeding primarily from isolation, secondarily from consciously-controlled imitation or study, and that the creative work of the artist is in its essence a reaction to a specific situation. As the conditions of the situation (location of economic power, ideology of social groups, restrictive action of traditions, and so on) change, so will his work.

It further implies that, if differences are bound up with the factor of isolation, as isolation in the modern world tends to become less, so will differences become less.

This direction is true of the whole of human activity, not only of art, and has manifested itself in the economic world in the growth of geographic independence and the gradual conquering of the necessities of life so that for the first time since man bestirred himself there is no longer a scarcity of food and material goods imposed by conditions to which he is a slave. Man stands on the threshold of a world towards which he has been moving [for] many years. This is the social situation in which the artist finds himself and it is in relation to this situation that our understanding of race and nationality takes on such importance.

In Germany in 1927, six years before Hitler came to power, there was already established a nationalist movement in art whose slogan was "Only German Art." It distributed graphic work in which a blond hero was shown demolishing temples labeled French modernism, American jazz, and so on. This movement was neither originated by the Brown Shirts nor in practical matters allied with their ruffianism. It was a manifestation of an attitude of mind that was developing in society as a whole due to the pressure of economic forces. It was the easy way out of a complicated emotional situation whose base was an impossible economic order. It offered a false solution to the problems of the artist, beclouded the objective situation with a fog of emotional attachments and accelerated the state of mind in the German people that made possible the political movement whose economic and cultural character is so indelibly written in the records of our time.

What implications are there in all this for American artists? We are confronted with a growing emphasis on race and nationality in art. We have many appeals for an "American art" in which the concept of America is very vague, usually defined as "a genuine American expression" or "explicitly native art" and sometimes includes a separation of American painters into desirable and undesirable on the basis of Anglo-Saxon surnames.

In the face of this, we should recognize that the real basis for an emotional separation between the member of the tribe and the outsider is to be found in more or less obscure feelings of economic rivalry and insecurity; that this separation becomes an effective barrier to a valid solution of the problems that face all artists; that just as the nationalist appeal in German art accompanied the rise of fascist reaction, a nationalist appeal in this country will inevitably contribute to a corresponding political movement; that finally the word "American" used in that way has no real meaning. It suspends a veil of fictitious unity and blinds our eyes to the fact that there can be no art in common between the Americans who own Rockefeller Center, the Americans in the Legion in Terre Haute, and the Americans in, as a symbol, Commonwealth College in Arkansas.

THE ARTIST AND HIS AUDIENCE

The Artist, His Audience, and Outlook
Max Weber

When it was suggested that I write a paper on "The Artist and His Audience" to be read at the Artists' Congress, I was at a loss to know what to say on a subject which by its very nature is so paradoxical. Museums, galleries and schools boast of considerable numbers of visitors to their exhibitions in the course of an art season. Still, when you consider the population of large communities, of large and small cities, the attendance is exceedingly small and more often quite negligible. I mean an audience that is heart and soul interested in the artist as a worker, as a human being with the same hopes and aspirations and needs as other workers.

The artist functions not only in a spiritual way but also in ways much as a machinist, bricklayer or cobbler does in the industrial sphere. But unfortunately art is still considered a luxury meant for the few, the privileged, for those "favored by destiny."

But if art is a luxury, why, in face of prevailing misery and poverty, are fortunes annually spent on antiquity and other ancient curiosities and historic souvenirs, and hardly anything for art by the living? The more battered and broken, the more fragmentary these antiques are, the higher the price. The more they dig, they more they find. With the modern derrick and steamshovel the archaeologists and the excavators are as prolific as coal miners, and the supply is inexhaustible, with ancient cities beneath cities. The volumes and historic opinions written on these finds that lie entombed in the cold and unvisited alcoves of the bibliotheques are getting larger and heavier with each succeeding decade. What are we living going to do about the undertakers in the museums and their funeral and embalming parlors—I mean the rooms of "recent acquisitions" with their "here lie" labels and eulogies? As artists and artisans we love and adore the authentic antique. Our gratitude to the museums is bountiful. Nevertheless, we living strongly resent being inundated, while so much of the dead past is excavated. Where is the logic, where is the balance? As for assurance of permanency, why exact and demand so much from the living artist and his work, when we see how fugitive, insecure and impermanent, yes even worthless, are many of the most expensive industrial products and even more so the contracts, treaties, and guarantees of honor and peace?

A few decades ago an artist was considered an outcast altogether, an idler, one who amused himself with the Muses, a dreamer, a shirker. Exhibitions, galleries, art lectures and museums were few and far between. In recent years, however, art interest has grown considerably, but is still slim compared to the audience an automobile or boat show enjoys. Even with this increase in the number of galleries and artistic activities, it is deplorable to contemplate the limited number of people an artist can reach. The art season is comparatively short, the opportunity to exhibit sadly limited, and consumption or sales nil.

Granting that an artist has an exhibition in a well located gallery, under favorable auspices and conditions, how many and what people can he reach in a fortnight or thereabouts? A few friends and relatives, a fair number of questful, serious art students, a few moneyless art-lovers, a sprinkle of bargain-hunters an hour before the close of the exhibition, a few esthetic art hairsplitters in search of the twenty-fifth (abstract) dimension during the quiet hours of the afternoon; others quite insipid and some so far advanced that they leave even Buck Rogers of the twenty-fifth century millenniums behind.

What happens at a one-man show happens at the large annual museum exhibition. A little review is written quite often by a biased, and more often still by a tired, dull and undiscerning critic, an insignificant mention of some trifle that suits his fancy, a little evasion, sarcasm, a grain of venom, derision and jealousy, a little playboy quibble here and there, a touch of gossip, a measure of superficial art jargon, and our leading newspapers find it fit to print. Such shallowness, insincerity and cheap auction-room appraisal passes for art criticism. And what can we expect from the average layman who seeks for light in the current reviews of art after reading such reviews. Of course there are exceptions. What interest can the greater portion of the mediocre press arouse in the reader and hungry art-lover?

It would be a waste of time to mention the traveling loan exhibitions, the prizes and juries, the prefaces in the catalogues, written by the erudite art directors of the mausoleums. I mean museums. And what do they do for the artist? Often as not, a note of thanks and a catalogue is sent to the artists, telling them what a great success the exhibition was, what it meant for the artistic uplift of the community. The pictures are returned, with a number on the too-often-smashed frames, with punctured canvas or broken glass. (Now pay your rent, buy your clothes and food for yourself and family with the note of appreciation from the well-groomed board of trustees of these museums and the salaried directors.) And with the publicity and prestige thus rewarded, the artist may gain admission to a seat in heaven.

It seems to me, my comrades and fellow artists, regardless of what innate talent or gifts we were favored with by the gods, in order to obtain a hearing and a return reasonably commensurate with our creative gifts, we must live in discarded places, lose our reason, cut off our ears and noses and finally commit suicide, if we hope for a considerable audience—half a century after our flight from this planet. (But it is tragic enough to starve and suffer the pangs of anxiety and fear in the midst of plenty.)

The causes of the neglect of the artist, and his limited audience are numerous, but the outstanding cause is the economic. For how many in the population of a given area can find the time and leisure for cultural pursuits? How pitifully few people can visit galleries and the out-of-the-way museums. The art dealer who deals in work by living artists is, by reason of the overhead expense and general maintenance, confined to small and cramped stuck-away quarters. He is compelled to curtail his exhibitions. His as well as the artists' activities and genuine ambitions are stifled and their programs minced and hectic. The palatial spacious day-lit galleries in prominent cosmopolitan centers are for the great dead and the masters of old.

The comedian, the hooligan, the wise-crack has an audience in the millions upon millions every hour, every day. The reason for this is simple and obvious. The joker is the Novocain in the struggle and agony of the daily existence of the great multitude. Indirectly he sells all sorts of trash, and announces tainted news and fraudulent commodities.

Compare the number of art lectures, art courses and publications, the number of art schools, with the carloads of pulp, variety and sex magazines and the bulk of the Sunday newspapers, the funnies, the radio propaganda of tooth-paste, hair tonic, cereals, macaroni and shoe polish, and the cheap, lewd movies, the pool-rooms and other demoralizing institutions.

Why, with so many vacant skyscraper lofts, armories and other spacious, unoccupied and centrally located buildings, should artists be driven to show their work and offer it for sale on the sidewalks of Greenwich Village? What impression can such a showing make on even the most sympathetic and understanding spectator? Pictures guillotined on iron railings, tossed by the wind, soiled by the dust and shouted out, as it were, by harsh out-of-door lighting; the grandest work of art would be mightily dimmed and its glow tarnished and cheapened, placed under similar conditions. These open-air art marts, while received good-naturedly, nevertheless call to mind the horror and sadness of the scenes of evictions in the slums.

High-domed edifices, veritable palaces in size and proportion, called banks, are built in the hundreds of thousands all over the land, of marble, granite, glass and brass for the mere counting of pennies and pieces of green paper, called money; for the housing in their cellars of military forts called safes, and a few desks and counters with clerks that look like ants in these vacant, space-wasted interiors, while art exhibitions, lectures, and musicals, with few exceptions, are relegated to improvised, dingy, cramped interiors.

Then we have the annual Independent Artists' Exhibition.

Another makeshift. At such unimpressive, temporary exhibition places, the yellow journals and their reporters find it expedient and easy to display, or give vent to their cheap vulgar wit at the expense of the bewildered, beaten and dispossessed artist and art student.

We do not seek the 57th Street gallery, robed in royal purple plush and trimmed with modern chromium, furnished with wrought-iron lamps and cushioned lounges. You don't see the staid art dealers display their pictures on iron railings, on dilapidated stoops, or in doorwards over ash-cans. No! They must have their plush, shaded light, uniformed attendants like Pullman porters, little hot-house evergreens, tropical plants in private nooks and cosy corners. A hushed atmosphere, a sanctimonious, ecclesiastical environment, engraved catalogues with introductions and forewords by French critics for greater prestige, a stamp of imported goods from abroad—such surroundings are more conducive to the sale of their wares to the industrial magnates.

In these palatial, life-lacking galleries, the art critic enters with humility and reverence. He is awed. A two or three column article with 6-inch square illustrations, headlines, captions follow. He is eloquent in his praise of the foreign and the dead, although truly bored and nagged with having to write and rewrite on the same subjects season after season. These grand, staid merchants of art have a special genius for resurrecting the dead and know how to keep the dead living. Only the profit system can breed such commercial wizards, parasites and opportunists. What chance have we? Where and how shall the living find an audience?

In the beginning of his or her career the artist is advised to make connecitons. We keep on connecting all our lives, and in the end most of us find ourselves connected with the poorhouse.

Still other and perhaps as grave impediments that tend to widen the gap between artist and audience are the million high-sounding manifestos of the countless prophets of the *isms*, the sly and copious self-appointed impresarios, the art-healers, art benefactors that confuse, antagonize and in the end repel an audience.

An outstanding factor that must be considered in an effort to augment the artists' audience is the perplexing question of subject matter as influenced and colored by the new social consciousness which, I believe, will be solved naturally through closer ties between artists and the steadily growing class-conscious proletarian population. Subject matter expressing and revealing the life, poetry and power inherent in the great toiling, awakening masses.

To achieve this we should reject and ignore idle intellection, dogma, sophistication and affectation of purity and naiveté. For an art as informing and mighty as archaic Greek and Assyrian sculpture and the sculpture of Elephanta, as elemental and rudimentary as the prehistoric frescoes of the bisons and reindeer in the caves of Altamira, we must strive. The spirit inherent in these works of art we must try to recapture. Though ancient in their titanic power, colossal scale and rhythm, these are nearer to modern dynamics and technical marvels, than are the trivial and roving interpretations and derivations of the art of our time. To hope for an art of similar plastic content and significance, we must first eschew the *isms* and *ists*, the maze of movements, theories and cults prefixed so often by the monosyllables *pre*, *sur*, *post*, and *neo* and what not, for identification and distinction in their zeal and expediency for supremacy, suggestive of the competition and greed in the market place or stock exchange.

Art for its own sake is doomed to suffocation and extinction, but art auxiliary to higher life expands and ever widens the bounds of human experience. It is then procreative, and not as art for art's sake which at best is a sort of celibacy. An art based on mere speculative and idle inferences, on mere whimsicality and caprice cannot endure and satisfy, as do the arts that are instinct with human beauty, social intimacy and divine inspiration. We must cast away therefore chameleon cleverness, and discard mental and optical illusions born of bourgeois decadence and ennui of a fast expiring civilization. This may sound dictatorial, assumptive and reactionary, but if you realize the meaninglessness and futility of the greater part of the so-called innovative or revolutionary art of the past twenty or thirty years, you will concede, I believe, that this may be good and timely counsel, suggested in utmost sincerity and with great humility, at a time when the very foundations of civilization are crumbling. The prophecies in art made two or three decades ago are now twice-told tales, and much of the art has become very stale. The same amount of energy and literary sophistication that was spent on initiating and hailing the *isms* is now being spent in pulmotoring efforts to save them from extinction and oblivion. But nothing can be saved when time itself becomes an opponent, and nothing can be kept alive on either sophistry or opiates.

By all means we should avail ourselves, and we do, of the innovative and contributive in modern art. But that does not necessarily preclude building an art as plastically organic and significant as the best of the abstract and at the same time endowed with richer informing spirit, cultural and social content, with greater appeal to a much vaster and more eager audience. This would obviate irrelevant controversy which so often leads to hairsplitting nuances in metaphysics or psychology and to argumentative twaddle and group snobbery.

Again, if these remarks seem imperative or coercive in character, let us consider the tyranny and intimidation of Fascism in art. Because we are in a struggle between darkness and light I appeal to the artist to abandon vagary and sophistry and to take hold of reality in order to strengthen his spiritual fortifications against enemies armed with the deadliest of weapons and the logic of the Devil.

At this crucial moment, even more than ever before, we workers in the field of the fine arts owe to this and future generations a legacy of as perfectly balanced a vision as our talents will afford. We must show the way from malady to health, from psychiatry and obscurantism to clarity. We must impress it upon the artist and layman in no mincing terms that this is no time for mental squander and debauch, no time to play with distractions, pantomimic graphics, with fossils or sea-shells, machine parts of no machines, with geometric forms that cannot conform, with immobile dynamics, with distortions of the convex and concave lens, with distorted perspective, with the occult and perversions of all sorts.

And while it would be ludicrous to prescribe or insist on a

proletarian art technique and curriculum, nevertheless, may we not aspire to create an art eloquent and unfailingly clear in its social import, as clear as is the religious meaning and decorative beauty in the frescoes of Giotto and Francesca or Uccello—an art so evocative and illuminating that it will not fail to bring new light and hope to the masses?

A truly modern art is yet to come, but not until the new life is here, and not before the imminent emancipation of mankind that we envisage.

By reason of the great and impending dangers we are morally obligated to look to the needs of the neglected and spiritually impoverished manual and mental workers in all fields, if we hope ever to link life with art inseparably.

In our effort at renewal let us also deviate from the academic and insipid nudes, and aristocratic madonnas of past centuries and tastes and ideals foreign to us in the twentieth century. Let us, instead, turn to the gladiatorial heroism, ambition, and tempo of modern beneficent and yielding industry, science and technology, to scenes of joy and verve of happy toilers in their own made environments, to the new home-life, nursery and school, to the new comradeship and brotherhood hitherto unknown.

For, our own palaces of art and industry and social and cultural intercourse we must build, and adorn them in conformity with our own conception and aspirations of freedom, justice and happiness. And who can deny or doubt that we already have our feet on the only path that leads resolutely to the new edifice (to the new arena); but we must not falter or fail to bring with us an art, a literature, a music, a philosophy compatible and consistent with our renaissance and its potential revelation and liberation. From obscurity and vagary to the opulent light of the very heavens we must turn.

And now my dear colleagues, I hope that I have been able, if only in a slight way, to point out some of the difficulties that confront us, as well as the unlimited satisfactions that await us, in solving the problems of subject matter in our respective arts; and in that effort, how to gain closer contact with, and how to avail ourselves of the new social and spiritual resources and ideology, so that our arts will spring from, interlock with, and serve the new humanity.

To reach this goal is our task and only hope, and not until we reach it can we afford to rest.

A Mural Painter's Conviction
Gilbert Wilson

Two summers ago I visited Mexico City. There I saw on the walls of the National Preparatory School some murals by Orozco. All the art I had seen before then had dealt with "grand" subject matter and "beautiful" things. Orozco's work stunned me. Perhaps it was because I had come fresh from the studio of Eugene Savage. But anyhow these frescoes on the walls of that school in Mexico gave me for the first time a sense of direction.

I found myself despising the nine years that I had been studying art. Despising it because in all those nine years nothing in any art school had taught me to comprehend the purpose of art as I saw it employed here on these walls.

Here were murals employed not simply as an enhancement for architecture, not as an aimless, meaningless, colorful pattern to decorate an interior, not something to please the eye or to relieve the monotony of an uninterrupted wall.

Here was art as I had never before experienced it; but from that moment on I knew it was what I wanted Art to be—a real, vital, meaningful expression, full of purpose and intention, having influence and relation to people's daily lives—a part *of* life. Here was the first *modern* art I had ever seen. At least, it was the first creative work done in my own time that seemed to have any need, any excuse for being.

That initial contact with those frescoes of Orozco made me see ever so clearly that I was interested in art as a social force. I decided (I think I read this somewhere) that murals, today, can contain one of two things, either the cruelty of emptiness or the cruelty of truth. And most murals will contain the cruelty of emptiness because the public taste finds emptiness more palatable than truth.

From that trip to Mexico, I returned to my home in Indiana very much desiring to obtain some wall space for a mural. I didn't have any particular idea in mind but I wanted a wall. I wanted it so badly that I put aside any thought of money for fear it might stand in my way of getting a wall.

I found an excellent space in the Science hall of the local Teachers' College. Much to my surprise fifty dollars was secured from the PWA to be used for materials.

I prepared a design—a simple massive figure of a scientist with a microscope pointing through an intense cobalt blue. The idea was rejected and it was suggested that I use another smaller space and copy some portraits of famous men of science.

I was stubborn, so I lost out.

Looking for another space, I found it in the Junior High School. I set to work on a new design and rendered it very much in detail. I took this drawing around to all the schools in the city for the purpose of getting the reaction of the students—from fifth-grade up to college—and each was asked to write what the picture conveyed to him. This proved an interesting investigation and helped me to clarify the idea that I was trying to set forth as a mural. My design depicted Science or Organized Knowledge liberating Youth from the menace of an abused machine age.

I then took up my proposition with the head of the city schools. He was quite favorably impressed.

Another request to the PWA for funds brought out the fact that I hadn't gone ahead with the project for the Teachers' College, so I was turned down. I told the school board I would furnish my own material. They were not very enthusiastic over getting something for nothing.

The promotion of the project dragged along wearily for eight months, during which period I think I must have given up at least a thousand times.

At last, I got a prominent minister and a business man to plead my cause. They were my friends and wanted to see me progress. They went before the school board and got me the privilege of using the space I desired, but with the understanding that the walls would be restored if my enterprise proved unsuccessful.

However, before I was permitted to go to work, it was requested that I remove the dollar signs from the eyes of the skull in my design. Also I was asked what I had planned for the opposite wall. I did not know then, but I described a wild idea expressing "Youth and the New Liberty." I knew they would like it.

The school built me a scaffold and I went gloriously to work. In four weeks I was finished with the first wall—18 by 28 feet. This was not simply because I worked almost constantly night and day, but mainly because I had discovered colored chalk, which not only made it possible for me to work swiftly, but was quite inexpensive. (I believe this medium has great possibilities.)

I tried to arrange a public "unveiling" of this my first wall in order to stimulate an interest in the work, but I was unsuccessful.

For three months I was held up on the removal of the scaffold. It was just enough for me to resolve that I would do what I damn pleased if I ever got back to work on the opposite wall.

Meanwhile, I had heard an address by Senator Nye and had attended a Youth Congress in Chicago and had received some ideas that I wanted to incorporate in the design of the second wall.

It happened that there were a number of people in the city that I admired very much, so I worked their portraits into my design. This fact helped me more than I realized at the time.

I had the wall about three-quarters covered with the charcoal sketch when the head of the city schools paid me a visit. He looked at what I had done and said it did not seem to express my original idea of youth and the new freedom. He asked me to give him a written explanation. So I wrote one out and sent it to him the next day, making a valiant effort to defend my ideas by putting in his hands a leaflet of the Methodist Church containing an outspoken report on the present economic situation. This proved a strong item in support of what I was trying to do.

Nevertheless, I went to work like mad, feeling that it wouldn't be long now. I jumped into the color execution of details even before the rest of the design was composed. Overnight I had all the local people's portraits done. Intuitively, I felt that these portraits would help defend my wall.

Fortunately, Dr. Oxnam, President of DePauw University, saw my work about that time and his good reaction made a very favorable impression upon the Principal of the school. This stood me in good stead.

I even got bold after that and introduced some ideas that I had been holding back. I was working almost constantly, sometimes sleeping at the school, and I was exceedingly happy.

With the walls finally completed, I took down the scaffolding myself and called in the photographer the same day.

The unveiling proved an encouraging success for the liberals of the city, and the trouble raised by the Legion and other reactionaries was overridden simply because their objections took such a ridiculously ignorant form—the prize, of course, being the quotation from the Declaration of Independence mistaken for an utterance of Eugene Debs. Nevertheless, flags soon covered the inscriptions. I went out one Sunday and put two more inscriptions on the wall and larger flags were secured. I was instructed to turn in my key.

The teachers and students of the school took up a collection and presented it to me. It exceeded the cost of my chalk by four dollars.

And now—if I may make a personal statement—I have concluded that Art, in this restless and changing day, has no right to deal with beauty, but must of necessity deal with a *preparation for beauty*, namely, the task of applying its powerful influence to the creating of an awareness in the mass-mind—an emotional awareness—of the significance of the great forces of social and economic change that are current in today's tempo. Surely, the betterment of human conditions in purely economic terms, in this day of depression-ridden unrest, transcends any need for such things as beauty or culture. Not that they are to be considered any less desirable, for, to be sure, they are the very heart and soul of that which we might call the more abundant life—but such things as beauty and culture and similar things of the spirit are being crowded more and more into utter inaccessibility by the present mad and furious confusion and by the relentless and tragic disruption of human living.

With Fascism sinkings its ugly roots more deeply into almost every part of the world, and with War, that must inevitably involve all civilization, becoming daily more imminent, how can we hope to know such things as beauty or culture in the face of such adversity?

Personally, I feel it is the task and obligation of every creative individual, whether he wields a brush or a pen, to raise a positive cry against these evils. To devote his creative energy to the expression of anything less than that high purpose is only to turn his talent to an inexcusably wasted end.

The Magazine and the Artist
John Groth

The relationship between the artist and the magazine is nearly always one of compromise.

The artist begins by asking for as much leeway as possible, and ends by taking as much as the editor will give him—he takes it, that is, if he expects to go on making a living at his job.

These compromises are bound to have some influence on the artist's work, and cause many to take the far less lucrative, and in some ways much more difficult, measure of doing exactly what they want to do.

Typical of the trials which beset the magazine illustrator is the following incident:

After a recent supreme court decision which nullified the Agricultural Adjustment Administration, a national magazine assigned a certain artist to do a page of drawings depicting a day in the life of a supreme court justice, and showing in a faintly funny manner—but not too funny, of course—just how a member of this august body might meet the slighter problems of every day existence.

The artist made the usual suggestions as to how he thought it ought to be done. The editor countered with the usual objections . . . and eventually the usual compromise was reached.

When the drawings were completed, came the inevitable "Audience Reaction" test. These methods of ascertaining potential public reaction consist of calling in the office help—and if he isn't too busy—the publisher himself.

Previously the idea had been pretty well gone over, and there were few, if any, suggested changes—that is—not until someone mentioned that he certainly thought it was a swell caricature of Chief Justice Hughes: "Looks just like an old fogey."

However well meant the compliment might have been, the reaction was a bombshell. It was all right, apparently, to do a polite satire on the nation's judicial body, but it most decidedly wasn't all right to make the Chief Justice look like an old fogey.

It might cast some reflection on his Honor's powers of perception, they said—and his ability to decide a major issue of more recent vintage than Dewey's capture of Manila.

The remedy suggested was a simple one. "All you have to do is make him look younger—more progressive—just take the beards off. That's all you have to do."

The beards came off—but that the Justice had very little chin after the operation was completed can hardly be said to be the fault of the artist.

This would seem at first only a temporary and superficial inconvenience to the artist. But there is an underlying social significance and this is evidenced by the fact that this same magazine—a few days later—asked the same artist to do a War Scene. "Not too realistic though," they cautioned. "Make it glamorous. You know, bombs bursting in air, and that sort of thing."

Here, as in the previous incident, was a situation that implied more than the artist's own professional pride and aesthetic instincts. And that some illustrators continue to make these com-promises does not mean they are influenced alone by the fact that it means their living.

There are those among us who realize that if *we* don't do the work—someone else will. We must realize that it is far better to inject even a slight suggestion of realism into a war scene than to let it be turned over to someone who will do just as he is told—and no questions asked.

That many fine artists have deliberately chosen their own ivory towers rather than subject themselves to momentary dis-comforts in the commercial field is regrettable. Genius under a bushel basket is not so important as bare talent which finds its way into thousands of homes.

One artist—probably the greatest satirist in the world to-day—and a master of caricature and composition—was sought out by the most successful "smart" magazine in New York, and asked to make a cover—a street scene, for example.

After having the preliminary sketch okayed, he brought in the completed job. Numerous changes were suggested by this and that editor until there was little left of the original concept.

Disgusted with this first experience among publishers, he has since refused to accept any further offers.

The result is that the work he might now be doing—a thinly veiled though none-the-less evident criticism of an inequitable social order—has no doubt been turned over to one less talented but considerably more tractable.

That such men as Gropper, Redfield, Gellert and others have sacrificed considerable revenue in favor of their convictions is indeed admirable.

Unfortunately, there are not enough liberal journals to allow more artists to follow their example.

There is, however, one course which more and better artists should follow in the war against War and Fascism. That is, to join the ranks of those who are now represented on reactionary publications.

No single drawing can contain the same amount of significance that is possible in more liberal magazines, but through innuendo it is possible to reach a larger and an otherwise misdirected and misinformed audience.

The so-called "Class" publications cater to a "Smart" audience. This audience will take an unlimited amount of what it might consider harmless satire, simply because it finds it amusing.

This type of reader doesn't mind at all if you take a financier or a politician for a nice, polite "ride"—just so long as you appear to be having your little joke with no harm intended.

The so-termed "Popular Publications" are somewhat different. Here there is no word other than glamour. The working man is a pink-cheeked, happy-go-lucky individual—and the boss a comparatively slim-waisted benefactor.

A war trench is as clean as a whistle, and even an occasional rat must have an air about him.

The girl who works in a "five-and-ten" looks like Joan Crawford, and is just as radiantly happy. The entire scheme is to set the stage for advertisements in other parts of the book. And this factor governs the pictorial and literary content of any publication in this field. Natives of Cuba must not look too dirty or a steamship line will cancel its "ad." An airplane crackup, unless it's a twenty year old plane—or a picket line, unless it looks like a group of Al Capone's henchmen—are both taboo. Revolutionaries must always wear beards.

The chief purveyors of glamour—artists like Flagg, Brown, Raleigh and La Gatta—not only form the necessary background for advertisers, but to a great extent dictate the art likes and dislikes of the public at large. When Mr. Average Magazine goes to the Metropolitan Museum, he looks for something that reminds him of Norman Rockwell or Leyendecker. It was the magazine that finally succeeded in creating a market for modern art. It is the magazine that will eventually educate the public to further advancements in what is still known as "Modernistic Art."

The artist who works on the magazine need not feel that he has prostituted his art. He is working in the tradition of Daumier and Forain. His romantic beach-scene assignment shows a maimed and crippled war veteran who watches children of the next war cavorting in the surf. He is convinced that the weapons of the movement against War and Fascism must be equal at least to the forces of the Reactionaries.

Graphic Art
Harry Sternberg

The social effectiveness of pictures may be said to be directly proportional to the size of the audience reached. For this reason the graphic arts have a special importance for the growing numbers of artists anxious to turn their talents to the service of the struggle against War and Fascism.

No other medium has the adaptability of the print, which can be produced rapidly and inexpensively in large quantities, and can be widely distributed at low cost.

The chief drag upon the development of the immense possibilities ready to hand in the print field today is the cult of rare prints. The fancy jargon of print connoisseurship is no more than a pretentious front for speculation with an artificially limited product.

Artists are induced to destroy their plates after pulling a ridiculously small number of proofs in order to appeal to the vanity of "connoisseurs," interested only in having things that no one else has. The steady contraction of this market with the depression threw the absurdity of the whole situation into sharp relief. As for those who still cling to the practice of limited editions with high prices, the quality and character of their work plainly show the depth and seriousness of these artists. You all know their cute babies, cunning dogs, flying ducks and picturesque cathedrals. This is the print tradition in decadence.

Among progressive print makers there is a healthy tendency to appraise the situation more realistically, and to enlarge even the hand-pulled editions to a point where the price may be drastically reduced and a new market built among those who still have some purchasing power.

As progressive artists become more concerned with reaching people, and as their work gains in breadth from a realization of the wonderful possibilities latent in the masses of people, ready to be developed through those social forms that meet their needs, then these progressive artists will want to go a step further and project their vision as widely as possible.

To do that they will adopt the mechanical methods of reproduction, printing etchings from the plate on power presses when the plates are steel-faced, printing lithographs from the stone on power presses, using zinc plate and photo-offset printing on power presses, metal line cuts that can replace the wood block, and even mechanical photo-engraving and printing of etchings.

The graphic artist of today who is not willing to be stultified must break with the tradition of artificially restricted output, and must join with his fellow artists in finding ways of breaking the barrier that exists between the independent artists and the broad strata of the people. Possibilities we scarcely realize may be gained if the way is found. Through the Congress we must lay plans toward that end.

THE ART MUSEUMS:
IMPOSING MONUMENTS TO OUR
NATIONAL DIVORCE
FROM THE ARTS
Ralph M. Pearson

The art museum, as it exists today, is a concrete illustration of a national misappropriation of esthetic energy.

This unfortunate situation is a natural result of the prevailing psychology of escape from first-hand creative experience and the fears, snobbery and ignorance responsible therefor. So deeply ingrained in current habits of thought are these negations of the normal creative life that they can be cured only by the major surgical operation—one that goes deep into the evils of an acquisitive, self-seeking society. A few preliminary curative steps are possible, not the least of which is a diagnosis of the malady and a plan for the rebuilding process. Let me touch on a few high spots of both.

The art museum is assumed to be a community institution. Its public function is widely recognized by the appropriation of public money for maintenance expenses and the donation of public lands for building sites. But, since its inception, the investing capital of the museums has been mainly derived from private endowment—i.e., from gifts and bequests by our barons of finance. In effect these gifts take on the character of votive offerings, of conscience-salving gestures of compensation for the sins of using private power to extract great wealth from the less

The subject assigned to Mr. Pearson was art museums, dealers and critics. Since there was not time to discuss all three Mr. Pearson centered his talk on the museums, merely touched on the dealers and referred the audience to his series of articles, "The Failure of the Art Critics" in *Forum Magazine* for November, December (1935) and January (1936).

aggressive citizens of the country. In other words, the private donations to art museums are not gifts to *art* for its direct, first-hand value, nor to the living creative minds which produce it, but to the Olympian goddess remote in time and space who can grant the magic favor—if only of respectability. The very act of worshipping the goddess confers distinction—is a kind of passport to that higher state which dollars alone and all their material pomp cannot achieve. Art is the measure of civilization. Let us, then, import great art from the past, house it in expensive copies of majestic Greek temples and, presto, we become certainly civilized. There can be no doubts about it as there might be if we financed contemporary art and possibly made a mistake in judgment. The old creations are certified. Incidentally, of course, in these art endowments, a monument is being raised to a Mr. Morgan, Havemeyer, Frick and Mellon which will far outlast their money-gathering fame and confer cultural distinction thereon.

So sired and mothered by a universal, even if repressed and vague, craving in the hearts of human beings for some explanation of and contact with the great mystery called art, the art museum was born and has grown lustily amongst us. It is because, in its major influence, it has deflected that healthy craving from living participation to vicarious hero-worship of the past and because of the taint of private cultural exploitation that the museum has become so revealing a monument to our national divorce from the arts.

Not only do its copied buildings and vast funds for the purchase of antiques with the attendant assumption that "appreciation of art" is caught, like a germ disease, by exposure to an outside source of contagion—the great art of the past, testify to this divorce; so does the personnel of control and management. Since the museum is the child of finance, the depository of large cash endowments and the home of multitudes of costly works, it must obviously be managed wisely by practical men—men who know money values, can conserve them, will inspire the confidence of wealthy patrons and so attract more private endowments. The fact that such financiers, even though they may have learned something *about* art, certainly have no hint of the meaning of the art experience, does not disbar them from the board of trustees; it invites them to membership. And they choose the director—a man trained in this school of divorce to satisfy cautious specialists in profitable investment and to infect the public with the germ of preserved art. The fact that some directors humanize and modernize this setting by adding art schools and exhibitions of contemporary work and so bring the storehouse alive, mitigates the falseness of the whole but cannot change the basic fact.

That these living activities have revivified the museums, have pulled greater crowds to the galleries, have added to their public service and consequent social value, have helped materially to justify the vast expenditures for salaries and other fixed expenses, cannot be denied; the very growth of such activities is proof thereof. The living artist is the source of these values. It is he who has contributed them to this wealthy, endowed, community institution. Have the museums acknowledged this contribution by any compensating support of living production, by any major diversion of funds from the purchase of antiques to contemporary creations? Aside from a few annual prizes and scattered purchases they definitely have not. Instead, their "practical" managements have assumed that *they* are "helping the artist with free publicity and housing." Within the year, they have officially refused to accept the policy of paying a rental fee to living artists for the use of their work in museum exhibitions. Even more devastating an indictment is the failure of the museums to spend the seventeen odd millions of dollars annually given to them "to further the cause of art," on production by living artists. See the report by William Zorach at the end of this section.

In their own words the incorporated function of art museums is to "promote art in the community." The conservative majority among them believe they can do this *without promoting the artist* as a professional and amateur producer. In other words they conceive of art as being a concrete thing existing in a finished product with a measurable value established by the average taste over a long period of time. They recognize this accrued value in dollars and cents and are willing to spend amounts up to $300,000.00 to purchase a single example of it "for the good of the community." They justify such heavy expenditures and all others of many millions for buildings and maintenance by the assumption that they are "supporting art" and that public appreciation and benefit will somehow bloom out of unfertilized adoration. The gentlemen of the museums who make these decisions are touchingly naïve.

The philosophy of knowing through doing is the new educational philosophy of the day. It is as sound in art as in any other department of education. It applies to appreciation as well as to production. It involves a reorganization of our entire art educational creed, machinery and personnel. It shifts the "source of inspiration" from the lecture hall and the glass cases of the museums to the studio and workshop, from the scholar to the artist. It rescues society from the intellectual clutches of the pretenders to the cultural throne—the various laymen "art authorities," including the interior decorator, and so frees it from an imposed slavery to styles, dogmas and literary concepts. Thus freed from the external, the intellectualized, the vicarious, it allows people to return to the participating experience of primitive civilizations—to sense, to feel, to thrill deeply to that invigorating adventure.

The museums of the country, generally speaking, do not understand this kind of participating appreciation any more than they understand the experience of creating and designing. They can't understand it. Expert knowledge of the making of profits or of historical facts does not help to such knowledge. Hence, even in those progressive museums in which there are art activities for children, art students or laymen, the teaching is predetermined to be external, intellectualized, factual—as in the case of all the popular copying processes, and so cold-blooded and remote from the warm, living experience of creation. This is inevitable under the present set-up. The only exception occurs when genuine, leader, creative artists are engaged as teachers—an occasional occurrence.*

The museums, then, are incapable of supplying the leadership in creative production and education which the country so sorely needs. This incapacity roots primarily in their inherent nature as expressions of the cultural camouflage of a private-profit society with its controls, both economic and cultural, in the hands of the profiteers. Because of such control the museums are incapable of the vision to recognize the importance of the creative experience for all people—professionals and amateurs, or the importance of the leader-producers whose genius is the most valuable resource of the nation in this field—infinitely more important than the eleven million dollar copies of Greek temples for storage warehouse purposes, and even of great *social* value than the masterpieces therein housed. In saying this I am not denying the historical importance of great creations of the past nor their cultural importance to specialists who make a specialized study and use of them nor their supplementary value to the general public; I am merely saying that the first-hand creative experience in its own right is of greater individual and social value than is the act of reverencing remote examples of that experience produced in other centuries when artists somehow had the chance to function effectively. If the museums were capable of recognizing this fact they would themselves be initiating such constructive practices as rentals to living creators instead of refusing to artist producers this minimum of tangible support. And they would be pressing for larger fees than the ones so far mentioned, especially for the most distinguished works, and continually searching for examples to subsidize in that healthiest of all ways—through pur-

---

*An exhibit of children's paintings recently gathered from the Saturday morning children's classes in a number of eastern museums and shown at the Newark Museum of Art, illustrates this statement. Out of a total of 213 paintings some 198 could be called either copies of subject or another art or a cold-blooded, intellectualized type of *learned* style, while only some 15 showed the emotional glow of genuine free creation.

chase. The very fact that they combat this move instead of supporting it proves the hopeless negations of the present situation.

On a reorientation of our accepted attitude toward art museums and on a reorganization of their entire structure and educational creed and procedure, probably as much as on any other cultural issue confronting us today, depends the character of the new society we are trying to build on the economic and human ruins of the old.

Understanding the issue clearly is the first step in reconstruction. Municipal art centers are a healthy substitute for the inadequacies and negations of the current, semi-private institutions— *until such can be made genuine community centers.* The rental policy is a necessary beginning toward forcing a revision of present practices and the courageous stand so far taken by two important organizations of leading artists must be maintained at all costs till the issue is won. The taking or giving of managerial responsibility to artists in art events (the Artists' Congress is such an assumption of collective responsibility) is a just and unavoidable allocation of authority where it belongs. And, finally, collective social planning that will eliminate the private profiteer and his hirelings from the misplaced respect and authority they now enjoy, replacing them with art activities which are a genuine expression of community life—as the constructive government art program of the past two years has been—all these are the ways and means which are now at hand for the rebuilding.

Proceedings and Discussion

In a general paper on "The Artist and His Audience," Jerome Klein showed that the awakening of artists to a consciousness of their relation to society has stimulated their interest in the kind of audience they reach. That in turn has involved a reconsideration of the whole nature and direction of their art, its intelligibility, and the limits of its appeal. Those most seriously concerned with reaching masses of people would necessarily occupy themselves only with those realities of greatest import to those masses. The relation of esthetic focus to outlet and type of audience was outlined with respect to the special problems in each medium, the easel painting, the mural, sculpture and the graphic arts.

Under this heading, William Gropper spoke briefly on the cartoon from the point of view of the revolutionary cartoonist.

MR. WILLIAM ZORACH: I have a little tale to read to you. It comes from the annual report of the American Federation of Arts.

(Reading) "We have been greatly impressed by the increased emphasis placed by educators upon the significance of the arts and of beauty in education and life. Considerable study has been given to the relation of this changing point of view to the attitude of those responsible for the spending of the vast sums now controlled by nearly 150 foundations at present operating in this country. Their combined capital, representing nearly a billion dollars, and their annual expenditures, of probably 60 million dollars, represent a power and an influence of no little significance.

"Before another report is made we will have gathered figures that accurately indicate the great sums donated, during the past fifty years, by people of means anxious to further 'the cause of art.' At present tentative figures are available only for the years from 1922 to 1932 inclusive, showing gifts totaling over 193 million dollars. For each of the eleven years this gives an average of over 17½ million dollars . . . . It is doubtful if any country or any race has ever known such an avalanche of private wealth for like purposes, given for the most part with so few restrictions . . . ."

I think these figures speak for themselves—louder than anything I can say. I leave you to draw your own conclusions.

All this money has been left to enrich the art life of this country. None of it has ever been spent for living art. At least, the percentage is so small it would take an Einstein to figure it out. None of it has ever touched the development of art in this country or been used to contribute to it in any way. No amount of concentration and worship of the art of the past will produce a living and abundant art life in the present. Only support of living art can do that.

MR. RASKIN: I would like to say a few words in connection with the paper read by Mr. Ward, about Race, Nationality and Art. I object to his point of view. He opposes the national idea in art because it may lead to some conflicts in society. It may be used as a way of estranging people through the differences of ideas. I say that if a thing can be used in a dangerous manner it is not the fault of the thing itself. A knife may be used for killing—it is not the fault of the knife itself. I say that national and nationalistic are not the same thing. Nationalistic means to use art to glorify a nation, but nationality in art means to glorify art. Whenever there was a great art it expressed deeply-rooted national ideas.

MR. WARD: I think there has been some misunderstanding. Nobody will deny that national differences do exist and have existed in the past. The point is that in the present world the direction is against the increase of those differences, and the direction is toward finding a common basis upon which the artists may stand.

MR. SCHAPIRO: One of the strongest points of Mr. Ward's paper was that there is no such thing as a nationally exclusive art, not only in a social and economic sense, but also culturally . . . . I am entirely in accord with Mr. Ward's insistence that the idea of national art is pernicious.

MR. LOZOWICK: I think the paper by Mr. Ward and support given it by Mr. Schapiro are excellent, but if to preach exclusive nationalism is a very bad thing, on the other hand, to preach exclusive internationalism, though not so bad, is still a great danger.

Let us consider the Soviet Union, where the national minorities have been given a chance to develop their culture. These nationalities have inherited cultures. Now, we cannot possibly doubt that this body of cultural heritage tends to give their expression a peculiar characteristic. This, instead of being suppressed in the name of internationalism, is supported by the Soviet Union.

Therefore, I say that to supplement the paper, which is undoubtedly excellent, we ought to make provision at this time for the acceptance and support of the culture of any minority.

MR. NAT WERNER: Meyer Schapiro's paper, I feel, has been completely negative. I would like to know whether he feels there are any artists today who do not fall into the classifications he has made.

MR. SCHAPIRO: I deliberately limited myself to the task I was assigned, namely to show how the social basis operates even with an art that seems to be an entirely independent art.

At the conclusion of the discussion, commissions on permanent organization, teaching, sculpture, artists' unions, etc. were set up to meet during the evening.

PROBLEMS OF
THE AMERICAN ARTIST
Second Closed Session
New School for Social Research
Jerome Klein, Chairman

TENDENCIES IN AMERICAN ART
Saul Schary

By the beginning of 1900 American art can be said to have come
into its own. There was a background of tradition and created
work and a sufficient knowledge of technical method to serve as a
foundation on which to build. From the time of the American
Revolution to the War of 1812 most of our painters had been
products of English training. Men like Stuart, Copley, and West
had brought back a working knowledge of the English school of
portraiture. This was the type of art most in demand by that class
of wealthy bourgeoisie which still looked to England as its cultural model. After the Revolution John Trumbull and others, influenced by a nascent spirit of nationalism, painted pictures with
such subjects as *The Battle of Bunker Hill* and *The Declaration of
Independence*.

The period of rapid territorial expansion immediately following the War of 1812 led to a cultural and economic decentral-
ization. The difficulties of transportation and communication
forced the far-flung communities of the growing republic to a
greater degree of intellectual self-sufficiency. This gave rise to a
folk and popular art which can be called truly provincial in
feeling.

After the Civil War we find a chaotic period of reconstruction having little time or interest in the pursuit of cultural activity. It was during this era that the tradition of the expatriate American artist began. Most of the outstanding artists of the decades before 1900—Whistler, Inness, Duveneck, and a host of others—went to Europe for their training. Winslow Homer, on the other hand, best represents the type of artist little affected by European currents, and stayed at home to interpret the American scene. Thomas Eakins, although he studied abroad, returned to express in his work the factual preoccupation. Here we have the crystalization of two divergent trends: Whistler would best represent the "pure" esthetic trend; Homer, the realistic.

The work of the next generation of painters—Henri, Luks, Bellows and others—had a tinge of social insight, though it appears mostly by inference. Bellows' social and political awareness did not prevent him, during the World War, from painting pictures of a violent chauvinist nature, based on atrocity stories created by the Allied propaganda bureaus. These men continue the tradition of the local and factual character of American art.

In the meantime there were new forces at work in Europe undermining the academic formula. Painters like Cézanne and Renoir and their followers, Matisse, Picasso and Derain, were exploring the art of the museums.

Most of the tendencies developed by these and other artists—Post-Impressionism, Fauvism, Cubism, Expressionism, and Futurism—were first seen by our present generation of painters at the Armory Show of 1913. This show, coming one year before the outbreak of the World War, marks, as did the War itself, the dividing line between the old and the new.

Few, if any, of our American painters today were uninfluenced by the healthy stir the Armory Show created. It swept away the mustiness of academic formulas and initiated an era of unlimited freedom of expression. The temper of the time was ripe for experimentation. It was during the time of post-war activity that many of our artists again went to Europe to study. Returning to America they carried on the tradition of European painting, modifying it according to the needs of their own personalities.

This was the heyday of "Art for art's sake." Various tendencies in this movement of "Art for art's sake," overlapping to a degree, may be distinguished.

Men like Preston Dickinson, Samuel Halpert, Henry Lee McFee and Bernard Karfiol worked in what might be called "the Cézannesque method." Others like Max Weber, John Marin, Charles Demuth, Joseph Stella, Stuart Davis, Arthur Dove, and Georgia O'Keeffe branched off in modified and personalized versions of Expressionism and Cubism. Frank realism, mostly characterized by sensitivity and taste, was not neglected. Such painters as Eugene Speicher, Edward Hopper, Charles Burchfield, Alexander Brook, Yasuo Kuniyoshi, and Franklin Watkins developed their personal vision to a high degree. A "realistic purism" was developed by Charles Sheeler, Niles Spencer and others. How far this work differs from realism may be seen in the work of Billings and Blume, who have, by a series of logical steps, worked out a form of American Surrealism.

With the advent of the depression the artist's dream of individual salvation through his art was rudely shattered. The laws of economic change intervened to awaken him to the threat of sterility contained in the blind alley of "Art for art's sake." His ivory tower, erected on the "economic plateau" of Hoover's delirium, was dispelled with the rustle of ticker tape and the crashing of markets. In his dilemma he turned to his fellow artists to discuss his problem and found that it was also their problem.

With the realization that as individuals they were powerless came the desire, on the part of some artists, to identify themselves in their work with progressive social movements. Now the romantic pictorial subjects of crowds in streets, vacation spots in the country, still lifes on tables, prize-fights and sports and the thousand and one amenities of modern life changed and took on a new meaning. A social consciousness appeared in easel and mural painting, in place of romantic realism, with its position of open or implied criticism of a system that tolerated poverty and other abuses.

We see this trend in the work of such men as the Soyer brothers, Nicolai Cikovsky, Joe Jones, Edward Laning, Ben Shahn, and among the political caricaturists, Hugo Gellert, Jacob Burck, and William Gropper.

These men should not be confounded with another group that has come into prominence with the depression, the painters of the American Scene—Thomas Benton, Grant Wood, and John Stuart Curry, who fostered a sort of intellectual back-to-the-soil movement, expressed in regionalism and an insistent nationalism. This is a familiar political phenomenon in times of stress and it is interesting to see its correlation in the field of art. The so-called painters of the American Scene have withdrawn before the issues implicit in their work and have veiled their attitude with the picturesque. When they show a farmer plowing under his crop, are we to infer that they approve the policy of scarcity in the midst of abundance or are they merely content to report on the passing scene? The answers to such questions will not be found in their pictures.

In the field of criticism, Thomas Craven, the most vociferous champion and apologist of the American Scene group, has gone even farther in his muddled thinking. He has made statements which in their nationalistic tendency show him to be congenial to fascism.

While, alongside these movements for a social orientation in American art, there persist the traditions of esthetic detachment, it is significant that even the latter are drawn into the social issues of the day. In the case of Surrealism, for example, some like Peter Blume and Walter Quirt, would use it in the service of the class struggle and others would use it as a means to escape that struggle.

To conclude, there now exists an appreciable body of American art easily distinguishable from European art. But when some of our nationalistically-minded critics call for an American art and inveigh against foreign influence in our art, they are following a fascist trend which is for nationalism against internationalism, for a limited culture as opposed to an unlimited one. The American spirit, embracing many nations and many creeds, is valuable in art or life only as it serves to give its own interpretation to the international struggle for freedom of expression against those forces of reaction which would strangle it.

TENDENCIES IN AMERICAN ART
Arnold Blanch

Here, where we have come together to discuss a common cause, it may seem both illogical and dangerous to speak of tendencies, or to try in any way to evaluate the various schools and directions of American art.

The reason it seems illogical and dangerous is because these personal or group characteristics have been a factor in keeping us apart. Wherever artists have gathered, it is their differences they have made important.

But now, we have come together humbly because we are faced with greater dangers than our esthetic dissimilarities. I do not want to emphasize our variations but I wish to defend them. I feel that only by a collective solidarity may real individuality be preserved.

It is my desire to prove, in a more or less general way, that being a member of the National Academy of Design should not necessarily denote dry rot, and animosity between the abstractionists and the "American Scene" painters does not have to imply the elimination of one or the other; that surrealism need not have to bring to our minds decadence and putrefaction, or that revolutionary art presupposes bad artistry. I would like to have you agree that the cartoon can contain art as well as propaganda.

And to many of us who are within or sandwiched between these dominant tendencies, I wish to prove it is not our fellow artist who is the enemy, but those who have made art the booty of exploitation, and who use it as a deodorant for war and fascism.

Before a fair analysis can be made of contemporary tendencies, it is necessary to outline briefly part of our immediate background.

In the period that immediately preceded the Armory show, styles were outwardly various but derived, for the most part, from various European sources.

In subject matter the academic artist depicted the more casual elements of nature. Through an insistent demand of conformity and precedent this tendency was the dominating factor preceding 1913, and it still maintains a contending position.

The organized revolt in 1913 was purely a demand for plastic freedom. The conflict, exploited by the press, was between artist and artist, modern and academic. The modern artist was "an insane anarchist," the academic, "sterile and superficial."

In perspective the Armory show was an important adjustment in our esthetic metabolism, but it did not (and could not) liberate the artist. If we are more wise today, it is because we realize that the greater barriers to plastic freedom are not within our profession.

After the Armory show there arose almost as many tendencies as artists, and it was true that in our effort for uniqueness and self-expression we neglected the art of being understood.

Many of us went to Europe because we thought America was culturally backward. This tendency to escape was a very general one, and it made little difference whether we painted abstract patterns, nudes, apples or workmen. The dominant attitude was the same. Rejecting our environment we lost ourselves in a revery of esthetic rationalization and snobbery.

I feel that one of the reasons underlying the escape tendency is the conception of art as a luxury. The effect of this luxury class concept has left its pattern in one way or another on all tendencies of contemporary painting and sculpture.

I hardly think it necessary to define all existing style characteristics, but I do feel it necessary to bring forth main current directions.

The recent exhibition of American art in Chicago established definite proof of the artists' tendency to break away from upper class domination. That they had done so was proven by the inane reactions of snobbish patrons and "lovers of art" in their search for a new popular realism.

We see other signs of change, of a new direction daily increasing its momentum. To quote from a very well known painter from the middle west:

"There is bound to be regional art. Let us hope it concerns itself with vital realism, and stops trying to prove its geographical superiority."

We find important American surrealists leaving their dream world behind them, and employing their fine and intricate crafts-manship in broader social objectives.

The studio painter has become conscious of the meagerness of his paraphernalia and the limitations of the anonymous pro-fessional model who knocks at his door. In attempting to re-vitalize his art he has come to his window to consider the world about him.

The seasonal changes, the effect of light and color, no longer seem sufficient for the landscape painter. He is becoming aware that his landscape is occupied by people who, like himself, are struggling with the problems of realization.

In the extreme left of the dominant tendencies of American art is the revolutionary artist. He has hit directly at the forces of exploitation. His attack has been crude but uncompromising. His capacity for growth will be and is being proven by his increased artistry. In his intent to reach the largest audience possible, he has been particularly successful in the medium of the newspaper cartoon.

In all these movements there is the constant problem of readjustment to traditions of art. It becomes a question of whether traditions use us or we use them.

In concluding, may I urge upon you again a collective soli-darity, based upon a realization that most of our differences arise not from our stylistic variations, but from economic rivalry. We are kept in this state of conflict for precisely the same reasons that other workers are sectionalized with conflict. We have come to this congress for the purpose of analyzing this condition and to take part in eliminating its sordid results.

GOVERNMENT IN ART

Government in Art
read by Arnold Friedman

Not more than four years ago, a noted art commentator, desiring some factual material on production of art in this country, wrote to Washington for a list of American products. The list he received contained everything from A to Z, from alfalfa to zinc—with one exception. Art was not mentioned.

Since that time art has attained an officially recognized position in our national life. The blessing given it by the federal government is the most progressive step in art ever taken by any American administration. Inadequate as the government program is, it is a step in the right direction. Whatever criticisms are made here are for the purpose of correcting administrative errors before they harden into set molds.

Inauguration of P.W.A.P. in November, 1933 marked the first attempt of any American administration to support unemployed artists in socially productive work. Over a period of six months, 3,749 artists were employed for periods ranging from one to six months at wages running from $27 to $38.25 for a thirty hour week. The government expenditure was $1,185,000.

Then the P.W.A.P. was permitted to lapse, and the artists employed on it were again out of work. Several art organizations, with the Artists' Union in the lead, began to press for project jobs. State administrations responded by rehiring a handful of former P.W.A.P. artists at the reduced wage of $24 for a thirty hour week.

This wage level set the standard for W.P.A., introduced later. However, insistence of artists for a union standard did gain a reduction in working hours from thirty to twenty-four.

About this time, the Procurement Division of the Treasury

Material prepared by Louis Ferstadt, Jacob Kainen, and Ralph M. Pearson.

Department created the Section of Painting and Sculpture and announced national competitions.

It was in the blackest depths of the crisis that the government manifested this sudden interest in art. The administration was rousing despairing, demoralized millions to new hope with the prospect of regeneration and security through the New Deal. Unquestionably it must have been felt in administration circles that artists could help fill out this promising picture.

Artists could find no objection to aiding the government's program, if given full right to express themselves, plastically and socially. But in the department bulletins appeared statements calculated to discourage social criticism, abstract painting, and the like. For instance, in the very first bulletin Admiral Peoples made the following cogent remarks:

"It has been said that among the reasons why Florentine painting reached such heights, was that the firm critical standard of those who ordered work was such that no artist dared to do a mediocre painting or piece of sculpture. Another was that the inhabitants, including the artists, were so imbued with the glory of Florence, that they would do nothing which did not enhance that glory. Without being sentimental, the Section of Painting and Sculpture hopes that in employing the vital talents of this country, faith in the country and a renewed sense of its glorious possibilities will be awakened both in the artists and their audiences . . . ."

This might conceivably be interpreted as a hint that socially critical art would not be tolerated by the Procurement Division. Such an interpretation can be substantiated by subsequent developments.

The Procurement Division's "firm critical standard" was brought into play with a vengeance in its national competition for Department of Justice murals. It was announced that "The subject matter of these murals should deal with some phase of the administration of justice in relation to contemporary American life."

Fifty-five nationally known artists, competing by invitation, sent in ninety sketches dealing with that subject. Every sketch was rejected and the competition closed without compensation to the artists. In reply to inquiries, it was stated that none of the sketches had been "adequate in composition"!

On top of that, when a director of the Art Students' League in New York asked permission to exhibit the rejected mural sketches, he was advised against it.

To invite artists to deal according to their honest convictions with so serious a subject, and then to handle their work in an arbitrary and secretive fashion hardly makes for confidence in the sincerity of those responsible.

By contrast, the action of the Treasury Department in approving the sketches of George Biddle over the veto of the Fine Arts Commission is a commendable liberal step. Acceptance of Biddle's sketch of the tenements and sweatshops of yesterday and a related panel looking to social betterment, marks a significant victory for the forces of social progress.

Much of the friction and dissatisfaction over disposition of the work of artists, both in Treasury Department competitions and government projects throughout the country is due to the predominance of laymen on juries.

The best contracts awarded by the Treasury Department were given without competition to artists selected by an Advisory Committee dominated by museum directors and administrators. Perhaps the Treasury Department was under the illusion that the seven museum directors were just as qualified as the four artists. Let the Treasury Department disabuse itself of such notions. Museum directors have very little to do with contemporary art; normally they are authorities on antiques. As such, they are out of touch with the problems of contemporary art.

To do justice to the interests of American artists as a whole, it is essential that juries not only be composed of artists, but of those recommended by artists' organizations, to whom the jury members would owe responsibility for their decisions.

It is likewise contrary to the interests of artists to enter competitions on a highly speculative basis. Each winner in the Post

Office competition was to get $3,000 for murals on two panels. This pay was to include the expense of installation, cost of materials, models, scaffolding, and in most cases, rental of studios in Washington. In the long run, the pay for the winners in the Washington competition is probably less per hour than the pay for artists on projects. And those who did not win got nothing for their preliminary sketches. Architects receive pay for designs submitted for Federal buildings. Why shouldn't artists invited to submit sketches be paid for their time and effort?

Since the further history of the projects under WPA is treated elsewhere, it is needless to repeat it here.

Suffice it to say, in conclusion, that the government is a major factor in American art today. It has the power and, insofar as the artists are unemployed, the obligation, to stimulate tremendously the growth of art in this country. We cannot doubt that the only fruitful course is that which lies in the frank and equitable treatment of artists, giving them a full measure of democratic participation in the administration of art enterprises, and the opportunity to work according to their honest convictions. We artists have a right to expect that of any administration truly representative of the American people.

Municipal Art Center
Harry Gottlieb

Today the artist is becoming increasingly aware of the inadequacy of the various traditional agencies upon which he has depended for contact with the public and for economic security.

Most of the dealers, because of their inability to cope with the situation, their adherence to policies determined by profit and speculation, and in many instances their antagonism to the artist's interests, have failed to be of any appreciable service to him and the community.

The failure of the dealer system plus the failure of museums to give tangible support to living artists make it imperative for muncipalities to accept some responsibility by establishing municipal art centers.

Such centers would stimulate public interest in contemporary art, encourage sales, and bring artists into closer cooperation with one another.

In New York City the question of a municipal art center, long hopefully discussed by artists, became an issue of the day with the First Municipal Art Exhibition. This was held under the Mayor's official sponsorship in March, 1934 at Rockefeller Center, only a few weeks after the destruction there of Diego Rivera's mural.

Feeling that this "harmony show," purporting to show [a] community of interest among all New York artists, was actually serving to whitewash Rockefeller vandalism, a group of artists refused to participate and picketed the exhibition.

Out of this protest there was formed the Artists' Committee of Action, to work for a municipal art program under democratic administration by artists, who would see to it that no private individuals or corporations would exploit such a program for their own interests.

Under the splendid leadership of Hugo Gellert, the committee drew up a complete plan, backed by the artists and by prominent liberals such as John Dewey, Lewis Mumford and Heywood Broun, who joined demonstrations that marched to City Hall on behalf of the program.

The plan, presented to Mayor LaGuardia on three occasions, March 20th, May 9th, and August 30th, 1934, contained the following main features: (1) a permanent art gallery for all New York artists, (2) a circulating library for pictures and sculptures, (3) a no-jury system, with no discrimination against any creed or color, (4) administration by artists.

At length, on January 6th, 1935, Mayor LaGuardia announced "his" idea for a Municipal Art Center. Ignoring those who had originated and popularized the plan, he put it in charge of a hand-picked "Committee of One Hundred."

In December, 1935 Mrs. Henry Breckinridge, chairman of

the "Committee of One Hundred," announced the forthcoming opening of a temporary gallery in a remodeled house at 62 West 53rd Street. Artists were to exhibit in self-determined groups.

Invited to show with one of the groups, one of New York's most prominent artists, Yasuo Kuniyoshi, was forced to turn back his entry blank when he found in it a clause limiting exhibitors to citizens. Because of Japanese birth, barring him from United States citizenship, he and other artists were shut off from any possibility of participating in the program.

The meaning of discrimination struck home to scores of leading New York artists when they found one of their own number, a man who had played a distinguished part in the art life of the city for nearly thirty years, thus affected by it. Indignant protests by more than a hundred prominent artists were concentrated through an Artists' Provisional Committee Against Discrimination, which cooperated with the Artists' Union in demanding withdrawal of the obnoxious clause. Artist members of the "Committee of One Hundred," credited with responsibility for the clause by Mrs. Breckinridge, contradicted her by denying it.

Faced with the prospect of picket lines at the opening of the art center, Mrs. Breckinridge announced a residence requirement which eliminated the citizenship ruling. Further, at the insistence of the Artists' Union, there was withdrawn a "hospitality clause" that would have permitted censorship of any art not satisfactory to the administration.

Nothing could have more dramatically revealed the urgent need for democratic defense of interests common to all artists. The discrimination issue at the Municipal Art Center precipitated the decision of several well known artists, previously hesitant to join the Artists' Congress [, to join] in order to work toward that goal.

It also completely vindicated the original stand of the Artists' Committee of Action for administration by artists responsible to organizations embracing the great mass of artists in New York. Such an administration is still to be gained.

Moreover, the temporary Municipal Art Center must be expanded. Another building should be added where a circulating library can be maintained for the rental of art works to institutions and private individuals, the rental payable to the artist, as specified in the original plans of the Artists' Committee of Action, and proposed in the Federal art bill sponsored by the Artists' Union. There should also be a school and a discussion forum.

With the temporary art center, New York artists have made a good beginning. This should be an incentive to all artists throughout the country to build municipal art centers in every city in the United States.

Status of the Artist in the U.S.S.R.
Louis Lozowick

To say that art has been encouraged in the Soviet Union is to make a true but tame statement about the actual situation. Of course art has been encouraged, but—and this is really the crux of the whole matter—the encouragement has not been intermittent, haphazard, depending on personal influences in high places or political exigencies of the moment: from the first it has been part and parcel of a *planned* policy inseparable from all other social and economic planning. Thus among the earliest government decrees adopted were those for the preservation of art treasures, for supplying studios and employment to artists, for progressive reorganization of schools. Responsible Soviet workers have always spoken of the strengthening and upbuilding of the three fronts—political, economic, cultural. Artists are considered part of the vast army of workers, physical and mental (a temporary distinction to disappear in the not too distant future) and as such an indispensable factor in the socialist reconstruction of the country. Full members of the trade unions, the artists carry insurance against sickness, accident, and unemployment. They are consulted on every issue that vitally affects the country. When we read, for example, of such a vast project as the ten year plan for the complete rebuilding of Moscow, the most gigantic scheme of city planning in history, we are not surprised to find artists actively cooperating.

It was inevitable that a revolution which abolished the private magnate in industry should also have abolished his blood relative the private dealer in art. Speculative manipulation of market values in art has been eliminated together with the institution so popular among the well-fed—the starving artist. Private patronage, while not illegal, has almost entirely disappeared and has been superceded by social and public patronage, constantly growing in proportion with the economic progress of the country and the cultural growth of the masses. Workers' clubs, cooperatives, collective farms, museums, educational institutions and government departments constitute both the new audience and the new patron. Here is a characteristic cross-section of such patronage during recent years: pictures for the Central Committee of the Bakers' Union; for the miners' club, Red Ray; paintings, sculpture, drawings on the story of the Red Army for the Commissariat of National Defense; pictures on the building of the Volga-Moscow Canal for the Commissariat of Transport; portraits and studies for the USSR Academy of Science; decorations for the newest Moscow Hotel; for the Institute of Mother and Child, etc., etc.

Whenever any artist agrees to accept an assignment of the kind enumerated, he signs a contract for a certain period on a salary ranging from five hundred to two thousand roubles per month, exclusive of travel expenses (the rates change, as in the case of other workers—five years ago they were from 250 to 500 roubles per month for the same kind of work). On the expiration of the contract the artist submits his pictures and stipulates a price from which the amount drawn by him in monthly fees is deducted. A Board of Estimates which for Moscow, for example, consists of representatives from the Society of Moscow artists, the Commissariat of Education and the All-Russian Artists' Cooperative, decides on the acceptance or non-acceptance of his price, while a jury of about twenty-five artists of various tendencies, critics and scholars, votes its approval or disapproval from the standpoint of the task assigned. The artist is invited to state, if he wishes, his aims and ideas and to argue the decision of the jury. I was present at a meeting while the work of such opposites as the conservative academician Grabar and the extreme radical Tishler were up for discussion. The spirit of tolerance is evident in the fact that both were accepted.

It should be added that a contract for any project as here outlined does not limit the artist to that project alone but leaves him free to engage in other work and thus augment his income. Practically every artist of talent has done work for the theatre, has taught, illustrated books, etc. Many times I asked: "Since the artists are all employed and since they are rather prolific, is there no danger of over production?" Invariably the answer was "No," because the circle of both producers and consumers of art is growing at a phenomenal rate. Not only are museums and exhibitions filled by factory workers, collective farmers and red army men but it would not be an exaggeration to say that there is scarcely a factory, a collective farm, a workers' club of any size without its theatrical, artistic, dramatic and musical circle. Non-professional groups in the various arts count membership by the hundred thousand. They offer courses from a few weeks to a few years; they meet in local, regional and national conferences, organize exhibitions on a national scale and not infrequently some of the more able members pass from the non-professional to the professional status. If we add the vast population of the national minorities whose education and interest in art [are] practically at [their] beginning, we shall see that the Soviet artist whether he works as a free-lance in his studio or under a contract for some institution, whether he does fine art or applied, his audience is well nigh inexhaustible.

The artists not under contract have their pictures in exhibitions which travel to all parts of the Soviet Union and from which provincial museums, palaces of culture and other local institutions acquire works. The thematic range of Soviet art varies from still-life and landscape to portrait and history, although the favorite subjects are naturally those with which the artist is most familiar: the new village and city, the new man and woman, the new ways of living and working. The artists are in continuous contact with other sections of the population, the factory workers, the collective farmers, the red army men, with whom they exchange visits, services and experience. Their social orientation might be summarized in a paraphrase of the familiar Marxist formula: Artists until now have *pictured* the world differently; we intend to help *transform* it.

Art in Fascist Italy
Margaret Duroc

Italian culture suffered a severe set-back when Mussolini made his dramatic entry on a white horse into Rome. A form of government was established which systematically set about lowering the cultural level of the Italian people. The decline has been very apparent in all the arts and sciences with the exception of aviation and the excavation of Rome and painting. At first, Mussolini scorned the Fine Arts. Taking his cue from Marinetti, leader of the Futurists, Mussolini said, "We do not want to be a nation of hotel-keepers and museum guardians." And "As for myself, I have been in a museum at most twice."

But Fascism needed money, and less bombastic people helped to mold the program. The Fine Arts, it was discovered, lent themselves very well to the imperialist program. It was pointed out that The Fine Arts were an unexploited source of income which was more valuable than agriculture. The result was that Mussolini soon started upon an ambitious career of opening museums and promoting the hotel and tourist business.

The promotion of Fine Art and Archaeology, while primarily for the purpose of bringing money into the country, also served another very important function: propaganda for Fascism. Art and Archaeology were used to establish the slogan that Fascist Italy is a continuation of the ancient Roman Empire and the glorious Italian Renaissance. The Fascist theoreticians decreed, therefore, that the art of Italy must be Classical in style.

One's first reaction upon seeing an exhibition of Italian art which has been arranged for the Tourists or for Foreign Exhibitions is that here is excellent craftsmanship. But the second reaction is that the work is pompous and boring. The artists attempt to portray the so-called eternal values. This simply means that there isn't a single picture of social content or a single picture which shows life under Fascism.

However, not all artists, only the best, paint for museums and export purposes. A different type of painting is used for public buildings. And in this work the degraded position of the Italian artist is most clearly revealed. At the MUSEUM OF THE REVOLUTION, for example, the artists were called upon to represent the "conquests" of the so-called Fascist revolution. The Museum is devoted exclusively to a glorification of Italy's part in the last World War and the March on Rome. That it happens that Italy did not play a victorious role in the war does not matter. The artists are called upon to win the battles which were not won.

One group of artists which has received official recognition does not belong to the Neo-Classical School: the Futurists, with Marinetti at their head. As early as 1909, the Futurists issued their first manifesto in which they proclaimed, "We wish to glorify war—only hygiene of the world!" These people found bomb-throwing a lyrical and mystical practice. "War," Marinetti has very recently said, "is beautiful, because it completes the beauty of a flowery meadow with the passionate orchids of machine-gun fire." The Futurists were attacked, though always tolerated (Marinetti was made an Academician and Senator). However, starting with 1934, their position improved tremendously. It is not surprising that on the eve of a new war the fascists should wish to exploit every agency which would propagandize war. Marinetti cooperated admirably. He turned the talents of all his young followers (the older ones had long since deserted him) to the glorification of the airplane.

Artists who pride themselves on being among the most progressive elements of any society, are in Italy nothing but salesmen and promoters of a regime of brutality and degradation. Mussolini has said, "Fascism rejects in democracy . . . the myth of happiness and indefinite progress." Instead of Happiness and Progress, Mussolini has substituted ORDER–AUTHORITY–DISCIPLINE. This slogan is one of his two favorite maxims which it was the sculptor's task to carve in the MUSEUM OF THE REVOLUTION. The other maxim is BELIEVE–OBEY–FIGHT. If the artist is nothing but a paid lackey, the sculptor will be content to carve such slogans and to make the Duce's features resemble Julius Caesar's; and the painter will be content to paint the nobility of men marching to slaughter and sea-shells for the Tourist trade. But if, on the other hand, the artist believes in Happiness and Progress, he will reject Fascism, and lend his talents to fight Fascism and build a better world.

Art in Nazi Germany
A German Artist in Exile

The Nazi State in Germany is based upon an authoritarian political ideal which dominates everything. What makes this authoritarian philosophy dangerous to the arts is its clear enmity to cultural values in general. True, the Nazis constantly speak of art and cultural values. Everything in Germany is national art and national culture. And, according to Hitler, "all leaders of present day Germany are artists." Indeed:

Hitler—a bankrupt painter;
Goebbels—a bankrupt poet;
Baldur von Schirach—a bankrupt poet;

Read by John Cunningham.

Goering—in view of his past and present—must be granted a talent for acting. These facts (and others like them could be cited) are adduced not for reasons of malice—everyone has a right to his own failures—but because the personal bankruptcies of these promoters of nationalistic civilization throw some light on the inferior cultural values which are being promoted. Afraid of the exposure to the truth, these "artists" suppress with an unwearied hatred every manifestation of freedom and independence in art as in every other domain of life.

And what is this new national culture in Germany? Let one of its leaders explain it:

"National Socialism is not an intellectual movement but rather a physi-emotional one; that is, a movement which has grown out of essential profundity, not intellectual sublimity."

"Essential profundity" leads us straight to the notions underlying Nazi policy in art, science or politics, namely race, blood and soil. Race, blood and soil qualify an artist to create national works of art. As a Nazi historian recently put it:

"Pictures have to have a certain smell of the soil."

The smell of the soil! How can one prove it? No proof is necessary. It is very simple—one just smells it, that's all! Fair girls with blue eyes, joyful workers carrying the swastika—who is not joyful in Germany today?—marching soldiers, old Wotan surrounded by his valiant heroes, portraits of the handsome Nazi leaders—these and similar national themes have the smell of the soil, provided, of course, the paintings look like colored photographs. In art history one calls it naturalism; the Nazi critics call it "steel-blue and hard romanticism." All other forms of art are Bolshevistic, international, Jewish, schizophrenic, syphilitic, feministic—in a word, no art at all.

Consider the burning of books, the military censorship of all creative expression, the fierce national discrimination, and try to visualize the reaction of the German artists. Some, quite many probably, have become "gleichgeschaltet"—one must live! Others went to prison, committed suicide, died of hunger. Still others found it safest to leave the land of their ancestors. To remain in Germany means to goose step, to march in public, in private, in art. The "intellectual beast" who does not wish to march must be exterminated. "Intellectual beast" was coined by Herr Hinkel, storm trooper and bankrupt journalist, now State Commissioner of Art. What follows, therefore, need not surprise us.

A Department of Culture was founded which, according to Goebbels, was to enlighten the German people and the artists "concerning the relationship between race, art, science, morals and military values." This body organized, together with the Society for German Culture, an exhibition in July, 1933, under the title, The Chamber of Horrors. It exists today as a museum in beautiful Nuremberg. Paintings "without the smell of the soil" were taken from other museums, removed from their frames, and a tag was attached to each carrying the name of the "intellectual beast," whether Jewish, part Jewish or Jewified, whether divorced more than once or insane. Homosexuals were, prudently, not mentioned. Most of these identifications were fictitious. Fantastic prices were cited which the poor German taxpayers were supposed to have paid for those pictures under the Republic. The whole exhibition, accompanied by all those inventions, was shipped through the country for the purpose of propaganda against the old regime.

Unfortunately, the Nazis themselves are forced to admit that Nazi art and the Nazi genius are still to come. As Herr Rosenberg says: "The dead heroes of the World War are the most noble witnesses of the eternal idea of race and folk. Out of this experience, one day, the artist of the Great War must be born, and out of this myth, one day, a new art and a new civilization must emerge." The Nazis are not backward about dragging out the martyrs of the World War to bolster up their monstrous myth of race, blood and soil, which thus far has been productive only of frenzied national discrimination, intellectual obscurantism, physical brutality, and an aggressive chauvinistic diplomacy which paves the way inevitably to future wars.

Let this be a warning to those intellectuals who can still make their choice for progress and against reaction, and let them throw the weight of their influence behind their choice.

FASCISM, WAR, AND THE ARTIST
Hugo Gellert

The major objective of our Congress is to take a stand against Fascism and War. To be able to combat Fascism effectively, we must know what Fascism is.

Spokesmen for Fascism never miss opportunities to refer to Mussolini's coming to power or Hitler's coming to power as "revolutions." And it is quite common to read about the Italian Fascist "revolution" or the German Nazi "revolution" in the press.

In a political sense (unless it is a mere palace revolution, the replacement of personnel by another personnel of the same kind) a revolution marks the transference of power from one class to another. Such was the nature of the French revolution, for instance. It lifted the reins of government out of the hand of the land-owning class, the feudal barons, and gave it to the class of bankers, merchants, manufacturers, in a word, to the owners of capital. That revolution broke the back of feudalism and definitely established the present social system as a new social form. Whatever the motives, nevertheless this new society made it possible to create the means of material well-being on a much vaster scale than the previous feudalistic form of society, and it usually allowed the distribution of these means among a much wider strata of the population. It accelerated scientific investigation and extended the field of learning and knowledge. For these reasons, it was a forward step in history.

Another example is our own revolution of 1776. That revolution severed this land from the British Crown and established it as an independent federation of capitalist republics. That revolution, however, was completed only at a later day, when through the Civil War Negro slavery was abolished in the Southern States, a necessary condition for the unhampered development of capitalism.

Let us examine Fascism in the light of this. Let us see if Fascism effects a change in the social relationship. Let us ask: Is Fascism a step in the direction of progress?

In the two typical countries, where Fascism is in power, namely Italy and Germany, the same finance and industrial capitalists rule today who ruled before Mussolini's "march" on Rome or Hitler's Third Reich. The only change is the increase in the intensity of exploitation and enslavement of the masses under the same rulers.

In Nazi Germany, as well as in Fascist Italy, the means of subsistence are steadily withdrawn from the people. That this is what the Fascists themselves expect of Fascism is borne out by an unguarded statement by Goering. When commenting on the shortage of butter and fats in Germany, he said: "We are making history, not butter." In "making history" the productive forces of the nation are forced into the service of destruction and are withdrawn from the field of useful endeavor, are withdrawn from the making of a more abundant, better life. Thus Fascism despoils the creative energies of the people living under it and menaces the peace and welfare of its neighbors. With modern technology and chemistry at its command, Fascism threatens the very existence of the human race.

It is plain that Fascism is not the inauguration of a new social order. It is not a revolution. What then is Fascism?

We must remember that in Italy immediately before Mussolini was put into power and in Germany before Hitler came to power, in both of these countries, the people were in open rebellion against the status quo. They were in open rebellion against the social system, which was so outworn that it was no longer able to provide those living under it even with the barest necessaries of life. They were forced to strike out, to change the social system, in order to insure their continued existence. The Fascists sought to side-track the revolutionary energies of the people. They promised employment and high wages to workers, security to the middle classes, land and freedom from debt bondage to the peasants and, above all, staged a sham battle against the bankers and monopolists, who actually financed them and whose tools they were. Thus Fascism secured the support of the most backward sections of the population.

Fascism came into power and the change to a higher social order was prevented. The role of Fascism is, precisely, to prevent that change from taking place. Fascism is counter-revolution. It is a most shameless attack by the most reactionary elements of capitalism against all the toilers. It is a terroristic attempt to intimidate the people, to force them to relinquish their birthright, to force them to forego the future. Fascism is an attempt to stop the clock.

But human society cannot be held down to a certain phase of its development without endangering its very existence. Fascism is such an attempt to arrest development. The social order immediately declines to the status of the Middle Ages. The pyre, executioner's axe, torture chamber, bigotry, racial and religious persecution are resurrected. Should Fascism continue to exist, its logic will lead back to the cave man.

It is not an accident that both Mussolini and Hitler point back to the pre-Christian era, to "the glory that was Rome" and to ancient Germanic tribal life, as examples to be emulated. Mussolini excavates relics of ancient Rome, while his blackshirts assault Toscanini for refusing to play the Fascist anthem. Hitler's lieutenant openly boasts: "Whenever any one mentions the word 'culture,' I instinctively reach for my revolver."

Mussolini declares that faith, not science, is the hope of mankind. Hitler says instinct, not knowledge, will find a way out. A reversal of progress, a headlong plunge into darkness: such is Fascism.

It is obvious, that under those conditions, no great possibilities exist for the development of art. Any enlightened, honest opinion would be a blow against such conditions. Therefore, honest expression must be strangled. It is strangled. The artist of integrity, deprived of civil rights, of freedom of expression, is doomed to non-productivity, under penalty of the concentration camp, if not death. The inevitable result is corruption and demoralization in art.

The threat of Fascism exists in the U.S.A. It is all the more insidious because it is disguised. Its advocates do not, as yet, come out openly in favor of it. A Mr. Seward Collins, Editor of the *American Review*, is an exception. In the current issue of *FIGHT*, in an interview with Grace Lumpkin, Mr. Collins says: "Yes, I am a Fascist. I admire Hitler and Mussolini very much . . ."

"Do you agree with Hitler's persecution of the Jews?"

"It is not persecution. The Jews make trouble."

"Does your group have the same attitude towards Negroes as towards Jews?"

"The same. They must be segregated."

"You have said, you wish to go back to medieval times. You wish to do away with all progress?"

"Yes."

"And do you wish to have a King, nobles, counts, dukes, etc. in America?"

"Exactly."

Such indiscretion is uncommon in America. It is necessary for Fascism to masquerade as a champion of democracy and liberty.

The vast American masses did not altogether put up with the poverty and degradation allotted to them as their share of the crisis. Under pressure of dire conditions and under continued attacks against their living standards, they learned the value of organization and action. This period witnessed labor struggles, which in scope and intensity are unparalleled in American history. Strike after strike flared up all over the country. The determination and unity of purpose of those partaking in them, despite bullets and tear gas, may be judged by the extent of the San Francisco general strike, which tied up that principal seaport of the West Coast for weeks.

Under such conditions, even that friend of Hitler, William Randolph Hearst, must pretend to be a pillar of Jeffersonian democracy. He must hide the club that strikes against progress under the cloak of Jefferson. His newspaper campaigns against our most distinguished educators, the foisting of the oath of allegiance on teachers to deprive them of the right to think and of the right to speak, are done in the name of democracy.

This period witnessed the rise of powerful organizations of

the unemployed of the cities and the pauperized farmers. These militant associations succeeded in wresting from the Government a measure of relief and protection against downright hunger and want. But reaction attacks even these meager provisions. The Federal Supreme Court annulled Acts of Congress, thus violating parliamentary representation, in the "defense" of the Constitution.

There is great discontent among the youth of the country. Their only prospect, becoming cannon fodder in order to stuff the coffers of bankers and industrialists, is not exactly alluring. The recent Nye Committee Investigation disclosed quite enough, by revealing the "high" motives behind war. It showed up the Administration of Woodrow Wilson as the cat's paw of the House of Morgan, traders in human life—for profit.

The American Liberty League criticizes Fascism as alien to American soil and denounces Communism as a foreign imposition. The assault against Communism is genuine. That is what should be expected from a League of munition makers, steel, automobile, finance and utility magnates. But the attack against Fascism is a fraud, as is the very name of the League, which should be called the League Against American Liberty, to be truthful, because its aim is to bring about Fascism in America and it leaves no stone unturned to attain that end. The League's connection with the various Fascist shirt-organizations is well known.

It should be noted here that as Hitler named his party the National Socialist Workers' Party, the aims and purposes of which were directed precisely against socialists and workers, so the purposes of the American Liberty League are directed against American liberty. Such is the road to Fascism.

The Roosevelt Administration offers no resistance against reaction. It is in constant retreat before it. By getting concession after concession, reaction is strengthened and emboldened. Nevertheless Fascism can be prevented. It must be prevented. But the artists cannot fight against it alone. We must have allies in other groups that fight against Fascism. But above all, we must ally ourselves with that most irreconcilable foe of Fascism, militant organized labor, against whom Fascism directs its hardest blows. Labor is the greatest organized body in the country. In it we find our most reliable and most powerful ally against Fascism. But there is another reason for closer relationship between artist and worker, namely the realization that while social forms and social classes may rise and disappear, labor remains indispensable as long as life itself exists. "Labor is a necessary condition of human existence . . . it is through the ages, a necessity imposed by nature itself, for without it there can be no interchange of materials between man and nature—in a word, no life."

To be isolated from the worker is to be isolated from the only vital, progressive force in society today.

Is Thomas Craven right when he says that the artist who found his way to the worker is a "political accomplice" and has "sold out to a social idea?" Is it necessary to be bribed in order to side with progress?

We artists may fulfill a very important role. We may point a way to the future. But our vision must not be blurred. We must have a clear outlook if we wish to claim the right to call ourselves artists, if we wish to claim a place as creative men in the front lines of advancing humanity.

ECONOMIC PROBLEMS
OF THE AMERICAN ARTIST
Third Closed Session
New School for Social Research
George Biddle, Chairman

ECONOMIC STATUS OF
THE ARTIST TODAY
Alexander R. Stavenitz

An artist who has been prominently identified with American art for over twenty-five years, who has won innumerable prizes and awards, and who has enjoyed fairly comfortable circumstances during most of his life, walked into the WPA work relief office to apply for a job. For over a year he had been living on borrowed money, and had just recently held an exhibition of his paintings. He had borrowed to meet the expenses of this exhibition, upon which he counted heavily to repay some of his debts. The net result of the affair was still another debt. For the first time in his life he had to resort to a relief agency for food and rent, and subsequently for a job. There was nothing else he could do.

An advertising art director who had been employed, for several years prior to 1930, at salaries ranging from $10,000 to $15,000 per year, presented his Home Relief card at this same office, as evidence of his eligibility for relief work. He had come down in the scale from owner of his home and a car, to a three-room coldwater flat for which the Home Relief Bureau allowed him $16 per month rent, and a food allowance of $5.40 per week for a family of four. He had not been able to obtain work for twenty-two months, and his application for relief was his last resource.

These men, one in the field of fine art, the other in commercial art, had come to the same place as a last desperate refuge from poverty and degradation. They had long been imbued with the traditions of "rugged individualism" and considered such application for governmental aid an admission of defeat. Forces beyond their control had brought them into the relief office. If I cite these two cases, it is not because they are by any means the most extreme examples available nor because they are rare, but rather because they are significant of a condition which is typical of an historic epoch. Here we have two instances of people highly skilled in their work, of recognized standing in their respective fields, yet unable to earn a livelihood in a normal manner. What is the explanation of such a phenomenon? If these were isolated and exceptional cases, one would look for the reasons underlying them in the individual backgrounds of the two people. But the condition they reflect is so widespread that it is to be found not only in the field of art, but in practically every phase of the country's industrial and cultural life, and requires, therefore, an examination of the historic forces that have brought it about.

The artisan of the Middle Ages functioned as a workman, specializing in the making of stained-glass windows, statues, altar-pieces, and similar objects of his time. He learned his trade during a long apprenticeship and was admitted, upon proper qualifications, as a member of a crafts guild which occupied an important place in the economic and social life of the community.

With the advent of the market and the slow but steady rise to power of the mercantile class, the artist was forced to adapt himself to new conditions. The Church was decisively defeated, reduced in economic and political power, and the new merchant class became the chief patron of the arts. In the process a different kind of art, under different methods of production, was made necessary. From the closely organized guild of the Middle Ages, with its stable position in the economic structure, the artist had been gradually pushed outward to a very unstable place on the fringes of society . . . a sort of scavenger, or as he is sometimes called today, a "free-lance." The direct relationships of the feudal artist to the user of his product had given way to the veiled relationships of the market. The artist now worked in isolation in his studio, seldom with any knowledge of the destination of his work. The stonecarver creating a statue for a specific niche in a cathedral, or the painter creating an altarpiece for a given church, had evolved into the artist who created sculpture and paintings for exhibition in a gallery, to be purchased by anyone who might have a liking for them and the money to buy.

By the middle of the nineteenth century the artist had become something approximating a recluse, an outcast, a misfit in the social and economic structure of his time. One need only mention such names as Rousseau, Van Gogh, Cézanne, Gauguin, to illustrate a commonly described condition of the period.

That the mechanism of the market has failed to solve the economic problem of the artist is amply attested to by history and literature, past and present. The phrase "starving artist" has become commonplace, and has been accepted for so long that many people have come to believe that it is a "natural" condition . . . a sort of biological law peculiar to artists . . . and not a few critics and writers have even attempted to argue that a state of economic poverty is a good thing for the artist, but very few artists share this view.

The most eloquent testimony, however, to the failure of the private buyer is contained in the developments of the last six or seven years. The crash of 1929 jarred the economic foundations of both commercial and fine arts so powerfully that thousands throughout the country were thrown into a disastrous condition shortly thereafter, and the general condition of artists became so acute as to force governmental intervention in their behalf. For the first time in this country's history a program of work was launched for artists, as part of a general nationwide relief program. Hastily improvised and inadequate, it was nevertheless an important step in the right direction. It marked the formal recognition of the inadequacy of the private market and the desperate need for a socially planned work program. A few short months after its inauguration the funds allotted for this program were used up and it collapsed, leaving the artist in a precarious condition. Not until the second government relief program was instituted, however, has there been such concrete and wide testimony to the desperate state of the artist. This was no question of competence. Many of the country's most distinguished and capable artists found it necessary to apply for direct relief, that is, food and rent. Nor was this confined to those artists whose work has had to contend with opposition from established convention because they attempted to break new ground. Here we are confronted with the phenomenon of even successful conventional artists . . . magazine-cover men, official portrait painters, advertising artists, trade decorators, calendar and greeting card designers—almost every category in the field—thrown into the unemployment heap. Clearly this condition was no matter of individual misfortune alone. The common denominator of widespread catastrophe and poverty threw a glaring light on the scene to reveal the fundamental cause as primarily economic. Out of the common misery and hardship of the artists arose an organized demand that the government come to their aid.

Profiting from the experiences of the first program, the present art administration has been able to plan much more comprehensively so as to broaden its scope and thus provide for a greater number of artists. The projects have been increasingly related to the life of the community, and mark a considerable advance in many respects over the first program. But while decidedly an improvement, the present program suffers from serious defects and shortcomings, most of which are traceable directly or indirectly to the impermanency that underlies the entire structure. This lack of a sense of security is basic and affects the whole program. Adequate and sound planning such as are necessary for more lasting benefits to the community and to the artist, are impossible under such conditions. Like a Damoclean sword hanging over his head, the fear of unemployment pervades the consciousness of the artist. Even before he starts to work he is aware of the date of expiration of his job. Such an atmosphere is hardly calculated to help him concentrate his energies and attention on creative work.

It should be obvious that the prerequisite for a healthily progressing art in this country is a permanent, government-supported program, conceived and administrated so as to make the efforts of our artists available to the public, to all the people. Within the brief space of about two and a half years the Government art programs have already demonstrated a means of bringing art to the American people in a manner and to a degree never before known here. Large sections of the population, primarily the economically underprivileged, are coming in contact with art for the first time in this country's history. Children of poor families, unable to afford tuition at private art schools, have been given free access to good instruction . . . in many instances by artists of the highest ability and standing in their field. In public schools, hospitals, and other public buildings, contemporary art is being brought to the public, without the intermediary of the museum's generally deadening hand. In hundreds of rural and semi-urban communities with little or no access to art, murals and sculpture have been placed in post offices, schools and other buildings. Although this represents little more than a beginning, there is conclusive evidence that it is effective as nothing else in this country's art history.

In making a permanent Government art program the focus of this paper, I am by no means unaware of the many other aspects of the artist's economic problems. Each category has its special as well as common problems. The exhibiting artist expends time, energy, and materials on the speculative chance that his work may be purchased. Museum and public benefit by his work but he receives no compensation for it; and a small, negligibly small, fraction of exhibitors sell anything. Miss Schmidt's paper deals in detail with the rental policy advocated by the Painters, Sculptors, and Gravers Society in an effort to obtain some sure return to the artist for his work. Only mention is here made of

ALEXANDER R. STAVENITZ

such aspects of the problem as multi-exemplar art, forms of organization, Municipal art centers, the special situation of the sculptor, and others, because they are dealt with specifically and in detail in separate papers.

Undeniably the most important single factor in the art situation today is the Government. Most of the other problems are either directly dependent upon, or indirectly affected by it, in varying degree. I am not alone in the opinion that in the people of this country are tremendous potentialities for a cultural Renaissance, such as we have never known, which could be greatly stimulated toward realization by a permanent, Government-supported art program. It is in the interest of all artists to support such a program.

ARTISTS' UNION REPORT
Boris Gorelick

The Artists' Union of New York today is an organization of eighteen hundred artists. On behalf of these artists I extend fraternal greetings to this Congress, and pledge their support to its objectives.

The issues which led to the formation of this Congress and which occupy our deliberations are War, Fascism, the Defense and Preservation of Culture. The wide response to the Call of the Congress is indicative of two significant facts: the emergence of the artist as a socially conscious individual, and the recognition by him of the necessity for organization.

The Artists' Union has played an important part in breaking down the isolation of the artist and in broadening his consciousness with respect to his social status. Artists of all esthetic perspectives have been welded together into a single union on the basis of common needs and common experiences. For two and a half years our Union has waged a continuous, determined struggle for the economic well-being of its members.

Originated by a group of twenty-five artists threatened with acute destitution, the organization has grown into a mighty body of national scope and influence. The closing of all channels of income, especially that of private patronage, which accompanied the continued crisis, placed before the artist an inescapable alternative: either to abandon his art and seek his subsistence in some other distressed field, or to build a new support for his creative activity. In order to perpetuate his art, in order to perpetuate his individuality itself, the artist discovered that he could no longer stand alone.

Some of you in this audience have, happily, escaped this bitter pressure. You have come here in obedience to the freer motives of social conscience and historical understanding. We of the Artists' Union welcome the opportunity to stand at your side, despite the fact that at the moment you may not be fighting in the same trench. The Artists' Union, too, has gone on record to resist with all its might Fascism and War. The dread powers of reaction, working to stifle even the limited liberties of the American people, have already aimed blows against our Union of Artists. In our effort to procure governmental support for art under the various Public Works Programs, in our effort to compel the Government to recognize its obligation to provide for artists, as producers deprived of their means of maintenance through no fault of their own, we have at all times been subject to the onslaught of those enemies of progress whom you have come here to resist. It is precisely in the economic life of the people that Fascist elements first manifest themselves. No program against Fascism can fail to recognize its tie-up with the struggle for economic security.

The Public Works of Art Project contained certain features which had been actively advocated by the relatively small group of New York Artists from which the Artists' Union arose. The creation of these projects recognized the major principal of our organization; the Government assumed responsibility for the welfare of the artist. It also acknowledged the principle of a so-called professional wage. The Public Works of Art Project, however, restricted its responsibility to certain hand-picked Grade "A" artists. It neglected the great mass of competent artists who, somehow, could not find their way into its original and sometimes even fantastic category of selection. Moreover, for most of those employed, the Public Works of Art Project lasted for a period of only six weeks to three months. The "Grade A" artists, who had been specially picked for preservation, were then thrown back upon their own resources, after those resources had been officially acknowledged to be non-existent.

The Public Works of Art Project "professional wage" was not food fallen from above. It was won by the persistent demands of organized artists. The brevity of its life attested to the fact that the strength of the artist was not sufficient to overcome the Government program of retrenchment. Projects for Class "A" artists alone can never be long-lived. In order to resist the never ending pressure of the reactionaries for Government economy, in order to maintain the very place of art in the social structure, it is necessary that all artists of professional status be supported in their need to work and live.

The P.W.A.P.'s brief career was over May 1934. Here in New York was have had since that time a continuing Art Project. Organized under C.W.A. it has lived through a whole series of administrative transformations: C.W.S., F.E.R.A., W.P.A. Today it employs in New York over 1500 artists, models and technical workers. It has created an unprecedented interest in art.

The development of this art program synchronizes with the development of the Artists' Union and depends directly upon its efforts. Every official gesture of retrenchment has been met by the firm resistance of our organization. The artists have learned how to make use of the defensive instruments of the Labor Unions. Met with a threatened wage cut, the artists adopted the weapons of a picket line, mass demonstration and stoppage. On the occasion of this proposed 10% wage cut our united action forced the retention of the previous scale. By these methods we have procured the lowering of our work week to 24 hours, and the allotment of a 25% non-relief quota in the interest of artists who had not reached the lowest level of destitution. The organization of the employed and unemployed artists into one union, the cooperation of this union with other professional groups, architects, engineers, photographers and musicians, the support of the organized movements against War and Fascism—all these methods of augmenting our strength and securing our position have been taught us by our experience.

During these two years of dealing with Government agencies we have learned in concrete, unforgettable terms the meaning of social reaction. Our picket lines have been attacked by police, our members have been jailed and fined, our artistic productions have been censored and destroyed by backward critics and art dictators. In the pages of Mr. Hearst's *Mirror* we have been presented in a disgustingly sensational fashion as a predatory gang of libertines and "Reds." From the very beginning our struggles have involved the need to protect the Negro and foreign born artists against discrimination.

At this very moment the Hearst Press, the Liberty League and all organized forces of reaction are crying for the abolition of the whole system of Relief and Government Projects. In their drive to lower the standard of living of the American people and to break the power of organized labor, these reactionary groups attack also the cultural and creative expression of progressive thought. The policy of the government in the face of these reactionary attacks constitutes a retreat which can be halted only by organizations like our own. We artists are met with a double responsibility—not only must we protect ourselves in our individual names, there rests upon us also the obligation to defend the advancement of culture.

What does the experience of the Artists' Union mean to all artists?

We can with the authority of this experience assert the following conclusions:

Organization of artists on a common basis is possible despite all esthetic differences.

Organized and concerted action is imperative in order to advance the interests of artists to defeat reaction.

Every improvement of the economic condition of the artist on government projects has been obtained through the existence, guidance and mass actions of the organizations of artists.

The fear that organization is incompatible with individuality is unfounded. It is precisely the existence of organization that guarantees the perpetuation of individual and esthetic freedom.

The establishment of arbitrary esthetic standards as a basis of organization is unsound and detrimental.

We, whose struggle against Fascism stems directly from our efforts to work and maintain ourselves as artists, feel certain that you will recognize the community of your interests and ours. The fight against War and Fascism for the defense of culture takes its most concrete form in the defense of economic standards. We hope and expect that out of this Congress will be formed a permanent organization with an aggressive program against the menace of War and Fascism. To such an organization we pledge our full and unqualified support.

THE RENTAL POLICY
Katherine Schmidt

I have been asked as Chairman of the Committee on Rentals of the American Society of Painters, Sculptors and Gravers to report to you on the rental policy adopted by that society. The rental question is first of all an economic question. The amiable and pleasant existence of the Society would not have been jarred into the projection of the Rental Resolution except for the economic collapse.

Financial hardships awakened members of the society to the realization that if the demand for the use of their work continued, it was high time they be paid for that use.

You are all aware of the fact that within our lifetime there has been a remarkable growth of exhibition centers in this country. Art is no longer shown in one or two metropolitan areas. Besides commercial galleries and clubs interested in the plastic arts, a string of museums has been built over the length and breadth of our country. These museums are large impressive buildings, monuments to the wealth and power of the nation.

The communities in which the museums were built were asked to support them. How could interest in them be stimulated; how but by bringing to them art which would interest them, art to which they would respond? As a practical matter only contemporary American art could consistently serve that purpose. Because of the high insurance charges on "old masters" and the heavy shipping costs for foreign shows, the average American museum (and even the wealthy museum) could afford such luxuries only now and then. Therefore, American shows, cheap in cost, began to be assembled and widely exhibited.

Moreover, museum directors discovered that the public is interested in American art. That fact produced a greater demand for American shows. Any artist of reputation can verify this out of his own experience.

The development of the exhibition field, just sketched, should once [and] for all dispose of the notion so frequently advanced from museum sources that the living American artist ought to be grateful to the directors of American museums for the opportunity to exhibit. With few exceptions (the Whitney Museum may be cited as an outstanding example) the choice was forced upon directors by the realities of the situation, and it was not made voluntarily from solicitous interest in the American artist. The museums' treatment of the living American artist can leave no doubt that this is the fact. For the most part the American artist's work is used only for exhibition purposes, to furbish up museum activities, and to keep the museums alive. The annual expenditures by American museums for purchase and encouragement of living American art are negligible. Here in New York City the reluctant and hesitant use of the Hearn Fund, a fund left to the Trustees of the Metropolitan Museum of Art, the income to be used for purchase of work by living American artists, is a shocking comment on the attitude of museum administrations toward the living artist. With some few honorable exceptions, this attitude is found the country over. What is old and well known, whether authentic or of dubious authenticity, for that museum funds are poured out—but for living American art, a pittance. This is not to imply that museums should not strive to bring the art of the past, or the art of other countries, to their communities. But there is over-emphasis, unreal preoccupation with art as ART, remote in time, fabulous in price, and not as a living force. It is that which leads to the preposterous notion seriously advanced—some of you may have seen it in Mr. Francis Taylor's open letter to the Society published in the *Art Digest* of October 15, 1935—that general funds of museums cannot be used for the encouragement of current American art because the sacred trust which the public reposes in museum trustees demands that these funds be used exclusively for the acquisitions of objects proven throughout the centuries to be of outstanding worth. A director who violates this sacred trust, stated Mr. Taylor—and I call your attention again to the fact that this is said to apply to museum funds marked for general purposes, not funds designated for specific purposes—risks a term in jail at the instance of the outraged public.

Faced with such projections, what response can living American artists expect when they attempt realistically to better their situation? They find what the Society found when it projected the Rental Resolution: intolerance and on many sides a stubborn refusal to alter no longer fruitful customs. The resolution was not hastily adopted. For two years prior to its adoption the Society discussed the question. The terms of the resolution were carefully worked out and agreed upon only after a great deal of deliberation. The resultant additional cost to museums for American exhibitions was of course not ignored in determining upon a rental scale. This was a practical question, and the Society sought to meet it in the practical way. With a minimum of one dollar and a maximum of ten dollars per month, 1% per month of the price of a work was finally agreed upon as being tolerably fair to the artist and not burdensome to the museums.

The overwhelming vote in favor of the resolution (87−7) is worth commenting upon. The Society is not composed of any homogeneous esthetic or political group. It embraces within its membership almost as many esthetic and political beliefs as are to be found in the country today. Yet the situation in which the members, with few exceptions found themselves, taught them that they must do something for themselves and for the other artists in the country.

Adoption of the resolution brought complaints from museum officials of hasty, ill-advised action by the Society, and of an attempt to foist an intolerable burden upon museums. It was further charged that the policy involved discrimination against younger artists who would "have to be excluded from exhibitions" (on the ground that it would be "unthinkable" to pay rentals to young, unknown artists). And it was even held that enforcement of the policy would bring an end to exhibitions of contemporary American art. Elsewhere we have answered these arguments and shown that the rental policy is not only feasible, but benefits young as well as established artists.

In response to our move, the Association of Museum Directors, meeting last May, discussed the Rental Resolution under the heading "Are Art Museums Indebted to the Dealers and Artists or Are Dealers and Artists Indebted to the Art Museums Because of the Exposition of American Painting in Art Museums?" But the directors declined to see the Society's representatives, and at the conclusion of their deliberations they solemnly resolved: "We unanimously refuse to take a painting, piece of sculpture or print to which a dealer's or an artist's charge is attached."

A few members of our Society, some of whom had voted for the resolution, hastened to resign upon learning of the museum directors' sharp disapproval of it. I think I am not doing some of these artists an injustice when I add that they saw a personal advantage in sending to shows to which others refused to send. The lightning of a prize or purchase might strike them the more easily now that others were staying out. Their obligations to their fellow artists sat lightly upon them.

The vast majority of our membership, however, has remained steadfast. During the current season we stayed out of shows unless a rental fee was paid. We recently elected more than thirty new members, all of whom prior to admission endorsed the Rental Resolution. If we continue to stay out of shows, and artists the country over do likewise, there is no doubt that the rental policy will soon become an established fact.

Not all museum directors are opposed to us. Some museums are paying rentals now. Directly or indirectly this is true of the Whitney Museum, Roerich Museum, the San Francisco Museum, the Grand Rapids Art Gallery, the Buffalo Museum and the University of Wyoming.

Museums must hold exhibitions and they need the artist for that purpose. In most cases it would not be a difficult matter for them to adjust their budgets to discharge their responsibility to the artist. Today the artist is the only creative person who is expected to go without compensation for the use of his work. The writer, the dramatist, the composer of music, all are paid when their work is used. And in the field of exhibiting art, everyone is paid except the artist. That condition the artist alone can terminate.

At the present moment the Society of which I am a member is leading the way to that end. Other artists' organizations (An American Group, the New York Artists' Union) are joining the movement. If you are a member of an artists' organization not yet affiliated with this movement, I hope you will help persuade it to do so. If you are invited to an exhibition, do not send unless a rental fee is paid. If we act collectively we shall assert our dignity as artists and our right to that consideration which every socially productive person deserves.

REVOLT IN THE COUNTRY
Francis Robert White

The artists' objectives in the face of economic crisis and social and cultural confusion are not to be defined in terms of population or sectional boundaries. The problems of artists in the rural midwest are similar to those confronting artists of the Metropolitan areas. In Iowa, the first organizational steps have already been taken to meet adverse conditions.

In presenting the case of Iowa, it is first necessary to discard the popularized version of the bucolic painter, milk pail in hand, and to realize that serious painters here as elsewhere are confronted with realities and are responsive to them. Of course there are Iowa artists living and working on farms, but they are not generally prompted to make pseudo-romantic halos out of the circumstances. There are also artists working in the small towns and cities, but they are not necessarily corn-conscious in their approach to art.

Iowa is not 100% Regionalist, publicity to the contrary notwithstanding. A majority of the recognized artists of this state repudiate Regionalism with its theme of opposition between city and country and are more closely aligned with the universal plastic idea. This is not to say that painters here do not make use of the contemporary scene. It is as inevitable that there should be evidence of barns, horses and farmers in Iowa art as that Fourteenth Street and Union Square should figure so prominently in the art of New York.

The questions which most vitally concern the Iowa artist center about the need for an assured place in society with the possibility of economic security in exchange for socially valid work.

The general machinery for art encouragement in Iowa, before the depression, consisted in local associations, Women's Clubs, art departments and a few endowed galleries. The Little Gallery of Cedar Rapids affiliated with the American Federation of Arts and under the direction of Edward Rowan was one of the most influential of these galleries. Fort Dodge and Davenport were also prominent. Traveling exhibits from the College Art Association, and American Federation, with a sprinkling from the Grand Central Gallery shows brought the art of urban America to Iowa. Local one-man shows and all-State exhibitions, with and without prizes, were additional features. While the cultural backwardness of the frontier has greatly lessened under this attack, the artist has remained on the fringe of society dependent for livelihood on outside sources, making his own spiritual and material investment against odds and without prospect.

The function of these Iowa art organizations since the depression has remained much the same as before, but on restricted budgets and with the almost total eclipse of purchases for permanent collections. The Little Gallery has inaugurated some changes favoring the artist and would like to do more; but the main problems have remained unchallenged except by the government.

It is impossible to survey the Iowa art field of the past three years without encountering the pervasive effects of Government patronage. Its influence has been salutary as a whole, despite what lapses in the local or central administration have occurred. Participation in art as a public act even from the relief angle has had power to stimulate new social responses in the artist and to raise the level of his aesthetic comprehension. Again the people of the State have profited from the creation of some significant public art works.

While the government projects have given the first instance of a national concern with the artist as a socially productive factor, the method and guarantees of such projects particularly in their local application are bound to require the leadership of artist groups. The experience in Iowa has proven both the constructive effects of such leadership when recognized by the authorities and the disrupting consequences which result from ignoring the group expression.

The organization in Iowa which has taken the lead in consolidating the artists' approach and in defending their legitimate interests is the Cooperative Mural Painters. This organization was formed on Labor Day, 1935, on the basis of common economic and cultural objectives. In calling the sixteen original members, the highest standards of technical and professional ability were consulted. The original members were all formerly connected with the PWAP. They were painters known to such national exhibits as the Chicago International and American Annuals, the Pennsylvania Academy annuals, the Los Angeles Museum, Corcoran, the Modern and Whitney Museums and other New York exhibitions.

The Labor Day session in Cedar Rapids received a 100% response from the artists called. A democratic form of organization was conceived, pertinent questions were discussed and group action has proceeded from that date, tangibly affecting the Iowa field.

An instance of the cooperative ideal can be seen in the operation of the group mural project under the Treasury Relief Art Project in Cedar Rapids. Five men comprise the mural team, one of whom is designated as master artist, but all of whom share equally in the designing responsibility and opportunity. The general subject matter outline was developed through conference among the painters. The architectural design considerations were solved so as to give definite and complete mural units for each artist's creative solution. Cooperation set a standard by which to regulate questions of scale and color harmony. The work has progressed with great internal harmony. This signal victory in collective enterprise has received the friendly cooperation of the chief of the Treasury Relief Art Project.

However, in meeting the larger State-wide problems, group action has been obstructed. When the Federal Art Project was first introduced it was necessary to protest the proposed appointment of a regional director on the basis of past experience and because all art authority would have been narrowly centered. An impartial representational plan of administration was urged for this region which would have represented equitably all the major Iowa groups and would have insured a comprehensive program.

This plan was rejected and correspondence on the subject was turned over, through breach of confidence, to the opposition. This introduced a confusion and reaction which has stultified the entire Federal Art Project for this State. The protested regional director finally declined the appointment, but politics came into play and the Iowa art project only recently limped into existence, tardy, restricted, inadequate, and administered by local politicians unfamiliar with art. It has not been very fruitful up to the present time and leaves unemployed some of the most authentic talent of this State.

Other questions in respect to the welfare of the artist both economically and professionally have been tackled by the Cooperative Mural Painters group; and throughout the State sympathizing artists are beginning to realize the significance of the organization and to desire admission.

It is possible that the further history of this organization may be qualified by such constructive steps as are taken by this Congress in furthering the cultural vitality of the nation and the well-being of the artist.

THE PRESENT IMPASSE IN SCULPTURE
Waylande Gregory

It becomes evident, upon analysis, that the basic cause of the present impasse in sculpture is due to economic disorder. Social and political discrimination are also important factors which prevent many from practising the expensive art of sculpture and limit the potential market. As a result, individuals and groups of artists have been forced out of the field of creative activity and have been turned into ghost sculptors. This gives cause for alarm!

The life of the ghost sculptor, like that of the ghost writer, is a life of hard work plus small financial reward and dissatisfaction. This must and can be corrected. An exmaple of a case where a cooperative group of sculptors could have successfully produced a monumental work is that of the pediment figures of the Pennsylvania Museum in Philadelphia. Instead, the terra cotta group of the pediment was designed by one artist. He made a scale model and received 50,000 dollars for his work. The rest of the work was done by commercial houses which paid coolie wages to their workers. The model was mechanically enlarged, molds were made and from these the terra cotta figures were reproduced. This procedure did not achieve its aim, in as much as the completed work looks like what it is—fabricated decoration. The finest works in terra cotta have always been directly executed. If the work had been done by sculptors working in collaboration with a directing sculptor, a ceramic engineer and the architect, a directly executed work would have been accomplished which would be true to the character of the medium.

Large civic sculpture commissions are repeatedly received by a very limited number of sculptors, who employ ghost sculptors to do most of the actual work for low wages. This constitutes a monopoly and presents evidence of discrimination and partiality which should arouse not only the disinherited and discarded sculptors but also the allied artists to defend the rights of sculptors and demand the correction of these practices which are leading to the impasse in sculpture.

Congress has within the last few years appropriated over a million dollars for sculptured work on only four buildings. On the Supreme Court Building alone 120,000 dollars was spent on the interior sculptures, and 230,000 dollars on the exterior, making a total of 350,000 dollars. Most of this money was received by a few select individuals.

It is interesting to compare these sums with paltry amounts set aside for sculptural projects on the PWA. However, the method of dividing the projects equally among the artists as done by the PWA is certainly a step in the direction of the greatest benefit to sculptors as a whole. But this is only a start, and it is up to the artists as a collective body to unite with all artists in demanding a permanent and adequate federal art project on a broader basis.

Sculptors must come to a full realization of the fast moving forces in our social life and take a definite stand in shaping its destiny. The sculptor is not vital unless he is observant and interprets life. Sculptors must become socially articulate and speak firmly and validly.

SURVEY OF ARTISTS' ORGANIZATIONS
Henry Billings

The painter seems to complete the same cycle again and again through the great periods of European art. As a romantic individualist he revolts from the existing order to follow a course of independent exploitation and this in turn invariably ends in the formation of a school or an academy.

The painter was the first craftsman to break away from the old guilds in the middle of the fourteenth century. Until the middle of the seventeenth century society still looked upon the artist as a master-craftsman, learning his craft through the usual system of apprenticeship which culminated in the painting of the *chef-d'oeuvre*, the acceptance of which entitled him to join the company of the Maîtrise. Under Louis XIV the old categories were broken down and the Royal Academy of Painting and Sculpture was established under the direction of Le Brun. Biennial salon exhibitions,—the first attempts of their kind,—introduced their work to the general public. At the time of the French Revolution, artists, impatient with the dictatorship of the Academy, demanded that David, the art dictator of the Republic, abolish the Academy. In 1795 it was replaced by the National Institute which included a new *Academie des Beaux Arts*. This organization continued the Davidian classic tradition throughout the nineteenth century, and has maintained its official authority although its professional scope and power have gradually diminished.

In the United States Trumbull was the first president of the American Academy of Arts in 1818. By 1828 a new society called the National Academy of Design had attracted wide support and by 1841 the old American Academy became defunct. Immediately after the Civil War American painters reaped a rich harvest selling their large uninspired canvases done in the Munich manner for ten and twenty thousand dollars. By 1880 art patrons had ceased to be interested in American art. Though the

Academy had ample financial support, the native painters "were encouraged to write about art, to teach it, to even exhibit, but rarely to sell it."

The real revolt came about through the famous International Armory Show of 1913. A wave of individualism swept the more vital painters away from the academic fold, separating them into tiny cliques. Since the war a great many societies, guilds, and clubs have been formed to sponsor art and the artist, but they are loose organizations and for the most part of a semi-professional character. Their interests and activities often overlap. For the sake of convenience they can be grouped under the following headings: (1) associations which combine semi-professional interests along with cultural activities; (2) groups and cooperatives for the purpose of exhibiting and selling art; (3) active associations and unions of artists which are realistically dealing with the economic, professional, and cultural problems of the artist under the depression.

Under the first grouping we might include the Mural Painters' Society, the National Sculptors' Society, the Water Color Society, the Society of American Etchers, the New York Society of Women Artists, the Print-Makers, the American Society of Painters, Sculptors, and Gravers, and the American Artists' Professional League. Some of these are held together by a common interest in a medium or technique. For the most part the activity of these organizations is limited to the holding of their annual exhibition.

Another group of societies is preoccupied solely with the holding of exhibitions. When the Society of Independent Artists was organized in 1917, it served a definite cultural need through its policy of "No prizes! No juries!" It is still run by professional painters, but its exhibitors are in the main amateurs. The Allied Artists and Salons of America are somewhat similar exhibiting societies.

In 1930–31 the situation became desperate for the artist. During this period the Artists' Aid Committee in New York arranged the out-of-door art exhibitions in Washington Square.

Finally even the so-called successful artists began to realize that private patronage would no longer support them, and that their aesthetic beliefs, [as well as] their personal direction, would in no way be jeopardized through group action. In 1934 the Artists' Union grew out of the Unemployed Artists' Group. It helped make possible the Public Works of Art Project of 1934, relief in order of registration rather than through "the merit system," sick leaves with pay, the Municipal Art Center, the recovery of back pay lost in changes of relief administration, and many other economic benefits. It has stopped lay-offs and the ten percent cut in relief. It fought the censorship of the City Art Commission. It helped to make possible the publication of the magazine, *Art Front*. It has 1600 members with affiliated organizations in Boston, Baltimore, and Chicago. So far it has dealt mainly with economic rather than cultural or professional problems and still does not have adequate representation among the more active well-known artists.

The American Society of Painters, Sculptors, and Gravers does represent the better known professional artists outside the Academy. In May of 1935 the new temper of the artist manifested itself when at a meeting of this society a resolution was unanimously adopted that a rental fee of ten percent per month of the cost of a painting, sculpture, or print be required of all institutions and museums exhibiting the work of the society's members. Other organizations are wholeheartedly supporting this rental policy and it seems likely that museums and art institutions will be eventually forced to recognize the validity of and the justification for a rental policy.

During the past century and a half the artist has had to fight his battles single-handedly, depending entirely on his wits. Society has made of him a recluse, an exquisite, a Bohemian, a romantic fellow in velvet trousers, a clown, and a bum. Always, however, he has remained a stiff-necked individualist. Today the artist recognizes the need for organization, for joining with his fellow-craftsmen toward a common end.

On what basis can he organize? The American Artists' Congress has supplied the answer. At a time like the present when our whole cultural tradition, our arts and technology, are threatened, no one can remain aloof. Especially must the artist who reflects and affects the immediate world around him strive to keep the channels of communication open. The vision of a better world which he treasures can only be preserved through united action.

Proceedings and Discussion

In a paper on "Art Colonies," Doris Lee pointed out that these communities, growing out of artists' efforts to find a perfect refuge, tended to foster dangerous illusions or else to degenerate into purely commercial resorts. Nevertheless, Miss Lee contended, the colonies could be made focal points for the interests of artists if realistic programs were developed, taking into account the artist's genuine need of an audience. Recent activity of a young Woodstock group was cited as an example.

A report was read from Erle Loran of Minneapolis on behalf of the Minnesota Artists' Union on the rental policy as a local problem. Though offering only minor benefits to the Minnesota group, the rental policy was supported by the union there because of its importance as a national issue, according to Mr. Loran.

Sidney Loeb reported on the problems facing the new Artists' Union of Chicago and held that the building of the Congress as a national organization would help strengthen unions in Chicago and elsewhere.

Frederic Knight reported on the activities of the new Artists' Coordination Committee in New York, the program of which is to act as a clearing house for information of vital interest to art organizations represented on it. The program also calls for direct power to be vested in the committee by organizations represented on it, to protest all forms of discrimination involving art and artists. Six New York artist organizations were listed as approving the preliminary plan for the committee.

MR. SIDNEY LOEB: A fortnight ago, the American Legion decided that a work of art painted two years ago and now in the

Roosevelt High School of Rockford, Illinois, a work that had been accepted by the United States government and the municipality of Rockford, Illinois, must now be removed because it is "communistic."

I didn't know where I could find the painter who had done this mural. He had left Chicago, but we sent a letter to his old address and in return got a three page letter sounding like a declaration of war, and ending with an application for membership in the Artists' Union of Chicago. We have undertaken the first fundamental defense of this work.

Herbert Rosengren, who did this mural, is not a lamb. If necessary he would fight this battle alone. But the case in Rockford is the beginning of a very definite, calculated attack on art that could very easily extend throughout the whole country. Members of the Artists' Union feel that if they are not effective in warding off the attack on this mural, the efforts they will have to expend in protecting any further work will be beyond their powers.

I hope that the Artists' Congress will send in a resolution and institute some program in defense of this case.

MR. LA MORE: I would like to raise one issue in connection with the report by Mr. Stavenitz. I think it is important for us to consider because of its connection with this New Deal agency. It is generally admitted to be the most pro-Fascist agency set up under the New Deal. They offered artists thirty dollars a month to go out to the C.C.C. camps and paint on a flat basis, to buy their own materials, and after the work was produced it was to be the property of the government. They came around with this proposition in the Fall of 1934. A number of artists went; they went because there were no projects and they could not get on relief, so they had no choice but to go.

I think this should really be discussed and it should be treated in some resolution. I would like to emphasize this question of the C.C.C. camps, mainly because of the character of the agency. Actually one artist who went out was not given an opportunity to paint, but was put on the road crew by the captain in charge of the camp.

REPORTS AND RESOLUTIONS OF DELEGATES AND PERMANENT ORGANIZATION

Fourth Closed Session

New School for Social Research

Peter Blume, Chairman

GENERAL REPORT OF THE MEXICAN DELEGATION TO THE AMERICAN ARTISTS' CONGRESS

read by José Clemente Orozco

COMRADES: First of all we shall render a report of the work carried out by our National Assembly of Artists. This Assembly was held in Mexico City, following your invitation to us that we send delegates to this Congress.

This report will simply be a summary of the main points taken up by our Assembly. A more complete ideological summary will be drawn up later for your consideration.

No less than twelve papers were read and discussed in detail at our Assembly. The principal points taken up by our Assembly can be separated into four divisions.

1. The artists' position as far as the problems of imperialism, Fascism and war are concerned.

2. The economic security of artists, including artists and craftsmen in popular arts as well as artists engaged in teaching.

3. The artists' and workers' organizations.

4. And finally, form and content in art.

We have felt it advisable not to include local problems in this summary, despite the fact that we reached important conclusions about these problems.

We shall confine ourselves to problems of international scope which affect all artists regardless of frontiers or nationality. Several months before the Assembly a conference was held in Mexico City in which problems similar to those being discussed at this Congress were taken up. The main achievement of the conference was the unification of numerous groups of artists and intellectuals in the fight against imperialism, Fascism and war. Since these three factors are common enemies which impede the development of new cultural forms, logically enough the conclusions dealing with this problem were unanimously adopted by our Assembly in the following terms: The artists' means of struggle against imperialism, Fascism and war consist fundamentally of Trade Union organizations, an essential point of which is the defense of all rights won by the working class.

The artists' means of struggle also include the open revealing of all crimes and criminal attempts practised against intellectuals and artists in fascist countries, and the waging of an intense campaign against the forces which are leading humanity toward a new massacre.

The artist's economic problem was taken up in four papers touching on the following groups of artists; all workers in the Plastic Arts, Artist-Teachers, and workers in the popular arts. In connection with this discussion a very interesting paper was read on the subject, "The Artists' and Workers' Organizations."

First of all we shall take up the problem of the artist-teachers in Mexico. Because of economic pressure the vast majority of artists are forced to lend their services as teachers of drawing and other manual arts in government as well as private schools.

Because of the artist's lack of pedagogical training, however, a great deal of his work as teacher is sterile and his own creative energy becomes atrophied in this activity.

The Assembly's conclusions on this problem were focused mainly on the necessity of removing artists without any pedagogical training from teaching jobs and instead, obtaining material and financial support for them to enable them to continue their work as creative artists.

How do we propose to do this? The organization of artists into trade unions and the relation of these unions to all other working class organizations offer the preliminary key to our plan of action.

The work of art is a commodity, subject like all other commodities to fluctuations on the market. Art galleries constitute the middle-man between the artist and his public, between producer and consumer. The crises through which art galleries are passing in the entire capitalist world, however, offer certain specific problems which must be clarified. The work of art has been considered an article of luxury accessible only to the leisure class. There is no doubt that the acquisition of so-called articles of luxury takes place only after the primary necessities of life, such as food, clothing, habitation, etc., have been fulfilled.

But is it true that a work of art is an article of luxury to be enjoyed by a privileged minority? Does not the work of art fill a higher function within the complexity of human relationships?

We shall go a step further. What should be the real function of the artist and his work today? If we accept the fact that the organization of artists into trade union groups is necessary for the defense of their interests, and if this organization struggles for economic betterment, is it not logical that the most direct way of placing our work, our art, before the working masses, should be through a system of inter-trade-union cooperation? Therefore we adopted the following concrete proposals:

The immediate establishment of a Cultural Section within trade unions and other syndicate organizations, these cultural groups to be under the leadership of members of the Artists' Union. The object of this Section will be to raise the cultural level of the masses by means of lectures, concerts, exhibitions, theatre performances, etc. Payment of the artists' services as well as the expenses entailed in the organization of this work, will be met by the works themselves by means of a cultural stamp to be sold at a minimum of five cents each.

Each worker will be obliged to buy one stamp every month. The amount obtained by this assessment will be used to finance mural decoration in the different trade union headquarters, to publish books, pamphlets in accord with the Artists' Union cultural program, and to give theatre performances.

All these activities will be directed by members of the Artists' Union, all of whom will be paid for their work.

This plan of cultural activity, destined to penetrate the ranks of the masses, has enormous possibilities in Mexico.

The League of Revolutionary Workers and Artists in Mexico and other organizations are already working toward the effective realization of this plan.

It is not our task to present the problems offered by this plan in detail.

You know your own environment and its particular problems. We want, however, to present the general idea for your consideration.

The outstanding advantage of this plan lies in the fact that it gives the workers in every field of art an opportunity to carry on their own work within a constructive system of cooperation, *intimately* bound up with the problems and struggles of the working class.

We are *submitting* a detailed plan of organization based on the general idea already expounded to the permanent committee of the American Artists' Congress for discussion and approval.

Resolution

THE CHAIRMAN: I have a commentary by no means irrelevant to make. United States Congressman Vito Marcantonio and other leaders were arrested in a demonstration of fifteen thousand WPA workers in this city this afternoon. I have before me a resolution which has been offered up by Mr. Blanch. The resolution reads as follows:

Whereas, the American Artists' Congress is a body of creative workers gathered to defend their interests in cooperation with other progressive workers, and

Whereas, the demonstration of fifteen thousand workers of the WPA in New York City today, February 15, in defense of their rights, was attacked by the police, be it

Resolved, that the Artists' Congress hereby declares its support of the WPA workers, and its condemnation of the arrests made of demonstrators and demands their immediate release.

(The resolution was seconded and carried. Telegrams were sent to Mayor La Guardia and Mr. Victor Ridder, New York WPA administrator.)

A paper was read from the floor by Stuyvesant Van Veen on problems of the revolutionary artist.

THE MEXICAN EXPERIENCE IN ART
read by David A. Siqueiros

Modern Mexican painting of revolutionary tendency arose at the same time as the Mexican Revolution and followed its contingencies. Thus the first unrest in art corresponded to the beginnings of social and political unrest. Towards the end of the Diaz regime, the thoughts of the artists were exclusively fixed on Europe. Their artistic tendencies reflected the mentality of the dominant feudal aristocracy. It was naturally at this period that unrest first appeared. The artistic unrest was manifested in the form of a movement for a folk art. Saturnino Heran, for the first time, took as his subjects scenes of popular life. In greater or lesser degree all other painters took the same path. Armed insurrection had already broken out in the North and South. In 1911 students of the School of Fine Arts—The National Academy of Carlos—organized a strike which included economic and political as well as educational demands. It called for the abolition of academic methods and the establishment of open-air schools. They supposed that they were expressing in this way their revolutionary position. They childishly abolished the black pigment from their palette as a revolutionary protest. Our strike insinuated itself into the struggle for land for the peasants, reforms for the workers, and against imperialism, but only in a more or less general manner. We received considerable support among the students of the National University. This was converted into a general protest against the existing methods of intellectual oppression in the universities themselves, and thus our strike assumed a definitely political character. Its leaders were arrested and the demand for their liberation became a matter of national interest. Six months later came the triumph of Madero and with it the fulfillment of our most elementary demands. In this way there appeared the first open-air schools and the traditional academic methods were replaced by impressionism.

Our Europeanism, the reflection of dying Porfirism, began to be replaced by a nationalistic aesthetic. We began to discover that Mexico had a great archaelogical tradition and also a rich folklore. Works by artists who had been ignored previously now assumed a very important place in our artistic thought. The popular drawings by Possados became highly esteemed; so did the paintings in the pulquerias (drinking rooms). We did not yet think about the political content of art. By 1913 there began to appear the first manifestations of social consciousness in our art with reference to workers, as, for example, in the works of Romano, Guillemin, Ortega, Furter and many others. This social art resulted in conflicts with the Ministry of Education. The growth of the revolution converted our first open-air school into a political center. Unanimously we joined the struggle of the masses against the dictatorship of Huerta. This made it impossible for us to continue work, and most of us entered the army of the revolution as soldiers. This fact put us for the first time in direct contact not only with the people, but also with the geography of the country. This converted the bohemian painters into a new type of artist. In a hiatus during the armed conflict of 1915 José Clemente Orozco and Goitia produced works of art which were important for the subsequent development of our Art. Orozco's anti-clerical drawings and Goitia's revolutionary scenes illuminated contemporary life, for the Mexican youth. A little later, in 1919, the work in the School of Fine Arts was resumed, absorbing a larger part of the youth restlessness. At the same time Siqueiros was sent to Europe by a similar group of artists that had emerged, in Guadalajara. This caused the contact between the restlessness of the Mexican youth with a certain degree of mature technique in Europe which was represented by Rivera. It made it possible to publish our manifesto *Vida American*—American Life—which appeared in Barcelona in 1921. Here for the first time Rivera and Siqueiros tried to express the theory of a muralist movement which developed a little later. This movement, however, had certain practical antecedents in the group formed by Dr. Atl called the Society of Painters and Sculptors which wanted to paint in a collective for the walls of the amphitheatre of the Prepatorium.

With the appointment in 1922 of José Vasconcelos as minister of education the impulse toward mural painting became a reality. Orozco, Rivera and Siqueiros obtained big contracts to paint murals, and various others obtained contracts to paint smaller panels. This circumstance produced groupings among the artists. Our manifesto talked about mural art for the masses. But the moment we began our actual work, having come to mural painting as easel painters we were primarily absorbed in new technical problems. We neglected the real problems of content and created murals of neutral or socially irrelevant character. As soon as we had acquired our technique we became more conscious of the social possibilities of our work and organized our revolutionary syndicate of painters, sculptors and engravers. It was then possible to give more consistency to our political attitude. At first our political confusion was a natural consequence of the uncertainty and confusion of the Mexican revolution as a whole and also our lack of revolutionary political education. None of us had had experience with trade unions, with strikes or social struggles. We gave little thought to questions of revolutionary strategy in the placing of our works. We were at this time Utopians in our conceptions of revolutionary art with little direct contact with the masses. The appearance of the organ of our syndicate, *El Machette*, was the beginning of our direct contact with the organized masses, and at the same time the beginning of our conflict with the government. Our murals were in places more or less inaccessible to the masses. But the moment we began to reach the masses through our drawings and prints the government became antagonistic to us. Our first audiences were students and teachers, only intellectuals; our second audience the large masses of people. This new broadening of contact in turn reacted on us to develop our political and social views and to direct our work along new lines. At the same time around 1924 and 1925 that we were perfecting the content of our work, some of us were little by little transformed from merely passive spectators of the revolution into active participants. This experience had enormous importance when we came to formulate a program for the artists' section of the League of Revolutionary Artists and Writers. This experience also enables us today to understand how the Mexican artistic movement fell into an opportunist and reactionary path with the declining curve of the revolution itself. It enabled us to understand how our art turned to the picturesque and adopted forms and contents attractive to the tourist spectator now coming in increasing numbers, which the influence of the new post revolutionary Mexican regime which supported the imperialist penetration of Mexico.

How can we explain that the newest generation of Mexican painters abandoned their recent tradition in mural art and occupied themselves with formal problems independent of social content? Several reasons have been given by the artists themselves—their reaction against the degeneracy of merely picturesque art made largely for tourists; their exclusion from possibilities of realistic mural art caused by the monopoly of Rivera; their desire to establish mural art on a sounder formal basis through a serious study of aesthetic problems. But the fact to be remembered finally is that although these artists had for a time detached themselves from social content in arts they have maintained their allegiance to the revolutionary movement and today announce their intention to create works revolutionary in content as well as in form.

But a new movement that has grown out of all the past experiences has appeared already in Mexico. The new movement is impelled and organized by the section of plastic art of the League of Revolutionary Artists and Writers, which includes the majority of Mexican artists of all schools.

What is the new direction formulated by the League of Revolutionary Artists and Writers? The League has adopted the principle that revolutionary art is not only a problem of content or theme—but a problem of form. It has adopted the idea that revolutionary art is inseparable from forms of art which can reach the greatest number of people. The new line of art adopted by the League is founded upon the principle of discipline within the organization. It has adopted the principle of self-criticism as an instrument for advance. It has also adopted the principle of teamwork as distinguished from isolated individual work. Instead of painting in the official buildings far from the masses, the League wants to help the Mexican workers to find a form suitable to a graphic art of revolutionary propaganda. The League will develop an art economically accessible to the largest number of people. This will give us tremendous possibilities of creating new forms of art. Only in that way can we eliminate archaic forms, old methods of teaching, and also the monopoly of production by the individual. The League desires to form real producers of functional revolutionary art. It believes that these objectives can be achieved only by the collective participation in criticism of all the artists involved in the work. This represents the viewpoint of the majority in the League, which is at present the outstanding organized group of Mexican artists. There are, of course, a few outstanding artists who do not accept the revolutionary esthetic of the League, but these men are in their way on the side of the Revolution, and—as in the United States—differences of esthetic opinion do not prevent us from uniting solidly on the all-important question of the defense of culture against the menaces, Fascism and war.

Proceedings and Discussion

Following the reading of the report for the League of Revolutionary Artists and Writers of Mexico by José Clemente Orozco and that of the National Assembly of Artists' Delegates in Mexico by David Alfaro Siqueiros, Julia Codesido brought greetings to the Congress from artists and writers in Peru, and A. Gattorno brought greetings as a delegate of exiled Cuban artists.

Reporting for the Resolutions Committee, Harry Sternberg brought in drafts of resolutions putting the American Artists' Congress on record: for an active struggle against the threats of War and Fascism; endorsing the rental policy of the Society of

Painters, Sculptors and Gravers; approving the introduction of the government art program and advocating its continuation and extension on a national scale; supporting the artists' unions and urging all artists to join unions; urging art teachers to join organizations in the fight against War and Fascism; urging art students to join organizations in the fight against War and Fascism; condemning the sending of artists into militaristic C.C.C. camps, at wages violating the federal art project scale; condemning all efforts made within the moving picture industry to use it as a medium for anti-democratic, Fascistic propaganda; protesting the attempt to secure the removal of Herbert Rosengren's mural in Roosevelt High School, Rockford, Illinois, and demanding its preservation; protesting the destruction, at the order of the President of the Republic of Panama, Harmodio Arias, of a mural in the National Institute of Panama by the Mexican artist Fernando Leal; protesting the imprisonment without trial of artists and writers in Brazil, and demanding their release and the restoration of their civil rights; protesting the Fascist terror in Portugal, and demanding the restoration of rights and liberties for artists and working class prisoners; greeting the artists of Japan and supporting their struggles against reaction; urging President Cardenas of Mexico to continue his support of the development of culture and defense of the rights of the Mexican people.

These resolutions were adopted by the Congress and the secretary directed to send copies of protests and messages to the responsible authorities.

Stuart Davis reported for the Commission on Permanent Organization.

MR. DAVIS: I wish to impress you with the fact that the considerations included herein were not the result of the actual discussion of a couple hours. The thing was gone into very seriously. Recommendations were made by the committee which had been in action for the past eight months. The fact that there has been a need for this organization, that this Congress has been called, is attested by the discussions and activities that the past sessions have shown.

The question why we need another organization has been clearly indicated by the speakers from the Artists' Union who spoke here today. If one artists' union were able to deal with all the problems that came up, we would not need this organization. The fact remains that a great majority of the artists are not organized. In the meantime, there are many other artists who do not feel like joining an artists' union at this time, but they are willing to join an organization which will be ready to defend the cultural liberty of the artists against all aggression.

The question is what type of organization will follow the interests that we have indicated. How will it be organized? How will it function? In the first place, its activities will not only be defense; part will be very definitely directed toward the development of the professional interests and orientation of the artists.

The Commission recommends that this organization be loose in character. In other words, we do not put down hard and fast rules regarding the active participation of members at this time. We recommend that a national executive committee be nominated and elected here today to carry forward the work of the organization. We have a slate to propose. (*Reads names*).

The Commission feels that this representation is a true one and fully represents the membership of the Congress. This committee will, by the very nature of things, meet where the greatest number of artists reside, which, of course, is New York City. This does not in any sense mean that the members from out-of-town will simply be mere figure-heads on the committee. They will naturally be immediately informed of the decisions taken at any meetings here. In the meantime they are organized outposts, making it possible for us to set up locals—member bodies all over the country. It is recommended that a minimum of five members in any given locality shall constitute a local unit of the organization. It will have autonomy in all activities, providing, of course, it does not conflict with the policies of the national organization.

Now, as to the question of what this organization can do, here are some of the suggestions that have been made. We will be active at all times in all cases within the field of art or related fields. We will be against destruction of freedom and repression of art works, and all forms of Fascist encroachment. We will be effective on all protests that we make according to the standing of our members in the localities they serve. We have an economic question in which our members are especially qualified to take leadership and that is the rental policy. The struggle for municipal art galleries is still with us, and we can take an active part in that. We can develop a wider audience, and directly linked with that would be the preparation of exhibitions.

It is recommended that the permanent organization be called "The League of American Artists." (*Subsequently the National Executive Committee decided it was preferable to continue with the name, American Artists' Congress.*) In the matter of dues, a nominal sum is suggested, two dollars a year.

I think this fairly describes the findings and recommendations of the Commission on Permanent Organization. I would like to move now that the recommendations of the Commission be adopted by the membership.

(*This motion was seconded, and after a short discussion, was adopted as read. A motion was made, seconded and carried to publish the proceedings of the Congress. A rising vote of appreciation and thanks was given Mr. Davis and the organizers of the Congress. The audience applauded vociferously.*)

MR. DAVIS: All I can say is that the artists who inaugurated this Congress are gratified with the results of their labor. I am sure we all feel it is beyond anything we expected. When we first started, we talked about fifty artists. (*Laughter.*)

I feel that the Congress has accomplished its purpose. It has brought together artists who barely nodded to one another on the street. Now they will meet and discuss their problems.

I feel very strongly the spirit that has brought the artists from out-of-town, and the artists from Mexico, Cuba and Peru, to show their solidarity with us.

I think we can close the session now with the feeling that something has happened here that has never happened in the history of American art before.

3
ILLUSTRATIONS

1. Diego Rivera, *Man at the Crossroads*, incomplete, destroyed, 1933.

2. Ben Shahn, *Prisoners Milking Cows*, 1934–1935, study for Riker's Island mural, New York City. Estate of Ben Shahn/V.A.G.A., New York, 1985.

3. Peppino Mangravite, *American Artists' Congress*, 1936 or later, collection unknown. On stage: Heywood Broun, George Biddle, Stuart Davis, Julia Codesido of Peru, Lewis Mumford, Margaret Bourke-White, Rockwell Kent, José Clemente Orozco of Mexico, Paul Manship, Peter Blume, Aaron Douglas.

4. Will Barnet, *Factory District*, included in "America Today
Exhibition," 1936, collection unknown.

5. Philip Evergood, *Portrait of a Miner*, included in "America Today
Exhibition," 1936, collection unknown.

6. Henry Glintenkamp, *Manhattan Backyards*, included in "America Today Exhibition," 1936, collection unknown.

7. Harry Gottlieb, *The Coal Pickers*, included in "America Today Exhibition," 1936, collection unknown.

ILLUSTRATIONS

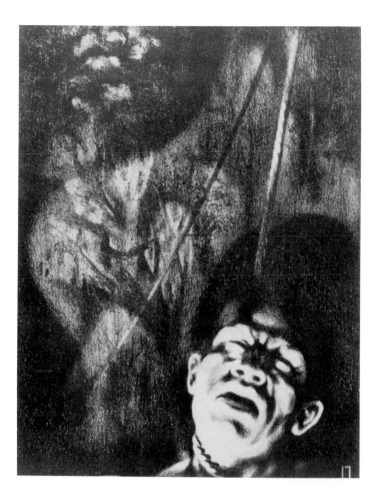

8. Louis Lozowick, *Lynching,* included in "America Today
Exhibition," 1936, collection unknown.

9. Andrée Ruellan, *City Market—Charleston*, included in "America Today Exhibition," 1936, collection unknown.

10. Harry Sternberg, *Coal Mining Town*, included in "America Today Exhibition," 1936, collection unknown.

11. Raphael Soyer, *Transients*, 1936, Archer M. Huntington Art
Gallery, University of Texas at Austin.

12. Stuart Davis, *The Terminal*, 1937, Hirshhorn Museum and Sculpture Garden, Smithsonian Institution.

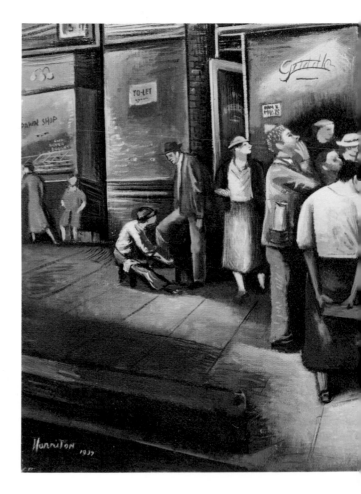

13. Abraham Harriton, *6th Avenue Employment Seekers*, 1937, collection unknown.

14. Francis Criss, *Still Life*, 1937, included in "First Annual Membership Exhibition," 1937, collection unknown.

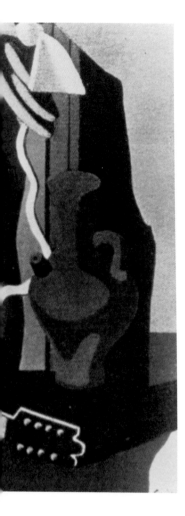

15. Adolf Dehn, *The Great God Pan*, 1937, included in "First Annual Membership Exhibition," 1937, collection unknown.

16. Gwen Lux, *Spanish Widow*, 1937, included in exhibition,
"In Defense of World Democracy," collection unknown.

17. Isabel Bishop, *Girl with Hands on Hips*, 1938, photo courtesy
Midtown Galleries, New York City.

18. Isabel Bishop, *Waiting*, 1938, Newark Museum.

19. Lucille Blanch, *Afternoon in Spain*, 1938, included in "Second Annual Membership Exhibition," collection unknown.

20. Mervin Jules, *Diplomats*, 1938, included in "Second Annual Membership Exhibition," collection unknown.

21. Max Weber, *At the Mill*, 1939, Newark Museum.

22. Eitaro Ishigaki, *Amazons*, 1939, included in "Third Annual
Membership Exhibition," collection unknown.

23. Georgette Seabrooke, *My Son and I*, 1939, included in "Third Annual Membership Exhibition," collection unknown.

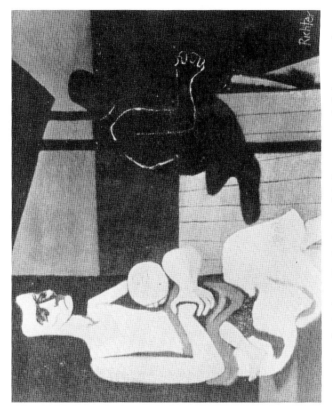

24. Mischa Richter, *Death of a Social Order*, 1940, included in "Fourth Annual Membership Exhibition," collection unknown.

25. Maurice Freedman, *Crossing to New York*, c. 1940, photo courtesy
of Midtown Galleries, New York City.

26. William Gropper, *Hostages*, 1942, Newark Museum.

27. A. J. Goodelman, untitled, 1943, collection unknown.

28. Aaron Douglas, *Power Plant, Harlem*, c. 1937, Harmon Collection, National Archives, Washington, D.C.

29. Mervin Jules, *Ditch Digger*, n.d., collection unknown.

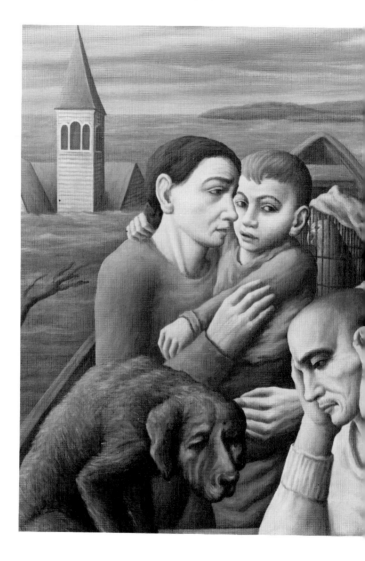

30. Paul Meltsner, *High Water*, n.d., photo courtesy Midtown
Galleries, New York City.

31. Doris Rosenthal, *Nude by Table*, n.d., photo courtesy Midtown
Galleries, New York City.

32. Louis Ribak, *The Man with the Bag*, n.d., collection unknown.

33. Philip Reisman, *Death of Sir Basil Zaharoff*, c. 1936, collection
ACA Galleries, New York City.

34. Mitchell Siporin, *Refugees*, 1939, Museum of Modern Art,
New York, purchase.

35. Harry Sternberg, *Insecurity. Economic.*, n.d., collection ACA
Galleries, New York City.

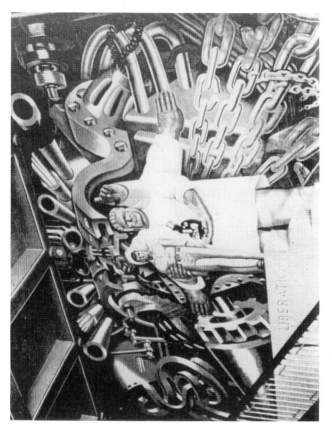

36. Gilbert Wilson, *Machinery Mural*, 1934, Woodrow Wilson Junior High School, Terre Haute, Indiana.

4
EXHIBITIONS
CATALOGS
BIOGRAPHIES

LIST OF CONGRESS EXHIBITIONS
IN NEW YORK CITY

1. "American Artists' Congress Exhibition," American Contemporary Artists Galleries (ACA Galleries) November 10–23, 1935. This original publication of the call contained three paragraphs that were subsequently deleted from other published versions. See Texts of Congress Exhibition Catalogs.
2. "Against War and Fascism: An International Exhibition of Cartoons, Drawings and Prints," New School for Social Research, April 15–May 6, 1936. See Texts of Congress Exhibition Catalogs.
3. "First Annual Competitive Exhibition," ACA Galleries, June 15–30, 1936. From these juried exhibitions, a young artist would later receive a solo exhibition.
4. "To Aid Democracy in Spain," ACA Galleries, October 11–18, 1936. Exhibition to raise funds for Loyalist Spain.
5. "America Today," December 1936. Exhibitions of prints which occurred in thirty cities. See Texts of Congress Exhibition Catalogs.
6. "Framed and Hung," ACA Galleries, March 1937. Satirical portraits.
7. "First Annual Membership Exhibition," April 1937. Simultaneous exhibitions in New York City, Cleveland, Chicago, Detroit, Los Angeles, New Orleans, Portland, and Philadelphia. The exhibition planned for Baltimore was canceled. See Texts of Congress Exhibition Catalogs.
8. "Second Annual Competitive Exhibition," ACA Galleries, June 20–27, 1937.
9. "In Defense of World Democracy: Dedicated to the Peoples of Spain and China," December 15–30, 1937. Simultaneous exhibitions in New York City, Baltimore, Los Angeles, Cedar Rapids, New Orleans, St. Louis, and Portland. See Texts of Congress Exhibition Catalogs.
10. "Second Annual Exhibition," Wanamaker's Department Store, May 5–21, 1938. See Texts of Congress Exhibition Catalogs.
11. "Christmas Exhibition," ACA Galleries, December 1938.
12. "Third Annual Exhibition: Art in a Skyscraper," February 5–26, 1939. See Texts of Congress Exhibition Catalogs.

13. "Sporting Man," New York World's Fair, Hall of Man, April 1939.
14. "Fourth Annual Competitive Exhibition," ACA Galleries, c. July 23–August 7, 1939.
15. "Print Exhibition," Hudson D. Walker Galleries, August 1939.
16. "Fifty Dollar Exhibition," ACA Galleries, December 1939.
17. "Joint Exhibition of Photographers with Photo League," Photo League Galleries, March 1940.
18. "Fourth Annual Exhibition: Art in Democracy," 785 Fifth Avenue, April 6–28, 1940.
19. "American Artists' Congress at the World's Fair," Contemporary Arts Building, July 28–August 15, 1940.
20. "Twelve Cartoons: Defending WPA by Members of the American Artists' Congress," undated.
21. An antiwar exhibition, 1941, no documentation.
22. "Third Annual Competitive Exhibition," no documentation.

TEXTS OF CONGRESS EXHIBITION CATALOGS

"American Artists' Congress Exhibition," ACA Galleries, November 10–23, 1935

[The following paragraphs were deleted from the call after its initial publication.]

The Artists' Congress, to be held in New York City, February 15, 1936, will have as its objective the formation of such an organization. Discussion at the Congress will include the following:

Fascism and war, racial discrimination; preservation of civil liberties; imprisonment of revolutionary artists and writers; federal, state, and municipal art projects; municipal art gallery and center; federal art bill; rental of pictures; the art schools during the crisis; museum policy in the depression; subject matter in art; esthetic directions, relations of media and material to art content; art criticism.

We artists who have signed, representing all sections of the United States, ask you to show your solidarity with us by signing this Call and by participating in the Congress.

"Against War and Fascism: An International Exhibition of Cartoons, Drawings and Prints," New School for Social Research, April 15–May 6, 1936

"Having eyes they see not"—these American millions they look at the photographs of fighting in Africa and Asia, of marching soldiers in many lands and war ships in many seas. But they do not see the war that will soon be calling for them. They read the headlines about our billion dollar budget for war preparations and think it is for national defense. They swallow this lie as easily as the one about ending war and saving democracy.

They see and hate the cruelties, the repressions, of Fascism in Europe. They say "It can't happen here—we won't let it." Yet in many communities their basic liberties are now being taken from them while they are being whipped to a blind frenzy of hate against the "reds." It is the high duty of artists to make these blind millions see and understand. It is their heavy responsibility to wake these sleep walkers while there is yet time to escape the destruction toward which they are being driven.

Harry F. Ward

There are a few people who have made a pot bellied living by the exploitation of labor, conveniently assisted now and then by that wholesale butchery of men, women, and children called War. There are millions of people who think that being slaughtered is Life, and that slaughtering— or being slaughtered—is its Heaven sent reward. Good: let them. So hurrah for Fascism!—and to Hell with the Human Race! Of the millions—and there are such millions—who want to pursue the cultivation of their garden which is America in peace and ordered security, art is the voice. For God's sake listen to it.

Rockwell Kent

The other day I was looking through a collection of caricatures attacking Gustave Courbet. The great painter and socialist and revolutionary had to swallow all sorts of jibes from the gentlemen who made satirical drawings for the French weeklies (with the approval of the French government). There were only a few good friends like Daumier who came to his defense. It struck me, looking through this book where so much stupid malice is assembled, that for more than a century the great mass of satirical artists have been on the side of the ruling class—not for any fundamental reasons connected with the nature of satirical art, but simply because the magazines able to reproduce their work and the galleries able to sell it have been bourgeois institutions. But the ways of satirical artists are dead and as forgotten as the hobble skirt. Meanwhile, a few independent figures like Hogarth (the artist of the middle class when it was still progressive), like Callot and Goya (with their sermons against war), like Daumier (the enemy of purse-proud philistinism), are still exerting an influence, are still teaching people to see the world through their honest eyes. May we honor them, both by remembering them and by following their example.

Malcolm Cowley

"America Today Exhibition," December 1936

For this exhibition of prints, which took place simultaneously in thirty cities, the book *America Today: A Book of 100 Prints* was published for the American Artists' Congress by Equinox Cooperatives.

The Origin of These Prints

In bringing together the prints reproduced in this volume the American Artists' Congress has made an important contribution to the new movement now manifest in the graphic arts in this country.

The one hundred prints here reproduced were selected from hundreds submitted by artists in all parts of the United States in response to the announcement by the Congress of a nation-wide exhibition of duplicate exhibits to be held simultaneously in thirty American cities during the month of December, 1936. The jury was composed of the following artists: Arnold Blanch, Stuart Davis, Ernest Fiene, Hugo Gellert, William Gropper, Wanda Gag, Yasuo Kuniyoshi, Margaret Lowengrund, Louis Lozowick, George Picken, Harry Sternberg, Lynd Ward, and Max Weber. Each juror was asked to include one of his own works in the exhibition. The method of selection was an innovation in jury procedure. It was the most democratic available. Each juror made an individual selection of one hundred prints, and then their written lists were tallied for the hundred prints receiving the highest number of votes.

The exhibition, as a whole, may be characterized as "socially conscious." It reflects a deep-going change that has been taking place among artists for the last few years—a change that has taken many of them not only to their studio window to look outside, but right through the door and into the street, into the mills, farms, mines, and factories. More and more artists are finding the world outside their studios increasingly interesting and exciting, and filling their picture with their reactions to humanity about them, rather than with apples or flowers. Even in the case of artists who have been working in abstract design, it is interesting to note their concern with social issues and subjects, at least as a source of inspiration, as indicated by their titles.

This revolutionary change occurring among artists has a complement in the changing attitude of a growing public toward the print. Many are learning to appreciate the fine possibilities inherent in this medium for humor, tragedy, satire, and full-bodied depiction of life. They no longer regard the print only as wall decoration, but as a form of contemporary expression, whether it be hung on the wall or studied in portfolio. And as more people embrace this new attitude and interest, more artists understand the importance of making their work accessible to this larger public. They realize that it is as wrong to destroy a fine plate or block after pulling a small number of proofs, when thousands of people would like to own such prints, as it is to create an artificial scarcity of food by destroying pigs and wheat while hundreds of thousands go hungry.

In arranging for the simultaneous showing of these thirty duplicate exhibitions, the American Artists' Congress is attempting to help the artist reach a public comparable in size to that of the book and motion picture, and to bring the artist and public closer together by making the print relevant to the life of the people, and financially accessible to the person of small means. It is trying to bring about that healthy interaction between artist and public which alone can develop a great popular movement in American art and reestablish the high traditions of such masters of the print as Durer, Callot, Rembrandt, Goya, Hogarth, and Daumier.

Alex R. Stavenitz

These Prints and the Public

The American Artists' Congress, in this, its first national exhibition of contemporary American prints, presents an issue of far reaching importance to the American public.

Shall the American artist manage the production, distribution and education in the field in which he is a specialist, or shall he continue to be the pawn of various lay agencies which have neglected or used him in the past for reasons dictated sometimes by idealism, sometimes by whim, sometimes by profit, or social prestige?

The artist needs autonomy. He can assert autonomy, as he has in this exhibit, but he cannot make such an assertion effective without public support.

In 1910 the Chicago Society of Etchers inaugurated autonomous action by artists in this country by staging its own exhibitions and publishing its own books and print editions. Similar efforts were undertaken by the Brooklyn Society of Etchers, the California Society of Printmakers and other organizations. The American Designers Gallery and the American Union of Decorative Artists and Craftsmen made brave attempts at such management in 1928.

The American Artists' Congress and its varied program are the result of cumulative pressure toward constructive action to satisfy a deeply-lying cultural need, accelerated by the depression. Direct contact between the layman who uses or might use works of art and the individual artist who produces them, together with the recognition of the artist's authority to choose and manage his own exhibits, is a healthy and fruitful condition. The present divorce of user and producer, encouraged and fostered by middlemen, for whom there is a specious respect, is an unhealthy and constricting condition.

By direct contact with his audience the artist avoids the censorships proceeding from both the profit motive and lay officialdom. He also gains the inspiration which arises from a sense of usefulness, which is inherent in that contact. Responsibility for the support or neglect of his work is placed squarely where it belongs—on the community. No honest mind of maturity and strength needs more nourishing, beyond the physical, than the challenge of this condition. The Government Arts Projects, in addition to the necessary physical support, provide such direct contact and elimination of the middlemen (except where they have drawn in lay art officials as regional directors). This characteristic distinguishes the Government program as one of the most significant steps in building a national culture ever undertaken by the American people. The artist, for the first time in our history, has his chance to produce with the sure knowledge that his work will be used by the society in which he lives.

The advantages to the general public of this direct contact are no less important. Art is taken out of the studio, the gallery and the art museum and put to work in the homes and public buildings of everyday. The artist ceases to be an ornament of the pink-tea, a playboy companion of the dilettante patron, a remote hero with a famous name. He becomes, instead, a workman among workers. He paints murals on a scaffold of planks and ladders. He prints his etchings, lithographs or woodblocks with hands which know ink and the rollers and wheels of his press. He works. He produces. He lives.

Ralph M. Pearson

The Woodcut

The oldest example of this, the earliest form of engraving—which has been used by the Chinese for over a thousand years—is from the middle of the ninth century, A.D. But the woodcut as we know it first appeared in the middle of the fifteenth century. It very quickly became more popular than any pictorial medium then in use among the common people, which is a marked contrast to the present day limited and signed proofs for the dealer, collector, and speculator in fine prints.

The list of artists who have made woodcuts, from Dürer to our own day, is a very long one. A preoccupation in the eighteenth century with the engraved metal plate was followed by a revival in the following century and a subsequent decadence into magazine illustration. With the invention of photography and photo-engraving for reproduction on a mass scale, the woodcut almost ceased to exist. During this low ebb, small groups of artists on the continent and in America kept the craft alive until, at the turn of the present century, a new interest burst forth. Today, a great tradition in the art of the woodcut is being established.

Technically, the woodcut requires not only a knowledge of drawing but skill in a distinct kind of craftsmanship. Much more than "hacking" at the wood is necessary. Clarity in design and expression in both line and area are most important. The wood*cut* is done on soft wood, the long-grain plank of apple, pear, beech, cherry—and also linoleum. All woods used are type-high, planed flat and sandpapered very smooth. The design is either drawn directly or traced upon the block, and the method, roughly is to cut away all white or light areas, leaving the black lines and areas raised, so that, when inked, they will print on paper under pressure. A knife or carver is used for incising the line and chisels or similar tools are used to clean out superfluous wood.

In wood *engraving* a hard, closely-grained wood—such as box or maple—is used. The block is cut across the grain of the tree, and an entirely different set of tools must be employed—burins or gravers and tint tools of different sizes and shapes whose capacities for varying degrees of fine lines and large spaces allow more profuse tonal and color variations than is possible in the woodcut.

Printing, as in all graphic arts, requires a great deal of skill. Perhaps the best method is with the Washington-Franklin proofing press, or the flat-bed press. But good proofs have been made with the burnisher, the back of a spoon, a Japanese baren, a roller, the old-fashioned letter press—and even the foot.

H[enry] Glintenkamp

Etching

Etching is printing from an acid-incised, inked plate. It was first done early in 1500; Daniel Hopfer is generally considered to have been the first known etcher. Albrecht Dürer, who produced etchings only a few years later, was the first important artist to use this medium. The first plates were of iron; red-lead was used for stopping out: the prints were pulled in wooden presses. These great technical handicaps were magnificently overcome. Modern etchers command not only superior metals, standardized acids and grounds, but also, in the steel-plating process, the means of overcoming the wearing-away of the metal itself.

The mediums of art have certain innate qualities. No one would think of doing small easel paintings in fresco, just as no sensitive artist would think of doing a water color on an etching plate (miscalled color etchings). And basically, because it is a reproductive medium, etching is meant for wide distribution.

The incisiveness of the bitten line demands that something be said with that line. The greatest masters of black and white have used the medium naturally and normally, line and tone telling the artist's reaction to his time. The prints were widely distributed and sold cheaply. For the most part the plates were used until they began to wear down.

Rembrandt's sympathetic renderings of the Jew, Goya's moving depictions of the horrors of war, Forain's sympathetic pictures of the people and his caustic criticism of the courts, Hogarth's biting comment on the morals of his time, and a host of others are examples of great artists utilizing the normal function of this medium.

Lately the print has been perverted into a false, unhealthy, unnatural preciosity. What is said—with tools an artist devotes a lifetime to master—has become unimportant. The plate itself is deliberately destroyed, sometimes only after ten proofs have been pulled, in order that rarity may be the chief selling point. Prints become a display of technical acrobatics, as meaningless and functionless as a tightrope walker juggling twelve balls at once. And people are cunningly misled into paying two or three hundred dollars for such a print, while a good Daumier or Goya can be gotten for twenty dollars.

Society has forced the artist into playing this game, into trying to catch with special tricks, special techniques and especially limited editions, the eye of the few who can pay. Such perversions have resulted in the spiritual death of many artists and almost in the death of graphic art.

Fortunately, some artists have been forced, by the none too gentle jolts of the times, to open their eyes. They have awakened to the realization that they have lost touch with actual life. As a result, prints are now being produced that portray the vital aspects of contemporary life. Editions are now unlimited. Prices are now low—not low enough yet—but even so more available to the huge new audience.

The hundred prints in this book move in this direction. They represent the beginning of a renaissance of graphic art.

Harry Sternberg

Lithography

Lithography is the youngest of the graphic arts. It was invented about a century ago by Aloys Senefelder (1771–1834). Reduced to simplest terms, the lithographic process consists of the following steps: (a) drawing with grease-containing pencil, crayon or ink on a flat surface of limestone; (b) chemical treatment of the stone (weak solution of nitric acid) so that the parts covered by the drawing are made receptive to ink and impervious to water, while, contrariwise, parts unoccupied by any drawing become receptive to water but impervious to ink; (c) feeding to the stone the ink, which is absorbed and repelled in the manner indicated; (d) putting the stone in a press and transferring the drawing to paper.

From the standpoint of technical procedure, lithography is the most flexible graphic art. Its great virtue is the range of tone which it makes accessible to the artist—from the softest, most delicate grays to the deepest, richest blacks, which are given a specific, textural quality by the surface of the stone. The finest line of etching, the grain of aquatint, the bold strokes of woodcut, the transparency of wash—all are attainable by the practiced lithographer. A slight hint of the limitless possibilities for experiment in this medium is afforded by careful examination of the mutually differing lithographs by Biddle, Kent, Kuniyoshi, Gropper, Gag, Dehn, Fiene, Davis and others.

A knowledge of the medium, and mastery of technique, when combined with a gift for formal organization, will distinguish the work of talent from the work of mediocrity. But nothing could be more sterile than exclusive preoccupation with technical experimentation, and nothing more foreign to the best traditions of the graphic arts. During the Reformation, the French Revolution, the American Civil War, the Russian Revolution, the graphic artist played a tremendous role—with no detriment to his art. Certainly Dürer's wood and metal engravings, or Daumier's lithographs and woodcuts, are no less valuable plastically because they were used in the service of an idea.

This is especially important to remember now, when progress and reaction are contending throughout the world. The integrity of the artist and the very fate of art are threatened today. If, by a formally significant creative interpretation, the artist fastens the attention of his contemporaries upon a living issue, he continues in the present the work of the great graphic artists of the past.

Louis Lozowick

"First Annual Membership Exhibition," April 1937

The artist of our time has been inevitably and profoundly affected by two events in the world outside—the Great War of 1914 and the economic crisis that began in 1929. Into the quiet of the studio these forces beat with the fury of a storm and the artist found that despite his desires for peace and isolation, he could not remain untouched.

From the war he learned that the world of art, seemingly complete and self-sufficient and impervious to the winds that blow through other places, is in reality a structure so frail that it takes but the insatiate ambition of military men, the desire of industrialists to increase their profits, or the blunt intention of bankers to protect their loans, to send it tumbling to destruction—the sculpture of the Renaissance crumbles beneath airplane bombardment, the paintings of four hundred years ripped to pieces by artillery, the living artists of a country riddled with bullets like any other men and left hanging on barbed wire entanglements.

From the great depression he has learned that even in times of peace the foundations of the world of art are not secure; that an economic system that brings unemployment, hunger and suffering to millions brings a full measure of death and sickness to the world of art; that meager patronage on which he eeked out an existence in 'good' times can virtually vanish in 'hard' times; that his world is not a world in itself, that a thousand threads bind the artist to his fellow men.

The artist has learned, too, that those who control the state and boast themselves the guardians of civilization have, in the final analysis, no real concern for him; that if left to their own devices and programs they will cast him off to starve, and ask only that he do it without protest. These things have been made overwhelmingly clear to the artist in the years since 1929.

But the artist has learned other things, too. He has come to see that if he wants the world of art to live, he must work actively for those physical conditions that are basic necessities for any art activity, an economic relationship with society that will provide a room to work in, food for energy, ample supplies of canvas, colors, materials. The old order has demonstrated that by and large and for most artists it cannot supply these physical conditions. Hence the artist seeks new relationships, federal projects and patronage, new uses for art, new places for pictures, new audiences, wider audiences, audiences sought for and created through re-arrangements in the fields of content and prices. He sees, too, that if he wants the world of art to live, he must fight for something beyond these physical conditions. That something is freedom, not just an abstraction or a word in a song, but with a very precise meaning. The artist must have complete freedom of expression, freedom to deal with any aspect of life without hindrance. He must be free to bring his work before people without the barriers that rise from official censorship, attacks by hoodlums and vigilantes, or prohibitive costs of materials and display space. He must have an audience that is in its turn free, not bound down by taboos and superstitions or kept from the contact with art by barriers of another sort, lack of education, lack of leisure, lack of money to buy and to own.

These then, are the things the American artist has learned about the world and about himself. Understanding has brought with it the compulsion to act. Because alone he can do nothing, because moreover, the conditions he wants are for all artists, not for a special group or clique, a new kind of artists' organization was needed. To meet this need the American Artists' Congress was formed somewhat over a year ago.

It joins artists of all races and aesthetic creeds in common action whose goal is the creation of those conditions that art must have if it is to live and grow. In the larger sense, this common action means complete and passionate opposition to those forces in the world about us that are moving toward another war, that seek to repeat the bitter formula wherein lust for power and privilege and desire for business profits work bloody havoc with the lives of millions. More specifically, this common action means opposing all censorships of what artists may paint and all attacks on what they have painted, whether these attacks take the form of physical injury to the work, as occurred in Los Angeles, or attempts to suppress the exhibition of a particular painting, as happened in St. Louis, and Rockford, Illinois. It means vigorous support of government art projects, since these projects, regardless of what immediate reasons impelled their establishment, represent the most significant step towards a sound economic base for art that has occurred in this country. It means working out new relationships with the public, as was done in the Congress exhibition of graphic art shown simultaneously in thirty cities all over the country. It means working with all other groups whose goals are similar to the goals the artist seeks, whose enemies are the enemies of the living artist, who are fighting restriction on civil liberties, who seek a higher standard of living for the workers of the country, who want more freedom and a more abundant life for the people of this land. With all who walk this road, the artist makes common cause, and this exhibition, because it springs from the deep desire of artists for a world in which there shall be both peace and freedom, is in itself a voice raised against war and against fascism, and a force for the advancement of culture.

Lynd Ward

"In Defense of World Democracy: Dedicated to the Peoples of Spain and China," December 15–30, 1937

A Note on the Exhibition

Participation of hundreds of artists in the American Artists' Congress is an indication that creative workers are no longer content to work out their problems in the isolation of their studios. Through the Congress they have asserted their collective solidarity with other progressive groups in opposition to the constantly increasing threats of the war-inciting Fascist forces active on a world-wide scale.

One of the significant differences between the Second Congress, opening in New York, December 17, 1937, and the first one, held in February, 1936, is that a large exhibition by the New York membership (paralleled by local exhibitions in Baltimore, Cleveland, New Orleans, St. Louis, Los Angeles, Portland, Oregon, and Cedar Rapids, Iowa) is an integral part of the current Congress.

Approximately two hundred painters, sculptors, photographers and graphic artists are contributing works to this show—"In Defense of World Democracy: Dedicated to the Peoples of Spain and China."

Thus the artists now make it clear, as they were hardly prepared to do at the time of the first Congress, that there is no essential difference between what they have to say on the platform and what they express in their artistic media.

This exhibition is the first definite showing of this kind held solely by the members of the Congress. The dangers to peace, democracy and cultural progress as manifested by Mussolini and Hitler through their direct 'sand-bagging' of the democratic countries of the world with threats of war and intervention in the Civil War in Spain gave impetus to the central idea.

The first exhibition, "Against War and Fascism," held in April, 1936, was much more general. Artists who were not members of the Congress were invited. The subject was treated historically and it covered a period of 400 years.

Although the original plan of the present exhibition was comparably modest, the increasing aggression of the Fascists and the Imperialist Fascist government of Japan warring an 'undeclared war' on China, the exhibition took its present form.

Although the fundamental idea "Against War and Fascism" was retained, the character of the exhibition, as its title suggests, was so broadened as to include curtailment of civil liberties, strikes, police brutalities, etc., as relevant subject matter. In fact, any work depicting undemocratic procedures and the exploitation and enslavement of labor was included. All schools of painting are represented and no censorship has been exercised as there was no jury. Two relevant items included in the show, although extraneous, are Picasso's etchings, "The Dreams and Lies of Franco," and anti-fascist drawings by the school children of Madrid.

That this particular exhibition comes within the scope and purpose of the American Artists' Congress goes without saying. That it is a necessary exhibition at this time must be self-evident to all those who believe in Peace and Democracy and those who hate Fascism and its counterpart, War.

H[enry] Glintenkamp

Foreword

This exhibition by members of the American Artists' Congress together with the Annual Congress sessions now current at Carnegie Hall and the New School for Social Research announce a new day in the world of American art. Artists, by these events, are acknowledging their responsibility as members of a cultural profession to act on issues affecting the national well-being. They are abandoning the easy policy of laissez faire. They are clarifying their philosophy, planning and carrying out a program. They are assuming the dignity of leadership in the department of human life wherein they are equipped by professional practice for meeting the rigors of the esthetic winter needlessly impressed on the nation by the thought habits of our times.

The national and local community in this country has lacked such leadership in its long history of neglect and cautious support of the arts. The antiquarian mind, the profit motive, the average layman art authority and the general ignorance of the art experience may fairly divide credit for the caution and the neglect. Artists as members of an organized profession have never essayed this situation and prescribed a remedy. The American Artists' Congress is essentially a facing of responsibility to do just that. And the vastness of the task is a direct challenge to the intelligence and integrity of the profession and its ability to meet and overcome the many obstacles which inevitably obstruct the new way.

The National Government in its art program (initiated in the relief department at the suggestion of American Artists' Congress member, George Biddle, and in its Treasury program by an artist, Edward Bruce) has taken the most important step in the Nation's history toward reconstruction of the esthetic ruins of our age. The Artists' Congress has supported and will continue to support that program. Also it will demand for the artist a voice in present and future policy and management. Participation is the only possible means to effectualize reconstruction plans.

Government action, however, must by supplemented and directed by professional action. The artist is now, as he has always been in the great producing periods of the past, the creator, the designer, the leader. Exhibition of current works represents one section of his responsibility. This exhibit, because it is shaped entirely by artists on their own resources, is symbolic of the new day in American art.

Ralph M. Pearson

"Second Annual Exhibition," May 5–21, 1938

The American Artists' Congress has taken a leading position among contemporary artists' societies and since it is only a little over two years old it is interesting to examine the sources of its strength. As a non-profit making, non-political cultural organization, it has attracted to its membership rolls over 800 artists of recognized standing in all sections of the United States, and its activities have been the result of the democratically determined needs of these members.

The Artists' Congress was formed as the spontaneous expression of the growing social awareness of American artists wherein art and culture were recognized as aspects of social development as a whole and not mere isolated forms of human activity. The social awareness among artists was accelerated in the world wide economic depression of the 30's, and by the attitude towards art and culture in those western European countries which have abandoned the democratic principles of government.

The economic depression destroyed the private patronage of the artist and threw him into contact with the desperate millions whose livelihood has also been taken away from them. The artist became familiar with pauperism and the demoralization of living on relief.

In those western European countries were democracy has been repudiated, books were burned, paintings ridiculed and destroyed, music by great composers forbidden to be played, and the right to studentship in the arts denied except within the barbed wire limits of a mystical and militaristic political censorship. In place of democratic rights and freedom of expression the artists in those countries were ordered to celebrate a rabid and false nationalism and racial hatred, or to concern themselves with the sterile academic forms of the past. Where democracy has been repudiated, the meaning, form, and content of art affirm and predict only one thing. Death.

In the light of these facts, which forced themselves into the consciousness of many American artists, it became clear that existing artists' societies were in themselves inadequate to express programmatically the present position and correct course of American art.

This was so because the artists' societies already existent were formed to promote the needs and interests of some particular section of the artist population, a section having either an economic, social, or esthetic objective in common. But the contemporary situation with its threat to democracy, art, and culture, was not directed at any particular section of artists, but was the concern of all artists, and so the founders of the American Artists' Congress issued a call to all artists of recognized standing in their respective circles to meet in a Congress to form a new organization which would represent their needs and interests. In issuing this call the founders did not in any sense seek to supersede or oppose the existing artists' societies, but they proposed the formation of a supplementary society in which broad social and cultural interests, common to all artists, would be the basis of unity.

The first American Artists' Congress was held at Town Hall, New York City, in February, 1936, and given permanent organizational form a few days later by a National Executive Committee, elected at the Congress and composed of artists from all sections of the United States. Since that time the Artists' Congress has carried on activities far beyond the scope of any other single existing artists' society. These activities include a number of general and special topics of social, cultural and esthetic importance; the publication of several important books, and a quarterly bulletin; it has raised a collective voice in support of democratic and progressive legislation which was of direct concern to our cultural future; it has given support to other artists' societies on issues which were the concern of all artists.

These organized activities and the direction they have taken toward preservation and development of democracy in culture, imply a new concept of the meaning of art and its role in society which is important. This concept can be described briefly as follows: art is one of the forms of social development and consciousness, which is in constant interaction with other social forms in its environment. The character of art at any given time stands in definite, although complex, relation to the social environment which makes that environment including its political, social, economic, cultural aspects, a matter of direct concern to all artists who wish to develop as rational human beings.

Art develops wherever the culture of the people is sufficiently broad to permit it and the resources of modern democratic society hold the potentialities of an artistic culture immeasurably greater than any in history. But these potentialities are blighted by the destruction of democracy and the narrowing of the base on which culture can develop, a truth amply demonstrated in several parts of the world today.

In contradiction to this conception of art as a particular but integral part of the social structure, there are some artists and critics who prefer to think of art as an isolated activity having its own history which is determined by the talent of an aristocracy of genius throughout the centuries. Such a viewpoint limits the meaning of art to a matter of fine taste in certain relationships of form and color and ignores the fact that these relations always refer to a concept of natural relations. These idealists observe that works of art have the most diverse subject matter: people, landscapes, still lifes, spatial relations—and they conclude from this that subject matter has nothing to do with art. This is exactly the same as arguing that since we observe life in people, in trees, and in apples, that people, trees, and apples have nothing to do with life, and thus they look for life in the "form" of a disembodied essence, a "non-objective" life without material limitation.

Such a conception of the meaning of art has no value for the contemporary artist because, ignoring reality, it can offer no real program of artistic and social development and becomes a befogging obstacle in the path of the artist searching for a fruitful direction.

Then there are artists and critics who, accepting the conception of art as a socially determined form, at the same time refuse to adopt a program based on that conception. They agree that a free society can best provide the conditions in which a great art can develop, and they argue that the repudiation of democracy destroys the very hope for the cultivation of a fruitful artistic soil, but, "alas," they moan, "there is no method whereby we can even hope in our lifetime to see that happy day when pure art will be loved by all. Reactionaries, Progressives, and Radicals are all equally doomed. But the artist must be brave, stubborn, even nonchalant, if possible, and work hard in martyred solitude with only the occasional solace of a few trusted friends who have not yet turned reactionary."

This type of socially conscious artist has nothing to contribute to the solution of the problem of contemporary artists except demoralization. He betrays his own social thesis and ends up in non-objectivity which in this sense means a non-existent objective.

But fortunately for American art these attitudes—that art is a non-social, absolute category awaiting the life giving touch of occasional genius, or that it is a social function unfortunately doomed by world wide reaction, only to be secretly preserved by martyred artist-priests, are not characteristic attitudes of the great majority of artists.

Instead we see an ever widening circle of artists expressing through the programs of the American Artists' Congress, and the various artists' unions, their faith in art and in the possibility of maintaining and extending the democratic conditions in society in which it can develop.

This Second Annual Membership Exhibition of the Artists' Congress is a concrete example of democracy in culture wherein artists of every sort of artistic and esthetic belief are showing their work to the people with the cooperation of the great commercial institution of Wanamaker's. It could not take place in a country where the principle of democracy in government has been repudiated. This exhibition has important social meaning with direct reference to art and culture, because while individually asserting many different social values in the various works, the entire display is dedicated to the principles of Peace, Democracy and Cultural Progress. This expresses a social decision by all these artists and a belief in the possibility of developing a democratic art, providing certain conditions are met.

The slogan, "For Peace, Democracy, and Cultural Progress," is not empty because it means that the members of the Artists' Congress are ready at all times to take whatever steps they can to preserve those objectives, and we believe that in this purpose we have the support of the great majority of the American people.

At the present time our program includes two main points: to work with support groups working against war and the spread of international anti-democratic aggression, and to work toward the permanent establishment of Federal support of the arts, based on the present Federal Arts Projects, which is the only guarantee for the development of a genuine democratic artistic culture in America.

This program is basic to the consideration of all other problems which confront the artist today. It includes as related questions, freedom of expression in art; discrimination; social content in art; abstract art; regionalism in art; art teaching; opportunity for art education; museum policy; dealer and artist relations; art as a free educational service to government; etc., and we invite all artists of recognized standing to join with us as members working toward the solution of these problems.

We also invite those interested in art and the artists' problems, who as non-artists are not eligible for membership, to join our associate membership and participate in our activities.

The American Artists' Congress wishes to thank Wanamaker's for their cooperation in the presentation of this exhibition which we feel to be representative of our collective determination to work toward the security of American art.

Stuart Davis, National Chairman

"Third Annual Exhibition:
Art in a Skyscraper," February 5–26, 1939

Peace, Democracy and Cultural Progress. What have they meant to the World in 1939? There have been wars; democracies have been engulfed by the aggressive march of fascism and culture has been blasted from the face of a large part of the earth. Does this mean that all our efforts have borne no fruit? Definitely it does not. While mankind in many countries has been succumbing to the scourge of this decade, the artist in America has not lost faith. Sorely tried, he has held aloft the banner of freedom— freedom for thought and freedom for expression. He has awakened a slumbering nation to its unrecognized heritage of culture and has brought into the field of the arts the first elements of a true democracy. The path of culture in Europe and Asia has been most difficult, and here we have not been without our troubles. Civil liberties, freedom of expression and true tolerance have not been free from attack and it has been only through the stubborn fight of those enlightened souls who saw the attacks in their true colors that today America has peace and democracy and that culture continues to progress.

Side by side with those defenders of democracy, the artist has fought. He has taken unto himself with true comprehension his responsibility as a creator and as an interpreter of the culture of today, but he has also recognized and accepted with understanding his role as a free citizen in a free country. He has not confined his struggles to his ivory tower or to his attic but has met the world on the highways and in byways. He has seen the life about him and has learned from it the real message of freedom and democracy. This message he has digested and through his newly found spirit of unified action has expressed.

Many of the peoples of the world have been deprived of the benefits of advancing civilization by reactionary regimes, which have perverted science and technique into instruments of destruction. The progressive artist has awakened to these threats. He has come to realize he is [a] functioning being in a society which has real need for the products of his labors. He has learned that, as in all other parts of society, so with the artist, the slogan "United we stand, divided we fall," has full application. All this the artist has seen, learned and taken into his being. All this has contributed to the fact that today the American Artists' Congress, founded in 1936 in a belief in Peace, Democracy and Cultural Progress, is holding its Third Anniversary Membership Exhibition. This exhibition is larger; the pictures and sculpture are vital because the artists have discarded their former aloofness and isolation and have rubbed shoulders with life and their fellow workers. This they have done through their works in the American Artists' Congress and the results are now on view not in some secluded edifice devoted to art as a fragile manifestation but in a modern skyscraper, itself a monument to the broader unity existing in the very roots of progressive America today.

Arthur Emptage

BIOGRAPHIES

GEORGE BIDDLE (1885–1973). Born in Philadelphia, Biddle studied law at Harvard. In 1908 he decided on a career as an artist and enrolled at the Pennsylvania Academy of the Fine Arts. He studied in Europe (Munich and Paris) between 1911 and 1914. He traveled widely as an artist, before returning to the United States in 1932. President Franklin D. Roosevelt was persuaded in part by Biddle to start the government art projects of the 1930s. He did several murals for the government projects. In 1939 Biddle published an autobiography, *An American Artist's Story*.

BILLINGS, HENRY (b. 1901). From Bronxville, New York, he studied at the Art Students' League in New York City. During the 1930s and early 1940s, he was employed by the government and completed murals for the Saranac, New York, Post Office in 1937, the Medford, Massachusetts, Post Office in 1938, and the Wappinger Falls, New York, Post Office in 1940. From 1935 to 1953 he taught at Bard College.

BLANCH, ARNOLD (1896–1968). From Mantoville, Minnesota, he studied at the Minneapolis School of Fine Arts from 1915 to 1917 and at the Art Students' League from 1919 to 1921. He joined the Woodstock Art Colony in 1923 and made his home there. During the 1930s, he painted government-sponsored murals in post offices in Columbia, Wisconsin; Norwalk, Connecticut; and Fredonia, New York.

BOURKE-WHITE, MARGARET (1904–1971). From New York City, she became a photographer in 1923. Between 1927 and 1930, she photographed architectural and industrial scenes for *Fortune*. She joined *Life* magazine in 1936 and was among the first to develop news stories in picture format. She was the only American photographer in Moscow in 1941 during the battle for that city and was one of the first to photograph the interior of the Buchenwald concentration camp in 1945. Her book, *You Have Seen Their Faces*, was published in 1936. Her autobiography, *Portrait of Myself*, was published in 1963.

BROUN, HEYWOOD (1888–1939). From Brooklyn, New York, he became a sports writer, book reviewer, critic, and war correspondent. Beginning in 1912, he worked for newspapers such as the *New York Tribune*, the *World*, and the *Telegram*. A founder of the American Newspaper Guild, he ran for the United States House of Representatives in 1930 as a candidate of the Socialist Party.

DAVIS, STUART (1894–1964). Born in Philadelphia, his early artistic influences were the realists of Robert Henri's circle. He was profoundly influenced by the Armory Show of 1913 and abandoned realism for modernism. In the 1930s Davis was politically active as a member of the Artists' Union as well as a staff member of its journal *Art Front*. He was also national secretary and national chairman of the American Artists' Congress.

DOUGLAS, AARON (1898–1979). Born in Topeka, Kansas, he studied at the University of Nebraska and in Paris with Othon Frieze. He painted murals in the 1930s for Fisk University and in New York City (under federal sponsorship) at the 135th Street Young Men's Christian Association and at the 135th Street Branch of the New York Public Library. He taught for many years at Fisk University.

DUROC, MARGARET (biographical data unknown). A signer of the Call for the Artists' Congress, as well as a speaker at the first meeting, Duroc also was one of the editors of the published *Papers* of the first congress.

FRIEDMAN, ARNOLD (1872–1946). From New York City, he worked most of his life as a postal clerk. Early in the twentieth century, he studied with Robert Henri and became a charter member of the Society of Independent Artists, exhibiting in its first show in 1910. Between 1935 and 1939, he painted government-sponsored murals in post offices in Orange, Virginia; Kingstree, South Carolina; and Warrenton, Georgia.

GELLERT, HUGO (b. 1892). From Hungary, Gellert was active in the congress throughout its life. He was a member of the jury for the ambitious exhibition, "America Today." In 1939, he also served as chairman on the Artists' Coordinating Committee for the World's Fair held in New York, where he painted a mural for the Communications Building. Gellert worked for the Works Progress Administration/Federal Art Project Mural Division in 1938 and 1939. He painted the first left-wing mural in the Workers' Cafeteria, New York City, in 1928.

GORELICK, BORIS (d. 1984). Active in the congress from its beginning to end, Gorelick was a signer of the original call as well as the call of 1941. Gorelick was also an active member of the Artists' Union.

GORMAN, FRANCIS J. (biographical data unknown). Gorman was vice-president of the United Textile Workers of America at the time of his address to the first congress.

GOTTLIEB, HARRY (b. 1895). From Romania, he moved to Ireland in 1901 and to Minneapolis in 1907. He studied at the Minneapolis School of Fine Arts. Gottlieb settled in New York City in 1935 where he joined the WPA as a graphic artist and became involved in the Artists' Union. In the late 1930s, he helped develop silk screen techniques and held the first exhibition in that medium in 1940.

GREGORY, WAYLANDE (1905–1971). Born in Baxter Springs, Kansas, he studied at the Art Institute of Kansas and at the Art Institute of Chicago. He was a private student of Lorado Taft and worked in Taft's studio. In the 1920s, Gregory traveled and studied in Europe. He returned to the Midwest in 1928 and worked as a ceramicist. He was for a time associated with the Cranbrook Foundation in Michigan. From 1936 to 1938 he was a supervisor of the WPA/FAP in Newark, New Jersey. He was well known in the 1930s for his sculpture, especially his *Fountain of Atoms* created for the World's Fair in New York in 1939.

GROTH, JOHN (b. 1908). From Chicago, he studied at the Art Institute of Chicago and the Art Students' League in New York City. He served as art director of *Esquire* from 1933 to 1936 and also worked for *Parade*. He illustrated several books including *Studio: Europe* (1945), *Gone With the Wind*, and *John Groth's World of Sport* (1970).

JONES, JOE (1909–1963). A midwestern artist, Jones was well known in the 1930s for his painting of scenes of radical political content. He was a signer of the original call as well as a signer of the call of 1941. Jones also served on the National Executive Committee of the congress.

KENT, ROCKWELL (1882–1971). Born in Tarrytown Heights, New York, he studied with several important painters including William Merritt Chase, Robert Henri, and Kenneth Hayes Miller. He was active in artists' organizations throughout his career and helped to organize one of the first exhibitions of modern art in the United States. He did mural work for the government in the 1930s as well as illustrations and prints. Kent served the Artists' Congress in many capacities. His autobiography, *It's Me O Lord*, published in 1955, recounts this work as well as his extensive travels.

LOZOWICK, LOUIS (1892–1973). Born in Ukraine, Lozowick first studied art at the Kiev Art School from 1904 to 1905. He emigrated to the United States in 1906, where he studied at the National Academy of Design from 1912 to 1915. He lived in Europe from 1919 to 1924, during which time he was associated with radical and avant-garde groups. From 1935 to 1940 he worked for the graphics division of the WPA/FAP. He is known for his prints of urban architecture as well as his writing about Jewish artists, Russian art, and the theater.

MANSHIP, PAUL (1885–1966). Born in St. Paul, Minnesota, Manship attended the Art Institute there before enrolling at the Art Students' League in New York City in 1905. He then studied at the Pennsylvania Academy of the Fine Arts and at the American Academy in Rome. In the 1930s he did several important public sculptural commissions, including the *Prometheus* (1934) at Rockefeller Center in New York City.

MUMFORD, LEWIS (b. 1895). One of his generation's major social critics, he is known especially for his writing on the relationship between technology and society. After joining the *Dial* in 1918, he subsequently wrote for other magazines including *American Mercury*, the *New Republic*, and the *New Yorker*. His books include *Sticks and Stones* (1924), *Technics and Civilization* (1934), and *The Myth of the Machine* (1967).

OROZCO, JOSÉ CLEMENTE (1883–1949). From Zapotlan, Mexico, he was a major muralist and easel painter. After studying at the Academia de San Carlos from 1906 to 1914, he made illustrations for newspapers. Revolutionary material appeared in his first murals in 1922 in the National Preparatory School, Mexico City. His American murals include those at Pomona College (1930), the New School for Social Research (1931), and Dartmouth College (1932–1934).

PEARSON, RALPH M. (1884–1958). A writer, teacher, and etcher, he became a supporter of modern art in the United States in 1914. His books include *Experiencing American Pictures* (1943) and *How To See Modern Pictures* (1925).

SCHAPIRO, MEYER (b. 1904). From Lithuania, he earned a doctoral degree in art history from Columbia University in 1929. Subsequently, he became one of the most important art historians of his generation. A specialist in medieval and modern art, his writings were collected in the 1970s and published in *Romanesque Art* and *Modern Art*.

SCHARY, SAUL (1905–1978). From Newark, New Jersey, he studied at the Pennsylvania Academy of the Fine Arts and the Art Students' League. He became an illustrator as well as a painter. For a part of his career, he was associated with the Daniel Gallery, which also included such artists as Yasuo Kuniyoshi, Charles Demuth, Peter Blume, and Niles Spencer.

SCHMIDT, KATHERINE (1898–1978). From Xenia, Ohio, she studied at the Art Students' League. She spent a major part of her career as director of the Downtown Gallery, New York City.

SIQUEIROS, DAVID ALFARO (1890–1974). From Chihuahua, Mexico, he attended the Academia de San Carlos in 1911. He then traveled in Europe from 1919 to 1922 before returning to Mexico to help found the Syndicate of Technical Workers, Painters, and Sculptors. The most politically active of the major Mexican muralists, he painted three sets of murals in Los Angeles in 1932 and conducted an experimental workshop in New York City in 1936–1937.

STAVENITZ, ALEXANDER R. (1901–1960). Russian born, he studied at the Art Students' League and the St. Louis School of Fine Arts. A graphic artist, he was active in the congress in several capacities. He was co-chairman of the Graphics Committee and as such was responsible in part for several exhibitions. He also served on the National Executive Committee. He worked for the WPA/FAP from 1935 to 1940. An active teacher, Stavenitz worked at the Pratt Institute, City College of New York, and the Museum of Modern Art.

STERNBERG, HARRY (b. 1904). Born in New York City, he studied and taught at the Art Students' League. During the 1930s, he completed government-sponsored murals in post offices in Chicago (the Lakeview Post Office), Sellersville, Pennsylvania, and Chester, Pennsylvania. He wrote *Methods and Materials of Etching* (1949), *Composition* (1958), and *Realistic Abstract Art* (1959).

WARD, LYND (b. 1905). From Chicago, he became an illustrator, writer, and graphic artist. He founded the Equinox Cooperative Press in 1931 which published *America Today* for the American Artists' Congress. Other books include *Song without Words* (1936), and *Storyteller without Words: The Wood Engravings of Lynd Ward* (1974).

WEBER, MAX (1881–1961). From Bialystok, Russia, he emigrated to

Brooklyn, New York, in 1891. He studied at the Pratt Institute with Arthur Wesley Dow. He became one of the earliest American proponents of modern abstract art. In 1905 he traveled to Paris where he studied at the Academie Julian, the Academie Colarossi, and the Academie de la Grande Chaumiere. He experimented with Fauvist, cubist, and Futurist styles, before developing his own figurative style. In the 1930s, Weber served as one of the national chairmen of the American Artists' Congress.

WHITE, FRANCIS ROBERT (biographical data unknown). White was director of the Little Gallery in Cedar Rapids, Iowa. In the late 1930s he was state director of the WPA/FAP in Iowa. In 1937 he served on the National Executive Committee of the congress.

WILSON, GILBERT (biographical data unknown). A midwestern painter, he wrote of his experiences recorded in a book entitled *Letters of William Allen White and a Young Man*, published in 1948.

INDEX